Tokyo
JAPAN
Kure
Midway
International Dateline
CHINA
Wake
NORTHERN
MARIANA
ISLANDS
MARSHALL ISLANDS
Saipan
GUAM
Ratak Chain
Rālik Chain
Kuwajleen
Sunday
Saturday
Manila
PHILIPPINES
Yap
Chuuk
Pohnpei
Kosrae
Mājro
FEDERATED STATES OF MICRONESIA
PALAU
Tarawa
Gilbert Islands
K I R I B
NAURU
Banaba
Ph
equator
New
Ireland
Bougainville
SOLOMON
ISLANDS
TUVALU
TOKE
PAPUA
PAPUA
NEW GUINEA
New
Britain
Santa Cruz
Islands
Guadalcanal
Rotuma
Wallis
&
Futuna
SAMO
FIJI
VANUATU
Vanua Levu
Viti Levu
Lau
Group
TO
Loyalty Islands
Coral Sea
Makay
NEW
CALEDONIA
Queensland
Bundaberg
AUSTRALIA
Brisbane
Norfolk
Kermadec
Islands
Sydney
Tasman Sea
Auckland
NEW ZEALAND
Chath
Isla
175°E
160°E
145°E
130°E
115°E

THE PACIFIC ISLANDS

UNITED STATES
Los Angeles
30°N
Oʻahu
Hawaiʻi
HAWAIʻI
MEXICO
15°N
Mexico City
North Pacific Ocean
Clipperton
Kiritimati
Line Islands
0°
equator
COOK ISLANDS
Marquesas Islands
Galapagos Islands
FRENCH POLYNESIA
Tuamotu Archipelago
15°S
Tahiti
Society Islands
Rarotonga
Austral Islands
Gambier Islands
Pitcairn Islands
30°S
Pacific Ocean
Rapa Nui (Easter)
155°W
140°W
125°W
45°S
110°W
95°W

My Land, My Life

Pacific Islands Monograph Series 31

My Land, My Life

Dispossession at the Frontier of Desire

Siobhan McDonnell

CENTER FOR PACIFIC ISLANDS STUDIES
School of Pacific and Asian Studies
University of Hawai'i, Mānoa
UNIVERSITY OF HAWAI'I PRESS • Honolulu

Chapter 5 was originally published in 2018 as "Selling 'Sites of Desire': Paradise in Reality Television, Tourism, and Real Estate Promotion in Vanuatu" in *The Contemporary Pacific* 30 (2):413–436. It has been shortened and revised for this volume.

Paperback edition 2025

Printed in the United States of America

First printed, 2023

Library of Congress Cataloging-in-Publication Data

Names: McDonnell, Siobhan, author.

Title: My land, my life : dispossession at the frontier of desire / Siobhan McDonnell.

Other titles: Pacific islands monograph series ; no. 31.

Description: Honolulu : Center for Pacific Islands Studies, School of Pacific and Asian Studies, University of Hawaiʻi, Mānoa : University of Hawaiʻi Press, [2023] | Series: Pacific islands monograph series; 31 | Includes bibliographical references and index.

Identifiers: LCCN 2023007260 (print) | LCCN 2023007261 (ebook) | ISBN 9780824894450 (hardback) | ISBN 9780824897192 (pdf) | ISBN 9780824897208 (epub) | ISBN 9780824897215 (kindle edition)

Subjects: LCSH: Land tenure—Vanuatu. | Land titles—Vanuatu.

Classification: LCC HD1125 .M336 2023 (print) | LCC HD1125 (ebook) | DDC 333.0099595—dc23/eng/20230707

LC record available at https://lccn.loc.gov/2023007260

LC ebook record available at https://lccn.loc.gov/2023007261

ISBN 9780824899165 (paperback)

Front cover art: "Paradise Found" real estate sign located near Eton Beach, Efate Island, 22 September 2014. Photograph by author.

Maps by Manoa Mapworks, Inc.

University of Hawaiʻi Press books are printed on acid-free paper and meet the guidelines for permanence and durability of the Council on Library Resources.

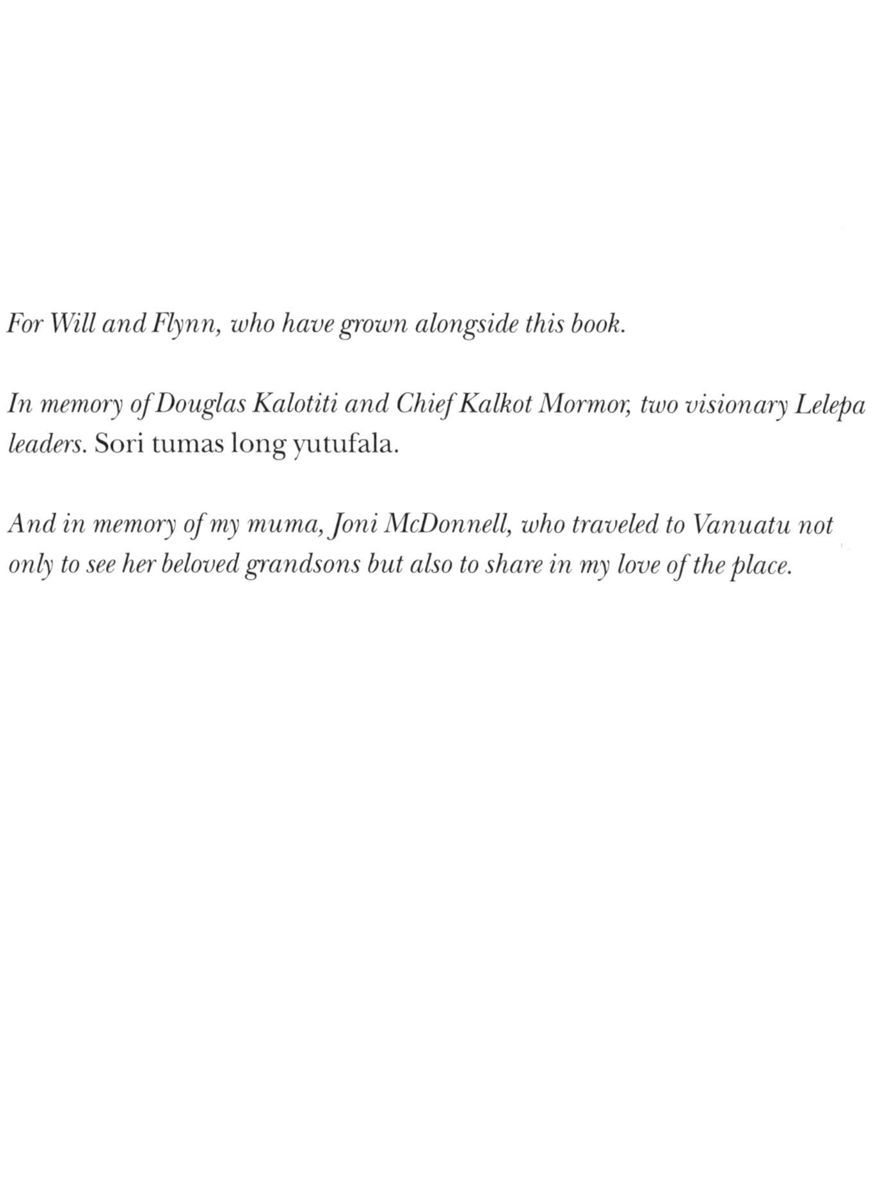

For Will and Flynn, who have grown alongside this book.

In memory of Douglas Kalotiti and Chief Kalkot Mormor, two visionary Lelepa leaders. Sori tumas long yutufala.

And in memory of my muma, Joni McDonnell, who traveled to Vanuatu not only to see her beloved grandsons but also to share in my love of the place.

The Pacific Islands Monograph Series is a joint effort of the University of Hawai'i Press and the Center for Pacific Islands Studies, University of Hawai'i. The series includes works in the humanities and social sciences that focus on the insular Pacific. A list of other volumes in the series follows the index.

Editor's Note

Across Oceania, land is important because it nurtures kinship structures and relationships between people, places, and the spirit world. It is a source of livelihood: it feeds and nourishes people's physical, cultural, historical, and spiritual needs. Land is therefore valuable, not only in its materiality but also as a site where cultures, histories, and genealogies are inscribed and identities are constructed and maintained. Land is life.

However, since the 1800s, many Pacific Island places have become intertwined with the global cash economy and the capitalist system that drives it. In this system, land is viewed predominantly as a commodity that can be traded or as a means of production vital to the creation of profit. Over time, this intertwining has led to a push to establish clearly defined and secured property rights, with colonial governments and private entrepreneurs—and later independent states—advocating for land registration that creates titles and thereby converts land into property. Registered titles to land can therefore be bought and sold or rented through fixed-term leasing arrangements. Examples of extensive land registration processes in the Pacific include the Great Mahele in Hawai'i in the mid-1800s, the *veitarogi vanua* (land registration) in Fiji in the 1890s–1940s, and the land reforms in Guåhan (Guam) under the Spanish and, later, US administrations. On gaining independence, many Pacific Island countries were encouraged to enact land recording and registration laws. This was driven primarily by the perception that customary systems of tenure were an impediment to economic development because records of rights to land were held in relationships and stories passed down orally from one generation to the next. Despite this, many Pacific Islanders resisted land registration. As a result, in some Pacific Islands, large percentages of land remain untitled, meaning they exist outside the purview of the state and are regulated by customary systems of tenure.

Some countries have established statutory mechanisms intended to protect Indigenous people's right to land. Solomon Islands' constitution, for example, stipulates that perpetual title to land can only be held by Solomon Islanders. Vanuatu's constitution goes further, providing that land can only be owned by Indigenous ni-Vanuatu who inherit ownership rights in accordance with *kastom* (custom).

In spite of this, customary land can be accessed through leasehold arrangements, often for long periods. In this volume, *My Land, My Life: Dispossession at the Frontier of Desire,* Siobhan McDonnell discusses how land-lease arrangements in Vanuatu have led to the dispossession of Indigenous customary landowners. Foreigners' desire for land and locals' desire to generate income through leasing has led to a "rush for land" and land speculations, especially on Efate Island, where the national capital, Port Vila, is located. This has led to the dispossession of customary landowners and huge profit by foreign leaseholders, who typically hold seventy-five-year leases. Nearly 50 percent of Efate's landmass has been leased at well below fair market value to foreign investors, who have subsequently subdivided and subleased land for 3,000–7,000 percent profit.

This book provides ethnographic insights into the processes of dispossession as they occur between investors, middlemen, and Indigenous landowners, as well as within Indigenous landowning groups, villages, and families. These include what McDonnell refers to as "acts of 'intimate exclusion' whereby chiefs and powerful men transact customary land without the knowledge or consent of the broader landowning group" (7). The exclusion is also gendered, as women are rarely involved in decision-making about land leases. McDonnell locates these local dynamics within global, regional, and national contexts and highlights forces such as neoliberal economic development actors and their policies that ultimately drive the rush for acquiring customary land in Vanuatu.

My Land, My Life contributes to the ongoing national, regional, and global discussions about land and economic development and the impacts on Indigenous landowning communities. It also provides a compelling analysis of how local communities at the "frontiers of desire" respond to, are influenced by, and at times influence the rush for land. This book is a valuable resource for academics and policymakers focused on these issues, and while it is framed by anthropology and legal studies, it has much to offer scholars and students in a range of disciplines given its multi- and interdisciplinary subject matter and research methodologies.

McDonnell does a marvelous job of providing the reader with an intimate insight into the intersections between global forces and local dynamics that influence access to customary land for "development" and the dispossession of Indigenous landowning groups. Such a comprehensive analysis is only possible because of the author's long-term and engaged ethnographic research in Vanuatu, especially on Efate Island.

The Pacific Islands Monograph Series is honored to publish this book. It will contribute immensely to discussions about land, economic development, and Indigenous landowning communities in Vanuatu, in the Pacific Islands region, and beyond. Land will continue to be important in discussions about livelihoods, cultures, histories, and economic development in Oceania and elsewhere. Land is, after all, life.

Tarcisius Kabutaulaka

Contents

Illustrations

Maps

Figures

Acknowledgments

Relationships are the foundation of all research. I have made it this far in large part due to the generous support of the Lelepa people, without whom there would not be a book. I remain indebted to the Lelepa people not only for the many years of care that they have given me and my family but also for the knowledge and wisdom shared over the fourteen years it has taken to complete this project. Four Lelepa men have been central to much of my work: Richard Matanik, Chief Kalkot Mormor, Douglas (Fonu) Kalotiti, and Pierre Makmar. Today only one of these men is alive, something that deeply saddens me. Two women, Leisara Kalotiti and Brigitte Laboukly, have influenced my work in North Efate, offering their insights into *kastom* and ideas of *ples*. With Leisara, I have worked on a range of issues and also mourned the death of her husband Kalkot Mormor, my adopted papa. With Brigitte, I have cried and belly laughed more times than I can remember. Brigitte is brilliant and capable, and my work in Vanuatu has often been made easier by her grace and good humor. These debts are larger and deeper than anything that could be adequately written into the procedural form that accompanies an ethics proposal; they are friendships and ties that bind. I would like to express my deep gratitude and pay tribute to all of the Lelepa people who have guided me in the work I have undertaken in Vanuatu.

As a lawyer and a fugitive anthropologist, I run land cases to win back Indigenous land. I have been involved in supporting Indigenous leaders by drafting negotiations over climate agreements and have been negotiating for many years in United Nations climate forums for the Pacific leadership. These are some of the rare and privileged spaces that I have been able to work in during the course of my career, for which I am truly grateful. I would like to acknowledge my colleagues from my time working in the Vanuatu Cultural Centre and in the Ministry of Lands. In both places I have worked with committed staff who have become friends as well as colleagues. I remain grateful to Ralph Regenvanu for the opportunity to draft the constitutional amendments and land legislation in Vanuatu. Ralph is a leader who stands apart from many other politicians due to his personal integrity and commitment. I have worked alongside him because I believe in these values and in his broad vision for Vanuatu. My work in Vanuatu has also benefited from friendships with Anna Naupa, Milena Stefanova, Brigette Olul, Leisande Otto, Howard Van Trease, Don Paterson, Joe Foukona, and Bob Makin. I am grateful for the comments made by Ralph and Howard Van Trease on earlier chapters of this book. I would also like to personally thank Garry and Evelyne Blake for agreeing to work alongside me and offer unfunded legal support to Lelepa people over a seven-year period.

At The Australian National University I have benefited greatly from being located in the Resources, Environment and Development Group in the Crawford School. I would like to thank my colleagues for their ongoing support particularly in these times of teaching and publishing during COVID and lockdowns. For the last four years, I have had the joy of convening and then co-convening alongside Maeve Powell a group of brilliant young Indigenous and non-Indigenous scholars in a "Decolonial Reading Group." This extraordinary group of scholars, including Maeve Powell, Sam Provost, Trish Tupou, Mitiana Arbon, Evie Rose, Em Fishpool, Bianca Hennessy, Oliver Liford, Kathy Jetñil-Kijiner, are very much the future of our disciplines in Pacific studies and Indigenous studies, and it has been an honor to be in conversation with them. Thank you all for teaching me so much.

I offer my deepest thanks to Carolyn Brewer both for her patience and diligence in editing this book and for her general good humor.

I would like to thank Margaret Jolly and Lamont Lindstrom for their insightful and generous editorial comments on an earlier version of this manuscript, which have no doubt created significant improvements to the overall structure and content of the book. This book began its life during my time in the School of Culture, History and Languages when I was associated with Margaret Jolly's ARC Laureate project and began thinking around land commodification and personhood, so I am indebted to Margaret in many ways.

I have been grateful throughout also for the editorial guidance provided by Tara Kabutaulaka, and would also like to thank Candice Steiner and the rest of the University of Hawai'i team.

In life I am blessed by the most extraordinary group of friends, too many to mention but who all have contributed to this work. I thank my parents Jonette and John McDonnell for their many years of love and care. Their love of ideas, books, art, and writing remain a constant source of inspiration.

Laurence relocated his life so that I could complete the fieldwork for this book. While in Vanuatu, he nursed me through dengue, watched me recover from a car accident, helped care for our dying friend Douglas Kalotiti, helped me rush friends to hospital, cared for our boys while I traveled on fieldwork, and managed numerous other domestic tasks while I worked obsessively. Laurence, I thank you for your kindness. And, to Will and Flynn, I have finally finished the book that I have been telling you about for all these years. I thank you *tufala pikininni blong mi* for your patience with your *muma.*

My Land, My Life

Introduction
My Land, My Life

> Why you wanna tell me I don't got what it takes
> to handle my birthright, my sole identity.
> The fundamental purpose of our independence
> is to bring back my forefathers' land to me.
> Instead of that you fall for personal judgements,
> while you sell our livelihood for a dollar and a dime or two.
> You got to know
> My land my life,
> affected by your propaganda and your lies.
> How long will we
> be silent while you sell our future to those rich, white-colored boys.
>
> Stan and the Earth Force, "My Land My Life"

As the moon rises over Vanuatu's Fest Napuan Music Festival, the hugely popular band Stan and the Earth Force takes the stage. The opening bars of "My Land My Life" start, and the crowd erupts; a wave of young people begins moving in unison singing the words of the song. It is a song of resistance, a song that speaks to young people's anger that their customary land "birthright" has been leased by chiefs, uncles, and fathers "to rich, white-colored boys." It is an open challenge to the political leaders who have been leasing customary land that people live and garden on, often without their knowledge or consent. And it is a song that acknowledges land as the foundation of Indigenous identity: my land, my life.

* * *

The starting point for this story is land is life. Access to land is central to ensuring the food security of current and future generations; to managing environmental issues and problems of environmental degradation; to ensuring the maintenance of complex Indigenous knowledge systems; to addressing the complex problems of relocation and resettlement; to providing options in relation to disaster responses and management; to addressing housing needs; to creating future development and infrastructure projects; and to ensuring cultural and language continuity. For Indigenous people, securing adequate access to land is central to adapting to the complex challenges caused by climate change impacts. Land is often central to understanding issues of conflict and resource extraction, functioning as a driver of both politics and the political economies of various states. Around the globe, contemporary neocolonial and enduring colonial processes focus on access to land and resource extraction.

Land has multiple, often contested, meanings. Land is not the same thing to an Indigenous subsistence farmer as it is to a speculative land investor, or perhaps to an Indigenous person who has lived and worked in an urban environment. Across Oceania land operates "as a shorthand for ties to locality, whether terrestrial or marine—[and] is the basis for membership and nationality" for most people (Ballard 2013, 48). In Vanuatu, shortly after independence, the first minister of lands, Sethy Regenvanu, famously stated, "For ni-Vanuatu, land is more than simply a commodity to be used for gain and to be disposed of when it has been stripped of its value. Land is an intrinsic part of themselves and their whole being. Land to ni-Vanuatu is what a mother is to a baby. It is with land that he defines his identity, and it is with land that he maintains his spiritual strength" (1980, 67). Here ni-Vanuatu relationships to land are contrasted with Western concepts of land as a commodity for use and transfer. Sethy Regenvanu described these relationships to land as reciprocal, as an intrinsic deeply maternal, embedded, spiritual connection to place that defines identity.

Across Oceania, people often describe the centrality of land to identity as spiritually nourishing and sustaining. Land is the mother. Indigenous Hawaiian philosopher Manulani Aluli Meyer wrote, "Indigenous people are all about place. Land/*aina,* defined as 'that which feeds,' is the everything to our sense of love, joy, and nourishment. Land is our mother. This is not a metaphor. For the Native Hawaiians speaking of knowledge, land was the central theme that drew forth all others. You came from a place. You grew in a place and you had a relationship with that place. This is an epistemological idea" (2014, 220). Land, and the kinship structures that it nurtures and sustains, is the basis for relational personhood across Oceania. But, as Meyer entreated, this is not simply a metaphor; this is a deep epistemological foundation for understanding meaning and knowledge. Within Indigenous knowledge systems, land is the basis for knowing yourself as well as understanding the material and spiritual world.

Concepts of place (*ples* in Bislama) are central to identity in Vanuatu. *Kastom* (custom) is largely understood as the "ways of the place," the proper way of behaving as an emplaced person. *Kastom* is often broadly defined as the contemporary practice of tradition. Margaret Jolly wrote, "*Kastom* is the Bislama word which loosely translates as tradition, but evokes not so much the totality of ancestral practices as a particular selection of such practices for the present" (1996, 176). *Kastom* forms much of the social fabric of people's lives in Vanuatu. *Kastom* dictates, among other things, the nature of relationships and appropriate marriage partners, gender and status, ways of meeting and mediating disputes, ideas of appropriate forms of speech and respect, ceremony and meaning, beliefs and being, hierarchy and authority, and the practice of *nakaemas* (the Bislama word for sorcery).

Across Oceania, concepts of land as foundational to identity exist alongside—and often in tension with—the formal market for land, which is nominally structurally regulated by the state. In Vanuatu, the period since 2000 has seen a dramatic land rush with over 10 percent of all customary land now held under long-term lease. This book offers ethnographic insights into the land-leasing processes involved in this rush at the scale of the village in the period between 2010 and 2014. It maps the relationships between investors and their middlemen with powerful local men at the frontier of desire for customary land. It also describes insights into the frontiers of capitalism, particularly as they relate to the dispossession of Indigenous people. It offers a multi-scalar and multi-sited ethnography of capitalism, not simply as a linear march toward commodification of the landscape by foreign interests, but as one that is replete with the gendered, fragile, and intimate contradictions associated with power and property—one that is, simply, much more human.

This is a story that begins with a song. Following the themes of the song, it explores the processes that underpinned the land rush in Vanuatu. It is a story that illustrates how property—as a cornerstone of capitalist relations—creates particular legal identities that enable powerful men to manipulate claims to land and entrench their personal authority, often without the consent or knowledge of the broader landowning group. In the words of Stan and the Earth Force, property enables these men to "sell our livelihood for a dollar and a dime or two."

Researching Capitalist Relations

Even in capitalist terms, land differs from other commodities. Writing in the context of the horror and global transformation of the Second World War, Karl Polanyi described land as a "fictitious commodity" in spite of its centrality to the operation of a capitalist economy (1944). This is because land is not produced for exchange in the way that other commodities are, and because land is intimately bound to social relations. Unlike other commodities, the uses and meanings of land are not stable and are regularly disputed. Land differs from commodities like oil and gas precisely because it is not mobile and "has an especially rich and diverse array of 'affordances'—uses and values it affords to us, including the capacity to sustain human life" (Li 2014, 589). The commodification of land can often be contentious, particularly where Indigenous communities live or are dependent on land for their livelihoods. The particular values and affordances that land holds mean that land transactions can have dramatic implications for societies. This led Polanyi to argue that land, labor, and money are not true commodities produced for sale in the market but rather "fictitious commodities." This is because if they were managed solely by the market, this could eventually lead to social breakdown.

Climate change impacts offer new insights into the value of land. We all know that land is intrinsic to our survival in that it supplies food, fresh water, and biodiversity. Globally humans have created massive environmental degradation, which is further impacted by climate change, particularly for populations in low-lying coastal areas, river deltas, dry lands, and permafrost areas, many of whom are Indigenous (IPCC 2019). Drawing attention to the colonial and capitalist legacies that created this large-scale environmental damage, as well as contemporary political economies founded on resource extraction and carbon emissions, Indigenous scholars are increasingly calling for climate change impacts to be located within the broader workings of capitalism, as linked to colonization (Davis and Todd 2017; Hromek 2019; Whyte 2017).

Anthropogenic climate change and the trouble it brings have further highlighted the multiple and contested meanings of land, as with so many other elements essential to our continued survival on the planet, such as air and water, that are increasingly disputed. What does it mean then for the practice of activism and research to live in such troubled times? In this age of uncertainty and of the prescient fears associated with living on a damaged planet, Donna Haraway suggested that as researchers and activists we "stay with the trouble." She describes staying with the trouble as "learning to be truly present, not as a vanishing pivot between awful or Edenic pasts and apocalyptic or salvific futures, but as mortal critters entwined in myriad unfinished configurations of places, times, matters, meanings" (Haraway 2016, 1). This is an important entreaty in the context of Oceanic landscapes so often mobilized either as paradisical or as apocalyptic sinking islands and drowning peoples, a recirculation of the trope of "paradise lost" (Alexeyeff and McDonnell 2018). But staying with the trouble also involves carefully studying the capitalist configurations that inform the trouble. It involves a deep dive into capitalist processes.

Further challenges to the practice of research in this time of trouble are provided by a growing cacophony of calls by Indigenous, Black, and people-of-color scholars to "let anthropology burn" due to the failure of the discipline to confront its colonial roots, adopt a meaningful decolonial practice, or contribute to critical theory on racism (Allen and Jobson 2016; Beliso-De Jesús and Pierre 2020; Brodkin, Morgen, and Hutchinson 2011; Jobson 2020; Shange 2020; Todd 2016; Welcome 2020). In the wake of the Black Lives Matter protests, scholars Aisha Beliso-De Jesús and Jemima Pierre critiqued colleagues for thinking that the challenges of white supremacy operate only in the streets rather than within the walls of the academy (2020). In a brilliant essay on the future of anthropology, reflecting particularly on 2020 with its attending cascading crises, Black Caribbean scholar Leniqueca Welcome wrote: "The world is on fire, anthropology as a discipline tethered to whiteness is on fire.... Anthropology aimed at material transformation is the only anthropological work that continues to be worth doing. Any other way of doing anthropology we can let burn" (2020). As anthropologists living in this age in which the "world is on fire" we must attend to scholarship that is involved in the dismantling of the multiple, interrelated systems of oppression that have created this time. Many of us have understood this as a time of acute precarity and realize that precarity is increasingly becoming *the* condition of our time (Tsing 2015). We have had to learn a new language for our grief, one commensurate with the trauma that comes from cascading crises. Like Welcome, I too believe that anthropology must contribute to material transformations of capitalist, colonial/neocolonial, patriarchal, ableist, and racist systems of oppression—or else burn.

In researching capitalist processes of dispossession, my starting point is that decolonization is not a metaphor (Tuck and Yang 2012). At its core, the practice of decolonial research and activism involves a commitment to the principles of Indigenous self-determination and to the repatriation of Indigenous land. In Vanuatu, I have undertaken legal and policy work to return land to Indigenous control and to end the large-scale leasing of customary land without the consent of the broader landowning group. This work has been undertaken alongside Indigenous leaders, organizations, and communities. My approach to researching land issues in Vanuatu has been a collaborative process woven out of this practical and legal advocacy work, conducted over twelve plus years, and it is ongoing. It is based on conversations, performances, and acts across many different stages and across multiple scales and fields, including two and a half years of fieldwork based with the Lelepa people of North Efate on Vanuatu's central island of Efate. In 2013, I became legal adviser to Minister of Lands Ralph Regenvanu, and in this capacity, I was also the principal drafter of a wide-ranging constitutional and land-reform package designed to deliver better Indigenous land rights and to halt the rapacious rush in customary land. My practice is one of fugitive-engaged anthropology. This book traces the continual spiral that informs much of my work—from research to praxis to scholarship—with each rotation building on the last.

The Speculative Land Rush in Vanuatu

Across Oceania, the overwhelming majority of land—over 80 percent in most countries—is held under customary tenure arrangements governed beyond formal, state-based arrangements. Like other parts of the region, in Vanuatu the vast majority of land (currently around 88 percent) is held under customary tenure managed by customary institutions governed by chiefs, or councils of chiefs, that determine use and access rights over an area of land in accordance with customary principles. Ralph Regenvanu described the operation of this "traditional economy" whereby people in Vanuatu live in large extended family groups, satisfy their food requirements largely through customary access to land and sea resources, speak a local Indigenous vernacular language, participate in custom ceremonies, and have disputes resolved by local leaders (2011, 30). Leasing customary land, particularly when it results in the eviction of the Indigenous population (as is increasingly happening in Vanuatu), has profound implications for the operation of customary systems and for the social and kinship relationships bound within these systems.

Removal of land from the customary system has been occurring since 2001, when Vanuatu began to experience an increasingly dramatic rush to lease customary land. This has resulted in over 10 percent of all customary land being leased (Scott and others 2012). On Efate Island, where the national capital Port Vila is situated, 43.6 percent of land previously held under customary tenure is now leased (see map 0.1). Many of these leases hug the coastline, with over 56.5 percent of the coastline of Efate Island now leased (Scott and others 2012). The coastline of Efate contains much of the most arable land on the island, land that is the best for growing gardens. Leasing on Efate has meant that the local Indigenous populations have lost access to gardening land and to adjoining coastal estates.

National lease data published in 2012 indicates that 46 percent of the Efate landmass is leased, but this statistic was compiled before the leasing of two large areas of customary land in North Efate (titles 12/0543/032 and 12/0542/001). After a seven-year court case, these leases were overturned on the grounds of fraud and mistake (see chapter 5).

Increasing academic attention is being paid to the practice of land grabbing—the changes in rural land use and accompanying social relations to land that have been taking place across many regions in the world. This literature focuses on large-scale land transformation—on a new scale and with a new intensity—resulting from processes of globalization, the liberalization of land markets, and increases in Foreign Direct Investment in land (Borras and Franco 2010; Deininger 2003; Li 2012, 2014; Sikor and Müller 2009; Zoomers 2010). In this literature, land is grabbed not only by high-wealth individuals but also by foreign governments demanding a supply of cheap food crops or arable land on which to grow biofuels and nonfood agricultural crops (Borras and Franco 2010; Cotula, Dyer, and Vermeulen 2008; Zoomers 2010). Nature reserves and conservation areas are also developed to achieve large-scale land transformation and dispossession of Indigenous peoples (Peluso 2012; Peluso and Lund 2011).

Much of the focus of this international literature is on global or regional geopolitical processes and drivers of land transformations. The actors in this context are multinational corporations, high-wealth individuals, and foreign governments. By contrast, this book offers ethnographic insights into the actual processes of dispossession as they take place within villages and family groups. These are the exchanges that occur between investors, middlemen, and Indigenous landowners at the frontiers of land transformations.

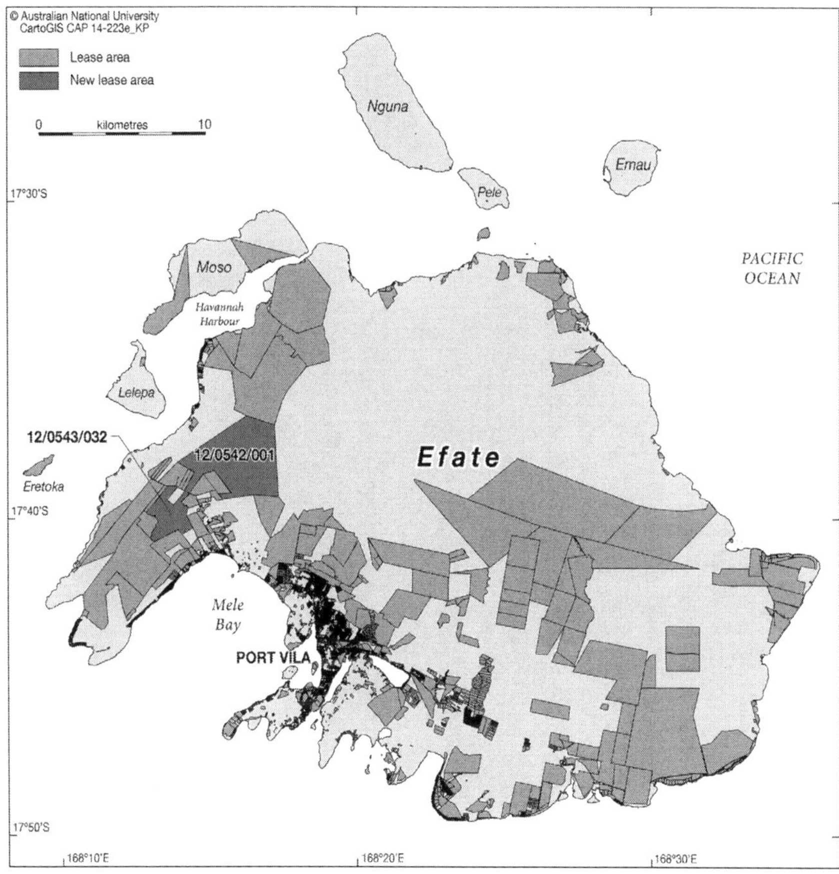

MAP 0.1. Leases on Efate Island, as of 2015. Dark gray marks a lease area. Data provided by the Ministry of Lands, Vanuatu. Map courtesy of CartoGIS Cap 14-233e_KP, The Australian National University.

They are often acts of "intimate exclusion" whereby chiefs and powerful men transact customary land without the knowledge or consent of the broader landowning group. To provide context for this detailed village-based ethnography of dispossession that informs my work, I first briefly detail the broader global, regional, and national context for the rush to lease customary land in Vanuatu.

Instead of referring to a land "grab," Tania Li advocated for the use of the term "rush," thereby placing land transformations in the context of rushes for commodities such as gold and agricultural crop booms (Li 2012; 2014, 594–595). The rush comes after the sudden, large-scale, visible, hyped interest in a crop or resource because of its newly "discovered" or somehow "enhanced" value and the "spectacular riches it promises to investors who get into the business early." Li wrote, "Hence the rush. Do it now before others spot the value, and the profit margins decrease" (2014, 595). There have been two periods of rush to lease land in Vanuatu. The first, from 1995 to 1997, was due to the shift in government policy to support foreign direct investment. An even more dramatic rush occurred between 2001 and 2014, fueled by speculative investment and the substantial returns to be made on the purchase of cheap customary land. At the regional scale, the land rush in Vanuatu can be interpreted alongside a similar large-scale land transformation that has taken place in Papua New Guinea through Special Agricultural and Business Leases, with more than five million hectares of customary land being leased to private companies between 2003 and 2011 (Filer 2011a, 2011b, 2012). With over 11 percent of Papua New Guinea's total land area now held under lease arrangement, this represents one of the largest land rushes anywhere on the globe.

In Vanuatu, speculative land investments involve the purchasing of customary land well below any fair market valuation, usually from a local man (or a small group of men) purporting to be the "custom landowner(s)." Once purchased by investors, the customary land is subdivided into smaller blocks, with each of these blocks being resold at substantially inflated prices, predominantly as sites for residential houses or tourism developments. My research for this book suggests that investors make profits of between 3,000 and 7,000 percent on these land dealings. This highlights the substantial gains available to investors associated with the rush to lease. In the period 2001–2010, an average of 608 leases per year were registered in Vanuatu: 895 new leases were granted in 2007, and 1,800 were granted between 2008 and 2010 (Scott and others 2012, 4). Most of these leases were for a seventy-five-year term, echoing the colonial legacy of issuing leases for the life of a coconut tree. The main legal mechanism used for subdivision during the land rush was the Strata Titles Act 2000 (Cap 266), which allowed for the subdivision of customary land based on government approval of a strata title plan, thereby bypassing requirements of custom-owner consent for a subdivision to occur.[1] Of the 13,815 leases in Vanuatu, 5,420 (or 40 percent) are residential subdivisions, with most subdivided land being located on Efate Island.

The transformation of customary estates into property is often entangled with processes of state formation. Ministers of lands have been pivotal actors in facilitating the land rush in Vanuatu, with the overwhelming majority of leases signed by ministers of lands located on Efate Island. In the thirty-year period from 1980 to 2010, of the 6,803 leases over customary land that have been granted, 21.4 percent, or 1,458, were signed by a minister as lessor. These figures, however, probably underestimate the proportion of leases granted by successive ministers of lands, as statistics for approximately 29 percent of the leases registered in Vanuatu do not name the lessor (Scott and others 2012, 7–8). However, this is likely an underestimate, as approximately 29 percent do not name the lessor. If we assume that the lessor in these cases was the minister of lands, then that would mean the minister acted as lessor on just under half of all leases during that period. The other half of leases over customary land were signed by "custom owners." For the remaining leases, the minister of lands truncated negotiations between local custom owners and investors by signing on behalf of the custom owners and consenting to the leases.

At the land rush's peak in 2004, the minister of lands signed just under 250 leases in one year over customary land (figure 0.1). Lease data for Vanuatu indicates that successive ministers of lands have repeatedly leased customary land without the consent of custom-owner groups. Numerous court cases and ombudsman decisions have demonstrated that successive ministers of lands have abused their powers by leasing customary and urban state land so as to grant land to themselves and to close family members, kin, *wantoks,* political associates, and close business associates (McDonnell 2017).[2]

In Vanuatu, political alliances are often formed around a coterie of individuals with shared interests, frequently at the behest of local or foreign-based investors with deep ties to the offshore financial sector. The windfall profits that can be made by investors from property transactions mean that investors are willing to make often generous illicit payments to state actors who help facilitate property transactions over customary and state land. The extension of state power over customary land is expedited through a "shadow state" network of national and international actors managing illicit flows of funds through the global offshore financial sector into local political networks. Shadow state networks also dominate ministerial leasing of state land. Further, development, planning, and environmental regulation are regularly subverted through alliances of investors with politicians.

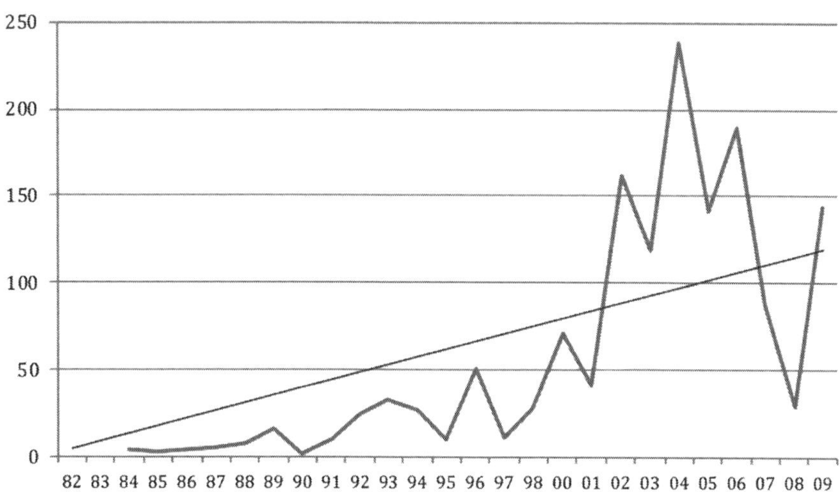

FIGURE 0.1. Number of rural leases signed by the minister of lands, 1980–2009. Reproduced, with permission, from Scott and others 2012, 7–8.

The rush to lease land in Vanuatu is part of a broader resource complex that encompasses the global world of offshore finance and money laundering. Offshore financial centers are tax-haven jurisdictions that are designed to accept deposit and investment funds to "to allow foreigners to minimise taxes, regulation, loss of assets, unwanted financial disclosure and forced disposition of property" (Van Fossen 2012, 341). Many Pacific Island states have used their postcolonial sovereignty to create and maintain tax havens. The most successful have elaborate legal structures that allow for the unregulated movement of foreign capital by maintaining the rights of private property holders and creating elaborate global financial networks of linkages to other tax-haven status countries (Van Fossen 2012, 11, 341).

Investors in the offshore financial sector remain extremely influential in the governance of Vanuatu. Any encroachment on the jurisdiction of the sovereignty of the tax-haven country has the potential to undermine the offshore financial sector, and investors regularly use their political influence to maintain the facade of sovereignty. Vanuatu's offshore financial sector, and the European Bank in particular, has long been linked with money laundering, "capital flight," and low levels of regulatory supervision of financial transactions (Van Fossen 2012). Accusations of money being laundered through Vanuatu continue, and in the last decade, the offshore financial sector has been linked to arms trading, drug dealers, and terrorism. Since 2005, Geoffrey Taylor, formerly the vice president of Tom Bayer's European Bank (1997–2007), has run the Vanuatu-based GT group of companies. The GT Group previously registered around 2,500 offshore shell companies linked to a network of clients spanning from the United States (US), the Caribbean, Russia, Ukraine, Cyprus, Hong Kong, Latvia, and Romania to the Seychelles (McGarry 2016; Ryle 2011). In 2009, a company registered by the GT Group, SP Trading Limited, was involved in smuggling thirty-five tons of North Korean weapons. The GT Group has also been associated with the proceeds of an A$245 million Russian tax fraud, involving the death of five people, and the laundering of A$479 billion from Mexican drug cartels (Field 2011).[3]

Pressure placed on Vanuatu's tax haven by Australia, the United States, and the Organisation for Economic Cooperation and Development led Tom Bayer, president of the European Bank and a key figure in the offshore financial sector, to conclude that business in Vanuatu was becoming increasingly "difficult," so much so that he had been forced since the mid-2000s to relocate many of his financial interests to Singapore, Shanghai, and Hong Kong (*Sydney Morning Herald*, 9 Sept 2006).

The entwined nature of land speculation and offshore financial dealings means that many politically influential investors in Vanuatu have links to the offshore financial sector and are involved in speculative land dealings. Evidence, such as that tendered in the infamous "Bribery case" that resulted in the jailing of fourteen members of Parliament for accepting individual payments of around VT 1 million, shows the ways that land dealings are used to transfer funds (*Kalosil v Republic of Vanuatu* [2017] VUCA 9; Civil Appeal Case 3797 of 2016, 7 April 2017).[4] During the trial, evidence was presented showing that the funds had entered Vanuatu from Hong Kong on 21 October 2014 and were deposited with the Westpac Bank of the Pacific International Trust Company (Pitco), with a sole sale of shares from the European Bank signed by Bayer. VT 35 million was then transferred from Pitco to Moana Kalosil's Australia and New Zealand Banking Group (ANZ) account. At the time Kalosil was leader of the Green Confederation and was trying to build support for a motion of no confidence in Joe Natuman's government. The funds were then transferred, based on an "Option Agreement" dated 27 October 2014, "for the sale and purchase of a leasehold property between Mr Kalosil's wife Mare Louise Miller and Pitco. The agreement was signed for Pitco by Mr Bayer. VT 35 million was paid for an option to purchase the leasehold title for a total end purchase price for VT 315 million. There were valuations produced showing the value of the leasehold title to be much less than the stated price" (*Kalosil v Republic of Vanuatu* [2017] VUCA 9; Civil Appeal Case 3797 of 2016, 7 April 2017). A few days later, Kalosil sent a letter to ANZ instructing it to make payments of VT 1 million to various people. On 18 November, a motion of no confidence in Natuman's government was submitted to Parliament, signed by the very same people who had received the VT 1 million payments.

The establishment of tax havens across Oceanic countries post-independence has meant that offshore financial sector interests have been inherent in the emergence of newly formed nation-states. The impact of this has increased the power of transnational corporations and enhanced the power of certain high-wealth individuals in the operation and affairs of the state. In Vanuatu, this has resulted in the emergence of a set of investors whose interests in land and sovereignty are neocolonial in design and who at certain times, and depending on political vagaries, exert a high degree of influence over the operation of the state. The political influence of these investors is particularly apparent in debates around land laws and land reform, as well as issues related to the regulation of Vanuatu's tax-haven status, citizenship, and flags of convenience.

Property at the Frontier of Desire

The market for land as a commodity is premised on being able to establish and maintain property rights. To hold a property right in land is to hold a right to use or access a benefit in the land. Property rights, as they exist both in custom law and in formal state regulatory arrangements, are therefore relational. Exercised against the rights of others, they include the right to exclude, to use, and to transfer rights to property (Blomley 2003, 121). Property rights are rights expressed by people in relation to others, rather than rights merely expressed in relation to claims to "things." Accordingly, property is expressed as a series of relations among social actors to an object of value such as land, a house, or a boat (von Benda-Beckmann, von Benda-Beckmann, and Wiber 2006). Throughout this book, the concept of land as property is held in tension with Indigenous understandings of the imbricated relationship between people and place.

Land transformation processes in Vanuatu are closer to what Karl Marx described as the process of "primitive accumulation" (1887), in contrast to other Melanesian countries' experiences of resource capitalism organized around the exploitation of a particular commodity. Marx's discussion of primitive accumulation involves enclosure legitimated by the concept of private property. David Harvey summarized Marx's description of primitive accumulation as "taking land, say, enclosing it, and expelling a resident population to create a landless proletariat, and then releasing the land into the privatized mainstream of capital accumulation" (2003, 145–146). Possession of private property enables producers to become entrepreneurs, whereas people who are excluded from access to private property become wage laborers (Marx 1887, 667–669).

In her own research on capitalist processes, Anna Tsing described how wealth is created through processes of alienation and the ability to ensure people and things "stand alone," removed from their entanglements (2015, 5). What is missing from Tsing's discussion of alienation is the concept of property. Historically, two distinct processes are integral to the capitalist alienation of people from land: commodification and individualization. Vanuatu's land transformation was driven by the legal arrangements attached to the ownership of property that enabled the individualization and commodification of customary land. By focusing on the processes of capitalist expansion, as described by Marx's "primitive accumulation," it becomes apparent that land transformations in Vanuatu operate on a resource frontier.

Frontiers are spaces of potential (Li 2014); they map processes of transformation and contain sites of desire. Throughout this book, the "frontier" of land transformation is discussed as both conceptual and real boundaries that reorder space and power. At the frontier of desire, new meanings are transposed onto landscapes. Frontiers are created by both technology and imagination and entail the plotting of a series of sites. Frontiers are instrumental in marking both the edge of regulation and also the supposed "wilderness" that stretches beyond the frontier (Li 2014, 592; Tsing 2000). Tsing wrote that frontiers operate at the edge of space and time as "a zone of not yet—not yet mapped, 'not yet' regulated" (2003, 5100). The map of Efate Island shows the tapestry of dark gray leases that mark the frontier of the transformation of customary land into property (see map 0.1).

The material transformation of the customary landscape through leasing can be understood only by considering both the idea of land as "property" and the protection by the state of property rights. In broad terms, the frontier of land control functions so that the access of Indigenous people to the land is restricted or excluded. Nancy Peluso and Christian Lund wrote that "new frontiers of land control are being actively created, through struggles involving varied actors, contexts, and dynamics.... They are sites where authorities, sovereignties, and hegemonies of the recent past have been or are currently being challenged by new enclosures, territorializations, and property regimes" (2011, 668). From the year 2000 onward, the speculative profits that could be made from land dealings, and then transferred following circuitous routes through various offshore bank accounts, marked the physical landscape as a new site of "discovery," an empty landscape awaiting possession (McDonnell 2018).

In material terms, the frontier is mapped by spatial markers of possession: real estate signs, walls, gates, fences, and signs to prevent trespass. Materially, the frontier functions as the territorial boundary of property and state formation. Inside the frontier, land is converted into property, mapped, marked, and regulated by the state. Outside the frontier lie customary landscapes, mapped and marked as *kastom* places that remain beyond the ambit of the state and managed under local authority structures. The cadastral mapping of place allows for land to be "seen" by the state (Scott 1998). Maps clearly delineate the frontier of property and state formation, the marked and surveyed patchwork of leases that hug the coastline of Efate Island. They are an increasing presence in the interior of the island. Beyond this encroaching frontier, landscapes continue to be governed under customary arrangements.

Before the landscape becomes commodified, it must first be saturated with desire. The *frontier of desire* for customary land emerges at the intersections of global capital, the idea of empty territory filled with foreign imaginings, and local demands for modernity and cash. Building from Tsing's work on frontiers, this book poses a number of questions. What are the processes by which a named and narrated embodied landscape becomes refashioned as property available for purchase? At the frontier of desire, who are the actors engaged in purchasing and selling leases? Why are Indigenous people actively involved in the rush to lease the landscapes so central to place, identity, and *kastom*? These questions can only be addressed by deep ethnographic research undertaken over many years and complemented with detailed legal research into the actual lease instruments. This book presents a localized study of capitalist processes—one that offers insights into both actual contract making and documentation and the individuals involved in this convergence of desire.

Gendered Performances of Property

Staying with the trouble of capitalist relations requires that we consider both the inequalities of capitalist processes and the effect these processes have on social relations and, in particular, gendered relations. In their 2015 feminist manifesto, Laura Bear, Karen Ho, Anna Tsing, and Sylvia Yanagisako argued for generative approaches to the study of capitalism that ask that, rather than assuming the economy is structured by a specific set of power relations, we consider the "fragile and intimate" contradictions that are present in localized studies of capitalist processes. Following this manifesto, our deep dive into capitalist relations must consider not only the formal procedures of capitalism, such as contract making and documentation, but also the informal aspects that shape the "performances of personhood" (Bear and others 2015, 1). Beginning with this understanding, this book adopts a feminist anthropological approach to consider some of the contradictions associated with late capitalism in Oceania—namely, how performances of property are gendered and enable the emergence of particular models of personhood.

Capitalism is not a linear process. It is rather more fragile and heterogeneous; capitalist relations are different depending on how people are positioned in relation to power (Bear and others 2015, 1). Li asked that we view capitalism not as a singular global force but rather as a series of localized entanglements held in tension with concepts of "Indigeneity" and "dispossession" (2010, 410). In Oceania, this tension takes a particular legal form, as the concept of indigeneity bound to land is recognized in property law as "landownership." Landowners have become increasingly central to the political discourse in Papua New Guinea, Solomon Islands, Vanuatu, and East Timor around law, customary land, and resource extraction. In Vanuatu, making a claim as a custom landowner is mobilized to establish the property rights associated with exclusive possession. These include the individualized right to lease land and to access the benefits or rental streams associated with leasing land—ideas I explore at length in this book. Concepts of landownership intersect with local leadership and authority in profound ways that influence land transactions throughout the archipelago. Across Melanesia, negotiations over what is "customary" function as responses to both the expansion of state formation and specific claims to resources by powerful Indigenous actors. Ultimately these negotiations have the potential to be socially transformative in that they change relational connections between people and place. Precisely because land is socially constructed and holds particular meanings, it is important to consider how property is performed. By this I mean not only who is enfranchised to perform property but also who is excluded and dispossessed from landscapes and how these processes are gendered.

Across Oceania, consideration of the localized performances of personhood in late capitalism requires attention to the ways that formal legal identities actively structure agency in processes of dispossession. Here I am building from Paige West's idea of the imbricated processes of dispossession and personhood:

> What emerges with processes of dispossession, both original and continuing ones, is not simply a new set of economic formations or structures. Nor is it just a new

> set of images that go along with the commodity economy. What emerges is a "new Symbolic order" and, connected to it, new modes of being, living, making, and knowing the world. . . . This process is constant and relentless. (2016, 27)

It is also a process that defines the performance of property, thereby redefining social relationships, and privileges certain masculinities over others. The ideology of custom landownership intersects with the agency of local actors and elicits a new model of personhood: a possessive individual property owner that I term a "master of modernity." Contrary to theories that posit binary models of personhood, the agency of the masters of modernity is actively contoured by the specific legal identity of "custom owner," as well as contested claims against rivals and the desire to assert personal authority over landscapes and people. To maintain their status within the village, masters of modernity must enact both individualized and relational personhood.

Following from the practice of activist scholarship, as well as a commitment to decolonial methodology, in chapter 1 I explain how this book is written out of a body of work that provided practical assistance to individuals, communities, and agencies. This has included writing land law; running land cases and legal clinics; providing free legal advice on land issues to Indigenous people and groups across Vanuatu; and working as a legal adviser in the Vanuatu Cultural Centre, to several of Vanuatu's attorneys general, and to the minister of lands. Politically engaged anthropology, as both an ethnographic method and practice, seeks to address social justice issues such as Indigenous dispossession. In this way, it offers an answer to the challenge posed to the discipline that it must contribute to material transformation or burn.

In chapter 2, I explore the *kastom* narratives that remain influential in the Lelepa people's construction of *ples,* including the idiom of customary land as a *saloa,* a wooden plate representing shared access and use rights to land, as well as the central ancestral figure of Chief Roi Mata. Lelepa people understand that the land is alive, replete with ancestral spirits who continue to inhabit place and who imbue the land with agency. These narratives are juxtaposed, woven against, the enduring colonial legal legacy that pervades the Oceanic region—the idea of land as property. Across Oceania, various colonial powers viewed Indigenous people's forested landscapes as largely empty or unused wastelands and proceeded to assert claims to the landscapes, turning them into agricultural plantations while also engaging in missionary projects designed to "save" local populations.

The local, particular practices of colonization in the New Hebrides are explored in chapter 3 with reference to land dealings and the "performance of property." Land titles made during the early colonial land rush in the New Hebrides became the basis for British and French claims of sovereignty across the archipelago. Often these colonial titles were entered into in dubious circumstances, with even contemporary commentators calling into question the tactics of title making by various colonial administrations. Despite a strong statement of Indigenous landownership in perpetuity in the Vanuatu Constitution at independence, the Anglo-Australian model of property and Torrens Title registration endures in the Vanuatu legal system, as elsewhere in Oceania, suggesting that postcolonial legal arrangements are informed by colonial legacies.

The legal identity attached to claiming land in Vanuatu, and to resource extraction elsewhere in Melanesia, is that of "landowner." In chapter 4, I explain how this identity centers on a foundational contradiction between the rights established in the *kastom* system—based on reciprocal and relational models of sociality and personhood representing overlapping claims to place—and those afforded by property as individualized rights over land. Landowners are central to political discourse. Across Melanesia, negotiations over what is "customary" function as a response to the expansion of state formation and Indigenous claims to resources. Increasingly the "ideology of landownership" intersects with the agency of local men and elicits a new model of personhood—a possessive individual property owner (Filer 2006, 68). In Vanuatu, this is also further complicated by the role of chiefs as the authors and arbiters of *kastom*.

Chapter 5 is about the way that frontiers locate sites of desire. A crucial element in the commodification of land is "the set of practices, relations and discourses that endow it with utility, value and price" (Li 2012, 6), which I describe in this book as *desire*. Transacting customary land is an exchange that takes place at the frontier of desire—a foreign desire to possess land and a local desire to lease land for cash. The process of rendering Indigenous landscapes as real estate—the picturing of land as empty and in need of possession—becomes central to the elicitation of foreign desire for customary land. The allure of the North Efate landscape is informed by specific narratives: "survivors" seeking a "last frontier"; real estate investors wanting to purchase and sell "paradise"; and conservationists inscribing the landscape as "World Heritage." Together these foreign imaginings have cultivated a landscape saturated with desire—desire made manifest in the rush to lease land.

Discussion among Lelepa people contrasts the acts of self-centered men who engage in leasing thinking only of themselves (*mi-nomo*) with the emplaced, relational agency of a *man-Lelepa* who acknowledges his obligations to the broader kinship group. In chapter 6, these discussions demonstrate how individual agency is held in tension with relational obligations. They highlight the dual models of personhood—relational and individual—that coexist in Lelepa people's expressions of agency. Using detailed ethnographic research, I argue that acts of leasing are better understood not as market transactions but as claims to personal authority in the landscape against the authority of rival men. The effect of investor demand for customary land has been to create new domains of agency that allow new sites for the production of masculine authority. In this process, a new masculine identity associated with land leasing has become entrenched—that of a master of modernity.

In chapter 7, I explain the ways in which performances of leasing land and the stages on which lease negotiations take place are starkly gendered. Discussions across Oceania often highlight the exclusion of women from decision-making around land leasing and natural resource management. This is not, however, the whole story. Sometimes, some women are able to speak about land. Women in Vanuatu offer complex and nuanced understandings about the operation of women's rights over land, demonstrating "vernacular" translated, local meanings of "rights." To be meaningful to women themselves, discussion of women's land rights in Oceania must be grounded in an understanding of local relational identities, power relationships, decision-making, and the gendered exercise of property rights and local authority over landscapes. Importantly, and perhaps to the surprise of some of the international nongovernmental organizations working on gender in the Pacific, these vernacular ideas of *raets* (rights) do not equate with Western, liberal claims to equality that inform discourses around individualized human rights.

"The Land Will Eat You"

Critiques of the performance of property by masters of modernity remind us that land transformations are never simply about land; they are integral to relational social kinship patterns and embedded in identity. They also speak to deep ontological understandings of the "ways of *ples*" as the correct ways of practicing *kastom.* Returning to Tsing's idea that the alienation of people and things—the ability to make things "stand alone," removed from relational social kinship—is central to the process of contemporary capitalism, we can see the impact of property in creating capitalist relations. Property is able to strip people from place to remake Indigenous landscapes. In effect, property is the tool by which foreigners can reassert neocolonial relations over Indigenous landscapes. Property enables dispossession.

One of the many contradictions that emerge in our deep dive into the capitalist processes associated with land transformations in Vanuatu is that the powerful men who lease customary land as masters of modernity must then reassert their relational status or risk retribution. Discussion of acts of sorcery and critiques by young men, women, and other community members all highlight the discontent associated with land dealings that are held not to have followed proper *kastom* practice. The ultimate critique is echoed in the curse aimed at men who have leased land that does not rightfully belong to them in *kastom.* Where landscapes are animated by ancestral beings, these men are told, "The land will eat you."

Chapter 1

Reciprocity as a Fugitive Anthropologist

In 2008, heavily pregnant and with proposal in hand, I walked the corridors of the mazelike Coombs building at The Australian National University to meet with potential supervisors in the hope of beginning a doctorate on land issues in either Papua New Guinea or Vanuatu.

On paper, my academic and policy background looked reasonably well suited to undertaking fieldwork. However, almost all the male academics that I met seemed taken aback when confronted with the physical presence of an eight-month-pregnant woman in their office. In one instance, I was the preferred candidate for a funded doctorate position in Papua New Guinea, only to have the position withdrawn at interview when I turned up pregnant and they realized that I was planning to undertake fieldwork with children. Fieldwork in the PNG Highlands with children, I was told, would be impossible.

* * *

For too long the archetype associated with fieldwork in Pacific anthropology has remained the Malinowskian-style image of a lone, white male living for a year or more in a "native village" (Stocking 1992, 59). Feminist, queer, and women-of-color scholars have critiqued this tired, "masculinist rite of passage," particularly as it assumes "an unencumbered male subject with racial privilege, to whom the field means a space far from home that can be easily entered and exited" (Berry and others 2017, 538–539). Many of us who engage in ethnographic fieldwork are not alone, or, for that matter, men. Even for those who are men, many seek long-enduring relationships in ways that belie a simplistic and narrow idea of the field or that complicate some of the power asymmetries often embedded in research. In challenging the violence of fieldwork and the academic hetero-patriarchal culture that sustains it, Maya Berry, Claudia Argüelles, Shanya Cordis, Sarah Ihmoud, and Elizabeth Estrada described fugitive anthropology as a critical transnational feminist practice, "grounded in black feminist analysis and praxis and inspired by Indigenous decolonial thinking" (Berry and others 2017, 560). Beginning with these perspectives, I explore my own style of fugitive anthropology, with its attention to an embodied pedagogy and its focus on issues of activist anthropology, through a critical examination of gendered and race positionalities.

Decolonial methodology requires that, as scholars working alongside Indigenous people, we are attentive to the imperialistic legacies of research and the centrality of anthropology to the colonial project. Māori scholar Linda Tuhiwai Smith described how research, "one of the dirtiest words in the indigenous world's vocabulary," has been inextricably linked to the practice of European imperialism, "implicated in the worst excesses of colonialism" (1999, 1). Many Indigenous scholars have critiqued the practice of extractive research that claims expertise about Indigenous peoples and that appropriates Indigenous knowledge. The role of research in the colonization of Indigenous peoples, as referred to by Smith, is, in part, the violence associated with representation. Research has the capacity to homogenize Indigenous experiences, to misrepresent Indigenous people "via generalization, misunderstanding, or distortion of knowledge, social meanings" (Nakata and others 2012, 128).

Indigenous scholars have critiqued not only the past practice of anthropology but also anthropologists' continued attempts to define and represent Indigenous people. Mohawk scholar Audra Simpson wrote of the ongoing colonization of Indigenous people through the discipline of anthropology: "To speak of Indigeneity is to speak of colonialism and anthropology, as these are means through which Indigenous people have been known and sometimes are still known. In different moments, anthropology has imagined itself to be a voice, and in some disciplinary iterations, *the* voice of the colonised" (2007, 67). Here Simpson's critique of anthropology is that as a discipline it speaks *for* Indigenous people.

Claims of Indigenous knowledge are rendered "valuable" by the state when they are attached to particular property rights, creating a role for anthropologists as the "ventriloquists" for Indigenous people (Tuck and Yang 2014a, 225). Waanyi novelist and scholar Alexis Wright challenged the role of lawyers and anthropologists who produce research in contexts that privilege the voices of professionals over those of Indigenous people. She wrote, "In other key areas of the Aboriginal world we have been forced to develop a dependency on professional people to argue on our behalf. Think of the bandwagon of academics writing and giving advice on Aboriginal issues, or the lawyers, anthropologists, historians, scientists, economists, accountants, doctors, health professionals, consultants and administrators who have been employed to give advice, persuade with their skills, knowledge, values and influence, and so have helped to reshape the Aboriginal story. But what is the Aboriginal story becoming, if other people are telling it for us?" (Wright 2016). Here Wright, herself a consummate, prize-winning author, cautioned against the overdependence by Aboriginal people on the professionals that pervade the Indigenous sector. She, like Simpson, argued that it is important who is telling the story and, equally, whose voice is being displaced.

Anthropology as a discipline can produce knowledge that renders Indigenous bodies visible, categorized, and knowable within the teleology of governmentality, while also effectively silencing Indigenous people themselves. Simpson argued that anthropology disciplines Indigenous bodies through both the production of knowledge and the modalities of the discipline and involves "categorisation, ethnological comparison, linguistic translation and ethnography" (2007, 67). Riffing off Simpson, Metis anthropologist Zoe Todd critiqued the way anthropology defines Indigenous people: "What I learn from Simpson's work, and from my own informal ethnographic study of the discipline, is that to speak of Indigeneity within anthropology is to navigate erasure of Indigenous agency, sovereignty, and self-determination (in all of their pluralities and complexities)—and to confront disciplinary conventions that frame Indigenous peoples in very specific ways. Ways that pose us alternately as cherished, noble informants (outside the academy), or nasty and brutish *problems* (within the discipline)" (2018, 6). The challenge posed by Todd to anthropology is to allow space for Indigenous agency, in all its diverse and plural forms, including within the discipline itself.

Recent work by feminist, queer, Indigenous, Black, and people-of-color scholars challenge both the research practices previously seen as central to anthropology and its disciplinary foundations (Allen and Jobson 2016; Beliso-De Jesus and Pierre 2020; Brodkin, Morgen, and Hutchinson 2011; Jobson 2020; Shange 2020; Todd 2016; Uperesa 2016; Welcome 2020). As a settler, non-Indigenous, cisgender scholar who is also a woman of color with Afro-Caribbean ancestry, I am concerned with how non-Indigenous scholars engage in ethical research with Indigenous people to attend to the asymmetries of power between the researcher and collaborators and remain conscious of the politics of representation. I am aware of the capacity of professional, anthropological voices of supposed expertise to displace those of Indigenous peoples, as critiqued by Wright. I am conscious of Todd's critiques that anthropology must offer ethnography that moves beyond simplistic stereotypes of Indigenous as "other"; that it must focus on Indigenous epistemological frames; and that as a discipline it must work to enable the participation of Indigenous scholars so as to challenge the elite "white public space" of the discipline (Todd 2018, 7; Brodkin, Morgen, and Hutchinson 2011; Kawa and others 2019). These are themes that I explore by reflecting on my own practices.

The Winding Pathway of Politically Engaged Research

Central to the practice of fugitive anthropology is the search for new pathways toward undertaking politically engaged research (Berry and others 2017, 539). This chapter is designed to extend the understanding of politically engaged anthropology as both ethnographic method and practice. Engaged anthropology is described as the practice of using anthropology "for constructive intervention in politics" so as to make anthropology "relevant and useful" (Kirsch 2018, 1). In practicing engaged anthropology, I have been a participant, alongside Indigenous collaborators, and directed by Indigenous leaders and groups in ways that transcend the increasingly outdated idea that anthropologists are simply engaged in observation (Low and Merry 2010, S212). Engaged anthropology seeks to address social justice concerns, such as structural violence or environmental degradation, that "are often rooted in colonial history and exacerbated by globalization and contemporary forms of capitalism" (Kirsch 2018, 3).

Engaged or activist anthropologists have often worked as participants in political movements or alongside political leaders of movements (Graeber 2009; Kirksey 2012; Powell 2018; Sawyer 2002; Speed 2007) and as experts in legal cases, including environmental cases (Bell 2002; Kirsch 2018, 2002). Engaged anthropology also considers a role for the anthropologist in promoting legislative reform (Fiske 2009). However, there is no discussion within the literature of politically engaged anthropologists instrumentally writing laws or running legal cases.

For many anthropologists, this is well beyond what they would consider standard practice, and at times I feel like a fugitive within the discipline, trying to contribute to projects to effect the material transformations so eloquently argued for by Leniqueca Welcome and others (Beliso-De Jesús and Pierre 2020; Jobson 2020; Shange 2020; Todd 2016; Uperesa 2016; Welcome 2020).

Anthropology as a discipline has not always looked kindly on the practice of activist or applied scholarship, suggesting it lacks objectivity or leads to thin ethnography because it relies too heavily on descriptions of heroes and villains (Hale 2006, 101; Kirsch 2018, 10). Anthropologists have long questioned the role of researcher as a disembodied "observer" of communities, as brilliantly articulated by Kirin Narayan (1993; see also Graeber 2009; Mosse 2005, 2015). In Vanuatu, the positionality of the researcher was redefined by Lissant Bolton in her work on Ambae as "participant engagement" (2003). In spite of these reflections, the practice of engaged fugitive anthropology challenges and complicates the practice of ethnography and extends the responsibilities and accountability of the researcher far beyond the boundaries anticipated within the academy or imagined by university ethics committees.

Returning to the opening vignette, my research has always necessarily been informed by an embodied pedagogy. As mother of a one year old and pregnant with my second child, my major concern in undertaking a doctorate was how I would complete the extended ethnographic fieldwork needed to understand land issues. With small, dependent children, traveling for an extended period was impossible. The solution, proposed by Chris Ballard, was that I undertake a year of volunteer work on land issues around Chief Roi Mata's Domain World Heritage site in North Efate. Formal fieldwork research could happen in the second year after the volunteer position was completed; in practice, these lines became blurred.

Indigenous scholars are increasingly articulating a decolonial approach that requires research to be undertaken *for* and *alongside* Indigenous people, to be of demonstrable benefit to Indigenous people by prioritizing their needs and interests, and to promote self-determination (Moreton-Robinson 2013; Rigney 1999; Smith 1999). Decolonial methodology demands that researchers privilege "indigenous knowledges, voices and experiences" (Smith 2005, 87; Nakata and others 2012). The practice of decolonial research involves a commitment to the principles of Indigenous self-determination and to the centrality of land to Indigenous peoples. Eve Tuck and K Wayne Tang argued that "decolonization specifically requires the repatriation of Indigenous land and life" (2012, 21). The importance of a politically engaged approach has been highlighted repeatedly by Indigenous scholars. For many Indigenous communities, ethnographic research may not always be the intervention that is needed (Tuck and Yang 2014a, 236), and Indigenous people often may request other forms of engagement. In Vanuatu, my volunteer position involved "land use planning" assistance. However, it soon became clear that community members and chiefs needed access to legal advice on land laws so as to better inform decisions around lease making. I was introduced by the previous volunteer as a lawyer who had come to help with land issues. This framed the understanding of my position both within the villages and in the Vanuatu Cultural Centre where the position was based. More than a year into my appointment and following the death of my close collaborator and fieldworker, Douglas Kalotiti, I began formal ethnographic research, such as conducting the recorded interviews that are the basis of the ethnographic sections of this book.

In Vanuatu, Ralph Regenvanu, in his former role as director of the Vanuatu Cultural Centre, repeatedly advocated for a decolonial approach to research centered on collaboration that included training for local ni-Vanuatu, researchers doing something of benefit for the community, and researchers providing copies of all research publications to those being researched. Regenvanu has critiqued poor research practice by arguing that "often the research that we do, that takes place in universities and academic institutions . . . does not really benefit the people of Vanuatu. Why? Because many people in Vanuatu can't read up to the standard that you use in your writing. And often researchers come into communities and take information; but it is important that they [the communities] understand that something comes back to them too." Regenvanu's idea of decolonial practice is structured around the reciprocal flow of benefits from researcher to the community, in exchange for access to the knowledge and time of the researched community, "because it is the way of our *kastom*—when you give something, there must be something that comes back" (R Regenvanu 2011, 130; see also McDonnell and Regenvanu 2022, 243). Conscious of these reciprocal flows, and the need to respond to requests, in my first years in Vanuatu my work was regularly directed by the Vanuatu Cultural Centre director and board, by my close research collaborators, or by chiefs, community groups, or family groups or was undertaken in response to specific individual requests. In practical terms, this work consisted of providing legal advice through mobile legal clinics, running legal advice workshops for villages and within the Vanuatu Cultural Centre and other organizations, collecting data and recording *tabu* (sacred) sites on Efate Island, providing legal advice and assistance to the Vanuatu Cultural Centre (including on significant matters related to the World Heritage site and various ongoing court cases), and engaging in legal work so as to break a number of leases for Indigenous landowners around the North Efate region.

To better explain the nature of my work in Vanuatu, I offer this journal entry from 2011:

> I arrive at the cultural center at my usual time of 8:30 am. . . . . Around mid-morning I get up and walk downstairs. Marcellin Ambong [then director of the Vanuatu Cultural Centre] sees me, he sees that I am in formal clothes, and asks: "What are you doing today?"
>
> I reply that "I am going with a Lelepa landowner to meet an investor and break his lease." . . . We talk for a while, Marcellin wants to know the details of the lease: where is the land, how much money will be exchanged, and how I know that I can break the lease. The idea that it is even possible to break a lease is met with a kind of quizzical exasperation. Most ni-Vanuatu don't believe me when I tell them that it can be done. Experience has taught them otherwise. They believe that I think it is possible, but they think that I haven't been in Vanuatu long enough to understand how things really work. . . .
>
> . . . Finally, Marcellin says, "It's not alright, you can't go." He explains that it is dangerous, that I am a woman, that I am young. He finishes by saying, "This is the XXX family, these are powerful people." He is resolved that I need protection and so we head to the desk of the large, burly Vanuatu Cultural Centre staff member Aminio David, who readily agrees to accompany me and the Lelepa landowner to the meeting. . . .
>
> . . . Later that day we arrive at the XXX family construction business compound. As we pull up in the truck, a number of dogs come to meet us. A few ni-Vanuatu staff are sitting outside the compound, which is full of building materials.
>
> We walk into the office, following the Lelepa man, who has clearly been here before. [The man] sitting behind the desk smiles and greets the landowner, then he sees me and Aminio and sits down again. The entire bearing of the Lelepa man changes. He removes his cap as we enter the office and moves to stand slightly behind me in the small office; his shoulders are hunched in a show of deference and respect towards the man sitting behind the desk.
>
> "What can I do for you?" the man behind his desk asks the Lelepa man.
>
> There is silence; tension blankets the room. The Lelepa landowner looks towards me; it is my turn to play the lawyer. I draw myself up to full height and pull out a folder with the lease instrument from my bag. In my most formal voice, I say, "We are here to break the lease." A look of surprise crosses the face of the man behind the desk. . . . [This was a loan instrument for which valuable *Survivor* beach land in North Efate was provided as collateral, with a lease to be entered into. The

> estimated value of the land was around US$200,000 and the value of the loan was US$1,500. If the loan could not be repaid, the Lelepa man would lose the land.]
>
> When the negotiations are completed, and the loan and lease broken, we are ready to leave. The man behind the desk turns to the Lelepa man and says, "You will be back." And then to me, in a patronizing voice, almost like explaining something to a child, "He will be back, next time he needs money for a court case, or his truck needs repairs, he will be back."[1]

Beginning with this account, I offer a description of my own fugitive-engaged anthropology as informed by my embodied experience, attention to positionality, issues of power and representation, and understandings of decolonial methodology. It is a path replete with the potholes and roadblocks associated with doing applied, politically engaged work. It is the path that I have chosen to walk alongside and at the request of long-term Indigenous collaborators.

Performing Research

The practices of both fugitive anthropology and decolonial methodology require careful attention to the power asymmetries in the conduct of research, as well as to reflexive practice and consideration of the privilege and position between researcher and those people and places being researched. Indigenous Australian scholar Aileen Moreton-Robinson critiqued the "God trick" through which the author makes a disembodied view of a subject. She argued that research is informed by the "standpoint" of the researcher—how "race, class, colonisation, culture, ableness and sexuality" shape the experience of the researcher and therefore the production of knowledge (Moreton-Robinson 2013, 339). Manulani Aluli Meyer entreated researchers to understand their own positionality as a central component of engaging in research: "Knowing that you are unique at this basic level will bring a keen understanding of the nuance of your own subjectivity. Begin to name it at this stage and write sharply about its impact in how you know and experience the world. . . . Your relationship to your research topic is your own. It springs from a lifetime of distinctness and uniqueness only you have history with. Be encouraged by this!" (2014, 223). Beginning with positionality brings accountability to the research and frees the researcher from having to tell the whole story (as if this were ever possible) by explicitly acknowledging how claims of knowledge are framed by subjective experience.

Research is an embodied performance. As researchers we move through a performance of multiple identities that often stretch across time and place. In Vanuatu, I have been, and continue to be, Siobhan, Toto Fakalé, *lawya blong yumi,* legal adviser to the minister of lands, Vanuatu Cultural Centre lawyer, madame, mother, sista, girl. Arriving in Vanuatu as a mother and a wife made my position as a foreign woman more culturally understandable than it would have been had I arrived alone. My identity in North Efate has always been linked to my husband, Laurence Wilson, and our children, Will and Flynn (figure 1.1). Nonetheless, my personal and working life in Vanuatu has included incidents of sexual harassment and attempted sexual violence, particularly from men who have viewed me as a "foreign woman" without knowing the context of my relationships with communities and people in Vanuatu or my status as a mother and wife. By contrast, I have always been treated with care and respect by Lelepa people and colleagues in the Vanuatu Cultural Centre, the University of the South Pacific, and the Ministry of Lands.

Across Vanuatu there are discussions about foreign women in which their inappropriate dress often signals to locals (men and women) their supposed immorality and sexual lasciviousness. Like Maggie Cummings (2013), I have repeatedly heard ni-Vanuatu critique the immodesty of young foreign (mainly Australian) women departing from cruise ships and walking around the main streets of Port Vila in miniskirts, shorts, and bikinis. To differentiate myself, I regularly wore *aelan dres* (island dress) to work at the Vanuatu Cultural Centre, on Lelepa Island, and in Mangaliliu, especially for the first two years. Later, working in the Ministry of Lands, I switched to more formal office attire. My ability to swap clothing, to change dress and location, to move easily in and

FIGURE 1.1. Our family in Vanuatu, 30 March 2013. *Left to right*: Laurence Wilson, Flynn McDonnell-Wilson, Siobhan McDonnell, and Will McDonnell-Wilson. Photo by Angela Whibly-Smith.

out of various "fields" as sites of work and research speaks to my "in-between" identity: in between the prescriptive categories of appropriate gendered behavior; in between the village and town; and in between expatriate and Indigenous spaces. Identity is also informed by privilege. Being a relatively wealthy Australian woman affords me mobility. Recently, in one day I moved easily from Natapau village on Lelepa Island, to Parliament House, to the Vanuatu Cultural Centre, to the Ministry of Lands, and back again to the village. In professional and personal spaces in Vanuatu, I am regularly the only non-Indigenous person and the only woman. The account around "breaking a lease" describes an illustration of the complex embodied positionality I hold at the intersections of gender, class, and race in Vanuatu.

Lawya Blong Yumi: Practicing Engaged Anthropology

One month into my volunteer position in 2010, after two preceding trips to North Efate, I watched various men argue over whose family would adopt me. This was less about creating a relationship with me and more about wanting access to a *lawya.* These arguments concluded with my adoption by the brilliant and charismatic chief of Mangaliliu, the late Chief Kalkot Mormor, whom I affectionately knew as my Mangaliliu Papa (figure 1.2). During the adoption ceremony, mats were exchanged, slit gongs drummed, and my new name was called out to the village. As Chief Mormor called out my new name, Toto Fakalé, he explained, "This name means that you need to be the mother for all the people of this *ples.*" He paused for effect in front of a large audience, "And mama Toto Fakalé, your children, they are crying, they need land" (journal entry, Aug 2010).

What is absent from this narrative is the other local marker of identity, the fact that all foreign women who work for an extended period in North Efate and who are adopted by Chief Mormor have been given the marker Toto as a first name. Early on when local people regularly forgot my name or confused me with former volunteer women, they could easily remember that I was a Toto.

Engaged anthropology highlights the importance of collaborative research as "an extension of the commitment to reciprocity that underlies the practice of anthropology" (Kirsch 2002, 178; Low and Merry 2010, S203). The methodology of engaged anthropology aligns closely with the importance of "working together" in Vanuatu (Taylor and Thieberger 2011). A moratorium was placed on all foreign research in Vanuatu from 1985 to 1994. The lifting of the moratorium involved a new process by which researchers individually obtained a research permit. Permits were approved on the basis of collaborative engagement between foreign researchers and local communities (R Regenvanu 1999, 98). To practice engaged anthropology, in my experience, often requires a "double time" of labor undertaken in addition

FIGURE 1.2. With my Mangaliliu papa, the late Chief Mormor, being handed a *saloa* in Lelepa Village, 20 July 2012. Photo by Brigitte Laboukly. Reproduced with permission.

to the academic work of teaching, research, university service, and publishing (Scheper-Hughes 2009, 3). My ongoing work on land issues in Vanuatu regularly includes preparing case documents, writing or commenting on legislation, writing briefing papers, running land cases, and providing legal advice on land issues. This is aside from my support of Pacific climate change negotiations and my long-term engagement as a lawyer supporting the West Papuan Independence Movement.

Soon after beginning work in North Efate in 2010, I was introduced as the *lawya blong yumi* (our lawyer) at various village gatherings. As I passed through the region—by car, on foot, or in a boat—small children would sing out *"lawya, lawya"* by way of greeting. Increasingly, in the weeks after I arrived, the full implications of local expectations became apparent. In response to this demand, I ran formal *likol kliniks* (legal clinics) complete with a portable solar panel and battery to run my laptop and scan legal documents (figure 1.3).

Overwhelmingly the people who visited my *likol kliniks* were men who had leased their land and came with the expectation that I would be able to wave a magic legal wand and cancel their leases. Some grown men wept; others became extremely angry on learning the details of the legal instrument they had signed. Much-vaunted joint ventures were often "joint" in name only, with benefits from the on-sale of the lease or subdivision accruing to the investors rather than locals. Employment clauses were often carefully worded to include no real obligation to employ. Verbal promises of scholarships for children

FIGURE 1.3. Running a *likol klinik* with a local chief, Lelepa Island, 8 August 2010. Photo by Richard Matanik. Reproduced with permission.

and payment of school fees were rarely included in the actual legal text of the instrument. Very few of the Lelepa men that I dealt with had received independent legal advice on the lease before signing. This is not to suggest that local people did not express carefully considered agency in signing leases.

Overlapping identities create multiple sets of relationships, and requests for my legal advice stretched far beyond the North Efate region. An account from my journal in early 2011 reads: "Today was Sunday, and I took the kids to the beach. I paid the entrance fee to the locals and sat on a mat watching the boys play energetically. A man appeared. 'You're that lawyer,' he said, 'that lawyer from the Cultural Centre.' It was a statement rather than a question. 'Please,' he asked, 'please can you have a look at this?' He placed the lease documents in my hand. His eyes entreated me with a kind of desperation."

With no other free legal advice service in Vanuatu, customary landowners may lose their land simply because they cannot afford the legal fees of private lawyers. Years before I became legal adviser to the minister of lands, local people (legal papers in hand) would hunt for me at the Vanuatu Cultural Centre or later in my office at the University of the South Pacific. People would ask me legal questions in minibuses, in *nakamals* at kava time, and on roads or beaches.[2]

Community and adopted family, friends and colleagues, expatriates and acquaintances were all in search of legal advice on land issues. When I became the legal adviser to the minister of lands, Ralph Regenvanu, in 2013, local expatriates increasingly requested legal advice and a "helping hand" with legal processes. A journal entry from 2013 reads: "Early this morning I went into Chantilly's for a coffee to be greeted with, 'Hey love,' by an Australian investor. 'Don't suppose I could discuss some of my land problems I've got with you, could I? I'm happy to pay top dollar.' He grinned assuming an expatriate camaraderie. 'I'm sorry,' I responded, in my most officious manner. 'I couldn't. It would be a conflict of interest. Feel free to make an appointment with me at the ministry though.'"

I have yet to work for an expatriate client. However, over the years I have read hundreds of lease instruments and legal papers. Managing the blurred line between professional work and research is the tension of politically engaged anthropology.

Navigating the Politics of Land and Representation

A decolonial approach to researching land must place "Indigenous epistemological and ontological accounts of land at the centre, including Indigenous understandings of the land, Indigenous language in relation to land . . . documenting and advancing Indigenous agency and land rights" (Tuck, McKenzie, and McCoy 2014, 13). Centering accounts of Indigenous agency requires complex, nuanced, and plural accounts of the many ways that people respond to land leasing in Vanuatu. Land disputes provide forums for performance of local politics of power, authority, and identity. Land and chiefly title disputes provide the stages for fierce contestations between powerful local men. Researching land issues requires a careful approach to avoid inflaming these contestations.

Working alongside local researchers is important to avoid some of the many contestations over land issues. The Vanuatu Cultural Centre's model for collaborative research often involves pairing foreign researchers with ni-Vanuatu *filwokas* (field-workers) who are culturally expert men and women many of whom have been conducting research for years. *Filwokas* serve as cultural advisers, as mediators between researchers and communities, and as experts in relevant *kastom*. I am extremely grateful that my work has been guided by *filwokas*. In North Efate, the late Douglas Kalotiti (chairman of the Vanuatu Cultural Centre *filwokas*), Brigitte Laboukly, and Richard Matanik (chairman of the Lelema World Heritage Site and Vanuatu Cultural Centre *filwoka*) have advised me and guided my work. Other Lelepa men and women who have expertly communicated *kastom* practice and landholding arrangements include *filwoka* Leisara Kalotiti (figure 1.4) and her husband, the late Chief Kalkot Mormor. I am deeply indebted to these people for the time and energy they have put into guiding my work on land issues over many years. This research is part of a broader woven mat of life that has included many

FIGURE 1.4. At the chief's *nakamal* for a land-use planning meeting with Brigitte Laboukly and chiefs, Lelepa Island, 8 May 2012. Photo by Sophie Ford. Reproduced with permission.

years of collaborative work. I am so privileged to have walked alongside these collaborators who are also my dear friends and my adopted family.

This book is shaped by my work and research across multiple, overlapping field sites. It is informed by work on land across many of the islands in Vanuatu. In traveling with and working for Minister of Lands Regenvanu, I have heard accounts or read land files and documents relating to leasing and land issues on almost every island in Vanuatu. In this regard, I led an eighteen-month-long Vanuatu Cultural Centre *kastom gavnans* (customary governance) project in Lamap on Malekula Island. While there is a broader base to my work on land issues in Vanuatu, the ethnographic accounts of land dealings in this book are based on research undertaken on land in North Efate—work that began formally in 2010 and continues. For two and a half years, I worked on a Vanuatu Cultural Centre land-use planning project in North Efate conducting ethnographic research that involved detailed interviews. I also ran workshops, focus groups, and large-scale community meetings to try to gauge key chiefs', custom owners', and community members' perspectives around the cultural landscape, land management, and land leasing in North Efate (see figure 1.4). Working alongside my collaborator and friend Brigitte Laboukly (manager of the Cultural Heritage Unit in the Vanuatu Cultural Centre), the participatory project involved detailed and lengthy discussions of contemporary land use, various *raets* (rights) of access to landscapes, chiefly titles, and dominions. Opinions around leasing and development are, of course, varied, divided, and changeable, but there was genuine concern that rapacious leasing, combined with rapid local population increase, would result in land shortages in the future. Many people were also concerned about the preservation of the core area sites in Chief Roi Mata's Domain World Heritage site, as well as important cultural sites (*ol tabu ples*) located on mainland Efate Island.

I have detailed how my approach to researching land issues in Vanuatu has been a collaborative process and has been guided by many local Indigenous people. Nevertheless, it is also an act of scholarship replete with the pitfalls of framing, analyzing, and interpreting the experiences of others. I wish to acknowledge that ethnographic accounts involve the production of knowledge, and as such they can have a "disturbing power" to represent people and places (Mosse 2015, 128). Professionals engaged in research must pay attention to the ethics of knowledge production and to the spaces of "refusal" as exercised by Indigenous peoples so they can place limits on conquest and colonization of knowledge (Tuck and Yang 2014b). This can include acknowledging how Indigenous people refuse to disclose, as well as our choice, as researchers, to decline to write certain stories (Tuck and Yang 2014a, 225, 239). Simpson wrote that these refusals are productive and central to the practice of research because they "tell us when to stop" (2007, 78), allowing us to move toward research that may more closely align with Indigenous peoples' own values.

In these complex and sensitive spaces of representation, my work builds analytical lenses through which I view agency and leasing from localized descriptions of behavior and meaning, rather than imposing theoretical framings on people. For this reason, the ethnographic accounts of land dealings in North Efate and my discussions of agency and personhood have all been checked and approved by local research collaborators. On Lelepa I have been guided by a small group of *kastom* experts and chiefs, under the tutelage of my Lelepa Island Papa, Richard Matanik (see figures 1.5 and 1.6). I am deeply indebted to this group of men for the many hours of conversations that we have had on Lelepa—on platforms under coconut trees, in houses, and in *nakamals* while drinking kava. This process began with numerous conversations with the late Douglas (Fonu) Kalotiti, whose death continues to be felt by all working on land issues and World Heritage in North Efate. Douglas's death has been keenly felt by my family and me, as he was living with us at the time. I have also been deeply saddened by the death of another close collaborator, Pierre Makmar, who for many years held the position of chairman of the Lelema Council of Chiefs and who spent many hours discussing associated issues with me with his trademark good humor and wit. With these generous collaborators, I have been privileged to hold long wandering

FIGURE 1.5. Just before dancing. With my Lelepa Island papa, Richard Matanik, at the National Arts Festival in Lakatoro Malekula, 22 August 2019. Photo by author.

FIGURE 1.6. With my Lelepa Island papa and mama, Richard Matanik and Leisara Kalotiti, at the National Arts Festival in Lakatoro Malekula, 21 August 2019. Photo by Brigitte Laboukly. Reproduced with permission.

conversations and discussions over weeks, months, and years around *kastom* and transformations, chiefly titles, landholding arrangements, and contemporary leasing practices. Similarly, ongoing dialogues around land issues have also occurred with a slightly more changeable group of older men in Mangaliliu, led by Chief Mormor and his *atafi* (assistant chief), Malesu. *Tank yu true yufala evriwan.*

I reported the major findings of my research in several ways: at a well-attended public seminar that was held in the Vanuatu Cultural Centre, at a half-day workshop to the male *filwoka* workshop, and during a broadcast (in Bislama) about my research on Radio Vanuatu. I left copies of my thesis with people who had checked my ethnographic and political-economy accounts, and a bound copy of my thesis is in the Vanuatu National Archives. I also ran a two-day workshop on Lelepa Island that consisted of going through all the major ethnographic material detailed in this book. This formal workshop was also dovetailed with numerous kava-drinking evenings of long, quiet discussion.

The attention that I have paid to checking and receiving approval for the ethnographic accounts offered in this book does not mean that these descriptions are without controversy. The book discusses the way powerful men manipulate *kastom* and legal identities to lease customary land, often to the detriment of wider kinship groups. Unsurprisingly some of these powerful men have been dissatisfied with parts of this book, and one or two have requested specific changes. Other Lelepa men and women have petitioned for these changes not to be made. As a result of these discussions, I have removed some sections. The final version has been checked by my close collaborators and *kastom* experts, but all mistakes remain my own. I offer this description as a way of acknowledging some of the many complexities associated with engaging in collaborative research.

Navigating Reciprocity and Reform

After living in Vanuatu for over two years, my family packed up to return to Australia. At our leaving ceremony (termed *go finis*) on Lelepa Island in July 2012, I was presented with two beautiful carved wooden *saloa,* the idiom for land. Chief Mormor then spoke, "You are a *girl-Lelepa* now. You will always have a piece of land here, but for now you must take these *saloa* with you to remind you that you belong to this *ples.*" These two *saloa* hold pride of place in my home in Canberra, reminding me, in a daily, practical way, of the meaning of land.

Although no longer living in the country, my work and research on Vanuatu has continued. Much of this continuing work relates to land law and land law reform. Almost as soon as I began living in Vanuatu, I delivered land law training, legal advice, and land reform work to government officers and agencies based in Port Vila. For two years I was employed by the Jastis

Blong Evriwan project (World Bank 2011) to deliver land-law training across numerous departments. From 2010, I also held the position of legal adviser to the Vanuatu Cultural Centre and worked on various legal matters. These included attempts to register the first sites of national significance under the Preservation of Sites and Artifacts Act, support for the Vanuatu National Cultural Council, and ongoing legal work on the Chief Roi Mata's Domain World Heritage site. This work involved several cases related to the acquisition of Artok Island (the central island in Chief Roi Mata's Domain World Heritage site). Work in the Vanuatu Cultural Centre also involved numerous lengthy conversations around land issues with staff of the Land Desk and *filwokas*. I also provided training on land law and cultural heritage. From 2010, I was appointed legal adviser on land law to the attorney general of Vanuatu and began work with Professor Don Patterson to review the drafting of the Customary Land Tribunal Act. This land-law reform work predated my work under Minister of Lands Regenvanu, which began in 2013.

In early 2013, having negotiated for the Ministry of Lands in the formation of government, Regenvanu asked me to begin work as his legal adviser in a position remunerated at local wage rates. From 2013, I worked as Minister Regenvanu's legal adviser, and I also became the principal drafter of a land-reform package. The new laws, gazetted in February 2014, involved a new leasing process and devolved power through constitutional reform to local *nakamals* and customary area land tribunals to identify the custom-owner group for an area of land.

In North Efate, Lelepa people celebrated having a *girl Lelepa* working with the minister of lands. Directly after my position was announced, Lelepa men began ringing requesting appointments with Minister Regenvanu and me to deal with land issues. However, initial celebrations were tempered by the perceived dangers associated with my new position. My two *papas* were particularly concerned for my safety. Knowing that I was a *strong hed* and a kava drinker, they hatched a plan.

> The sun is going down as the boat we are in lands at Mangaas. Matanik is in the boat with other chiefs and senior men. No one will tell me what we are doing. I am directed out of the boat and told to remain silent.
>
> We enter the clearing under the large banyan tree. There is a rustle of movement amongst the trees, and slowly the sound of the slit gongs rings out through the clearing. Everyone is grave, silent as a mark of respect for the sacred *ples*. The slit gongs echo, the drumming becomes faster, the frisson builds. We move forward. Slowly and silently, I am ushered behind the clearing to the walled precinct that once belonged to Chief Roi Mata.
>
> The singing starts, and chiefs appear from behind the bushes in *kastom* dressing of *nangria* leaf *eviv* and faces caked in mud. Slowly we move behind to the *namale* trees. Chief Mormor cries out and begins to speak in Lelepa language; he is calling on the *kastom* power of the place. Men point gravely as the trees begin to shake. A

> carved coconut kava bowl is produced, and all the men sing out in unison. Together they place their hands over my head.
>
> The ceremony is finished, and we drink kava. A new bowl has been carved for me by Matanik. Chief Mormor tells me, "We have called the power of Roi Mata to protect you. It's too dangerous, this land job of yours, being Ralph's lawyer, and you like to drink kava too much." Chief Mormor frowns at this point and reminds me that it is not good for a woman to drink kava. "We have been worried that someone will poison you! But it's alright now; just remember to drink from this bowl." (journal entry, April 2013)

Confronted with the perceived dangers of my position as the legal adviser to a minister of lands intent on reforming the political economy of land dealings, the chiefs offered me the *kastom* protection of the ancestral figure of Chief Roi Mata.

Navigating the Politics of Identity

The vignette of *kastom* protection by Lelepa chiefs is perhaps better understood in the context of various critiques of my role. Because of my gender, race, and nationality, my role as legal adviser to the minister of lands (2013–2016) has been regularly criticized as the perspectives of an "Australian woman." A letter to the editor of the *Vanuatu Daily Post* that appeared two months after my appointment provides an example:

> It is sad to find out that Minister Ralph has employed an Australian to provide legal advice to the Minister of Lands.
>
> The Minister has been a strong advocate for land coming back to ni-Vanuatu...why does he need to employ an Australian to give him legal advice? Is there no Vanuatu man or woman who is qualified to do this work? Or Vanuatu women do not understand land issues which means he must take an Australian woman?
>
> I find it disturbing to see an Australian woman who has come to sort out land issues in Vanuatu.
>
> My perspective is that Minister Ralph has contradicted his thinking and statements about land and how to solve the issues.
>
> Slowly GJP [Graon mo Jastis Pati] is becoming a party where they are using the language of transparency to say no to man/woman Vanuatu who could give advice or hold a political position and are using this language as a pathway to give work to Australians to work in Vanuatu.
>
> I hope that the Labour Department takes note of this issue of Australians who come as volunteers then come back to work in Vanuatu. It would be good if GJP and the Labour Department clarified her work permit details. I hope she has not used a different name. (Regenvanu 2013)

These critiques must be interpreted in the context of perceived Australian paternalism in the Pacific. The letter is a critique that recalls the fiercely nationalistic debates that occurred around race before independence—debates that were at the intersection of colonial oppression and land alienation. These debates continue to resonate in postcolonial Vanuatu in part because of the role played by Australian investors in leasing land.

The letter to the editor of the *Vanuatu Daily Post* was not an isolated incident. Sitting at the front of the Malvatumauri chief's *nakamal* during the 2013 Land Law Summit, I was told I could sit and hear the debate among the hundreds of participants about laws that I was drafting, but I could not speak. Eventually, among the dozens of questions on the first day, a man stood up and offered a long narrative of the evils of colonial land dealings, of land being stolen for tobacco and beads. His voice reached a crescendo as he came to his final question, *"Hu ia waet woman wea hemi stap sit daon long forhed long nakamal?"* (Who is the white woman who [dares to] sit down at the front of this *nakamal*?) (Chiefs' Nakamal, Port Vila, 15 Oct 2013). The narrative arc of this question creates a clear link between colonial land dealings and my supposedly "white" "Australian" identity. The cavernous *nakamal,* with its large, mainly male audience, was completely silent. I stood and responded respectfully in Bislama, thanking the audience for the question, and then gave an account of my years of working in Vanuatu. No more questions were asked, and after the session broke, a number of men came and apologized to me for the impertinence of the audience member.

Responding to the letter in the *Vanuatu Daily Post,* Minister Regenvanu, as the president of the GJP, wrote of my experience working on land issues with Indigenous people in Australia, as well as my expertise in land issues in Vanuatu. His response also described the role of foreign advisers in drafting the Vanuatu Constitution. He concluded with the paragraph: "GJP wanted to take the position of Minister of Lands to correct all the land issues, and now we are working on this. To do this work we need the support of everyone. Skin color or nationality is not important, 'competence' and 'integrity' we need now" (*Vanuatu Daily Post,* 23 April 2013). That a response was required that specifically addressed the issues of "skin color" and "nationality" shows how these markers of identity continue to resonate in Vanuatu, particularly when it comes to debates around land. Narratives of my identity as an "Australian" or "white woman," while informed by understandings of whiteness as privilege, are complicated by the reality that my skin color is not actually "white." I have origins that include European and Caribbean-African ancestry.

As anthropologists, we must attempt to navigate decolonial pathways that allow for the plurality and diversity of Indigenous voices, agency, and experiences and that create ethnographic accounts of Indigeneity beyond the caricatures of "noble informants" or "brutish" subjects critiqued by Todd (2018). As a non-Indigenous woman of color, I offer a winding account of my own style of fugitive anthropology, with its attention to embodied pedagogy and decolonial methodology. It is a practice of activist anthropology that also offers critical analyses of gendered and race positionalities. Beginning with this positionality, I have tried in this chapter to carefully articulate my own positionality in Vanuatu by exploring the ways I have been named and adopted through a series of reciprocal obligations and claims.

Names have power. In North Efate, Lelepa people articulate an ontology in which the act of naming has the power to transform and alter identity. Many years after my initial adoption ceremony, Chief Mormor returned to the *kastom* meaning of my name, carefully synthesizing it with my identity and agency:

> When you came to be with us, I watched you. When I looked at all your good work and how you spoke to people, I could see that you cared, meaning that you were like a mother.
>
> In the octopus clan—*wita*—we have the right to this name Toto; it means the daughter of our *naflak* [matriclan]. But from your good work on land, I thought hard about your name, and I realized that the name that I had to give you was this one, Toto Fakalé. *Fakalé* means you must take care of people; you must look after all the people. If there is a child of the *naflak* or the village, then it is up to you to care for that child; till he is grown you must look after that child. That is what your work is. That is what you do; you try and make sure every child has enough land for the future.
>
> I gave you a good name because I was thinking about land. All of your work here and in the big law that you have written in Vanuatu, it comes from this name. *Wan stret nem stret* [This is the right name for you, exactly the right name]. (Chief Mormor, pers comm, Nov 2014)

To Chief Mormor, it was his act of naming that transformed my identity, leading eventually to my work reforming land laws across Vanuatu.

Names have power. This act of naming established both the relational fabric of belonging and the obligations associated with being claimed.

Chapter 2
Weaving Narratives of Place

Beside the water on the coastline of Lelepa Island, a woman bends over a large pot slowly, rhythmically stirring black liquid that covers pandanus fibers. Her name is Trudi Kalotiti, wife of my close colleague and collaborator Douglas Kalotiti, and she is widely, somewhat enviously, regarded as the best weaver on the island. Later the dried black fibers will be deftly plaited against natural pandanus fiber to form a laced black-and-white-patterned *rong* (basket).

Across the Ocean, as I bend over my computer keys, I too attempt to weave a story of place. In this story, there are multiple voices representing the many strands of fiber plaited together with colonial entanglements—narratives intertwined as a white fiber against black.

* * *

Originally from Aneityum Island, Trudi traveled to Lelepa Island to marry Douglas at the invitation of her adopted father, Chief Kalkot Mormor, the former chief of Mangaliliu Village. Trudi waited twenty-three years before, self-funded through her weaving work, she went back to Aneityum Island. Returning was a shock; everything had changed. Words in the Aneityum language had so altered that children laughed when she spoke. She sounded like an elderly person rather than a forty-year-old *woman-ples* (meaning literally a woman of the place, a woman who has been born to a family group with connections to the land). With the presence of cruise ships regularly docking at Mystery Island, just off the coast of Aneityum, local people gain ready access to Australian money. Trudi remarked that local village store prices were now listed in Australian dollars and that people constantly listened to Radio Australia hoping to improve their English to earn more money from tourists. Finally, she said, "kastom hemi janis bigwan" (*kastom* has changed significantly) and, more damningly, "rispek hemi lus, hemi no olsem bifo" (respect has been lost, it is not the same as before). Trudi's comments suggest significant transformations in the practice of *kastom* in the space of one generation.

Comprehending the multiple meanings of land to Lelepa people involves understanding conceptions of place as marine and terrestrial but also as spiritual and ontological and as the basis of cognatic kinship. Practicing decolonial methodology means privileging Indigenous perspectives, voices, and ontologies; it means establishing the core foundational understanding of place. By building these understandings of local Lelepa people's conceptions of place, we can begin to understand their critiques of land leasing, as well as the national movement to resist and refuse the large-scale leasing of customary land.

Kastom is defined in this book as the proper and correct "ways of place." *Kastom* narratives of *ples* represent a careful weaving of past and present, held fixed against the proper ways of being a relational emplaced person. Place operates as a locus of social practice, imaginings, and meanings. The *kastom* narratives that remain influential in Lelepa people's construction of place include: (1) the idiom of customary land as a *saloa,* a wooden plate of shared access and use rights to land; (2) the central figure of Chief Roi Mata; and (3) the ancestral spirits that continue to inhabit place in North Efate and who imbue the land with agency. Together these narratives bind Lelepa people to place and inform a dialogue on the correct ways of being emplaced in the landscape.

Narratives of *kastom* remain central to contemporary claims to place and to being of a place, a *man-Lelepa.* The colonization of Vanuatu brought with it dramatic transformations in cultural practices that continue to influence the contemporary practice of *kastom.* In this chapter, I explore the influence of missionaries and colonial land leasing on narratives of *kastom* as the "ways of place." Early missionaries profoundly altered the practice of matrilineal landholding arrangements and chiefly title descent structures. Contemporary *kastom* dialogues around attachment to place continue to demonstrate the implications of these transformations.

Kastom as the Ways of Place

Kastom in North Efate is thought of as the "ways of the place," the correct and proper ways of behaving as an emplaced person, often described as *man-ples.* *Kastom* functions as the expression of *ples*-based identity (Bolton 1999, 43). The connectedness of people and *ples* in Bislama is something that pervades both discussions of land and broader questions of identity in Vanuatu. The term *man-ples* was also associated with this early nationalist discourse of *kastom.* Reverberating with important political meanings, "such imagery was not only crucial in reclaiming the land as inalienably attached to the people of the place, but proclaiming the people as necessarily in control of the place" (Jolly 1992a, 342). The symbiotic definition of person and place requires that everyone in Vanuatu comes from a place. To be without place is irreconcilable with Indigenous identity. Historically urban towns were unlikely to be considered a place by rural migrant ni-Vanuatu populations who had less *kastom* attachment to the landscape. Writing on this aspect of place in Port Vila in 1999, Gregory E Rawlings noted that people "identify primarily with their island or village of origin.... Very few rural migrants regard a town as their place" (1999a, 75). Rawlings recorded how towns, to this group of people, represented displacement and the term *man-Vila* was a term of insult, a declaration that a person is without a *place* (Rawlings 1999a, 75–76). More recently, work by Benedicta Rousseau (2017) has argued that urban residents engage in practices of "simultaneity" that evoke home islands through kava drinking, remittance incomes, sending children home, and so on, while also living in town. Writing about Freswota youth who are confronted with the idea that, because they have no access to land, they "float," Daniela Kraemer argued that a new kind of belonging has taken shape in which the young men call themselves "Roots Men" who are literally and figuratively putting down roots in Freswota as an urban locale. She concluded that Freswota is increasingly becoming reconfigured as a *ples* such that *man-Freswota* means the people of Freswota, as a recognized urban identity (2020, 52–53).

In North Efate, the term *man-Lelepa* describes the centrality of place to personhood. As former chairman of the Lelema Council of Chiefs Pierre Makmar, explained, "In *kastom,* the most important thing is the importance of *ples.* This is my *ples.* I am a man of this *ples.* The *ples* doesn't just mean the land; it is all the stories that are about the land. It's the meaning of '*man-Lelepa*' " (interview, May 2012). In North Efate, the synergy between people and place is expressed in cosmology, kin relations, narratives of community unity, a shared Lelepa language, governance structures, and the identity of being a *man-Lelepa* (or the less-used female-gendered term *girl-Lelepa*). A *man-Lelepa* also has many "concentric circles of identity expressed in place" (Rodman 1992, 648). Finally, matrilineal *(naflak)* kinship ties also bind Lelepa Islanders to other places through other members of their *naflak* group, located on Efate or in the Shepherd Islands, and to populations in Pango and Mele.

A *man-Lelepa* is also a *man-Efate* likely to have many ties to Port Vila through employment, schooling, and kinship networks. In spite of a reasonably small population base (around five hundred people at the time of independence) two *man-Lelepa* were prominent "fathers" of the Independence Movement and involved in the subsequent formation of the Vanuatu state: Donald Kalpokas (former prime minister of Vanuatu) and Peter Taurakoto (independence leader and former Vanuatu ombudsman). The involvement of *man-Lelepa* in the operation of the state continues, and in contemporary times, many *man-Lelepa,* who hold positions of leadership within the government bureaucracy, are lawyers or judges, teachers or health workers. The 2012 election saw local Lelepa Island man the late Gillion Kalotiti William elected to Parliament as a member for rural Efate.

Throughout Vanuatu, being is tied to landscape and encapsulated in the idea of *ples.* In his consideration of the word *kastom,* John Taylor is clear that place is a defining narrative of sociality for the Sia Raga in North Pentecost. Instead of the politicized Bislama word *kastom,* Sia Raga instead use the Raga-language phrase *alenan vanua* (Taylor 2008b, 10–11). *Alenan vanua* means not just cultural practices but "a more deeply felt sentiment of correctness of human behaviour and thought, one that is importantly merged with place... [meaning] all the correct ways and ideas belonging to a place" (Taylor 2006; 2008b, 10–11). Benedicta Rousseau similarly writes that *kastom* functions as "a measure of the correct or appropriate way of being. . . . In everyday life *kastom* operates as a critical tool in determinations of the propriety and legitimacy of behaviour, personality, relationship and intent" (2008, 16). In North Efate, being is tied to place and articulated through the proper form of human behavior, the correct way of being in the place, often discussed with reference to past practices. *Kastom* becomes a "matter of selective perpetuation from past to present to future, of distinguishing good from bad *kastom* between those practices thought worthy of continuity or revival and those which should be left to expire" (Jolly 2012b, 124). The value of *kastom* becomes entwined with the value of place, held in opposition to foreign ways of being or aspects of modernity that are regularly pronounced on, particularly by chiefs, as not *kastom,* including cash payments, styles of clothing and hairdressing, and types of food.

Understandings of past practice also demonstrate the entanglement of local histories with colonization. Lelepa narratives of *kastom* as the "ways of *ples*" continually reference the *taem bifo.* As one Lelepa chief explained, "*Bifo* we lived by *kastom.* The *kastom* way of the ancestors existed in the time *bifo.* We lived by it. Then in the time when Christianity came, it came to teach us all a new way, and then *kastom* started to divide. The time when we came inside and learned new Christian knowledge, that is when we lost many of our *kastom* ways of living. We let go of our *kastom* and moved inside the white-man system" (interview, Nov 2014).

Taem bifo is a descriptor of *kastom* based on temporal understandings of the time before missionaries as the *taem blong tu dak,* the time of heathen "darkness" in contrast to Christian "light." This echoes missionary accounts of the New Hebrides. The opening lines of Graham Miller's volumes on the Presbyterian Church in the New Hebrides read, "The people were almost all in darkness when John and Charlotte Geddie landed in Aneityum on 29 July 1848" (2001, 1). In North Efate, accounts of the *taem bifo* are interwoven with discussions of chiefly authority and the construction of moral narratives around the use of sacred power (Facey 1981, 304; McDonnell 2015). This descriptor is also informed by the pre-independence discourse of *kastom* as the "revival" of past cultural practices and many of the practices previously denigrated by missionaries as heathen practices.

Temporal understandings of the "past" permeate the present. Movements of the central ancestral figure of Roi Mata form a continuous circular narrative that opens concertina-like into the present before folding back in on itself, leaving behind the physical markers of ancestral figures etched in the contemporary landscape. Similar understandings of temporality pervade many Oceanic landscapes, connecting a chronological sequence with particular historical figures and their movements through specific places (Salesa 2014, 40). Recognition of Pacific temporalities allows the questioning of single unilineal historical accounts of past practices and events and lineal accounts of the transformations of local *kastom* practices that accompanied colonization in Vanuatu. Influenced by this work, my approach recognizes continuity while also acknowledging the transformations that have occurred to what are understood as precolonial customary practices and customary tenure arrangements. This is a narrative of transformation rather than loss of *kastom*. On Efate Island, these transformations have occurred largely as a result of the following events: epidemics in which a large proportion of the population died, missionary influence on the ordination of chiefs and on existing matrilineal landholding arrangements, and the impact of land leasing in the colonial period.

I seek to avoid the challenges posed by much of the anthropological writing around *kastom* in Melanesia (Keesing 1982; Jolly 1992b; Lindstrom 2008; N Thomas 1992; Tonkinson 1981a, 1981b, 1982a, 1982b). I do not seek to be an arbiter of *kastom,* as if such identifiable certainties exist or as if that could ever be my role. I am conscious of claims of *kastom* and transformation being interpreted with reference to the "persistent specter of inauthenticity" or loss (Jolly 1992b, 49). Instead, I wish to document divergent narratives of relationships to place—their tensions and contrasts—and document the impacts on place and *kastom* from land leasing. In this way, I am adopting former Director of the Vanuatu Cultural Centre Ralph Regenvanu's deceptively simple, repeated assertion to me that "*kastom* is what people say it is" (pers comm, June 2013). People say *kastom* is many different things. Understanding *kastom* requires a deep ethnographic approach that considers how people themselves think of their own *kastom* practices—not as fixed precolonial narratives but as part of the fabric of their lives and as an ongoing discussion of the "ways of place." In pursuing this approach, I am less concerned with consideration of representations of supposedly authentic *kastom* than the politics of representation—namely, who is empowered to speak about *kastom* and place and how these narratives work to emplace or displace other Indigenous people from landscapes. Narratives of place function as accounts of power and authority over the landscape and are therefore inherently contested and political.

The accounts of attachments to place and *kastom* practices in this book are those of Lelepa people (who reside mainly in North Efate on Lelepa Island and in Mangaliliu Village). I reference only in passing the narratives of Tongoan people, who also make claims to the landscape of North Efate. Tongoan claims center mainly on the island of Artok and the ancestral figure of Roi Mata (see, eg, David Luders's 2001 article supporting Tongoan claims and critiquing José Garanger and Jean Guiart, as well as Guiart's 2004 response). These claims remain salient in the contemporary politics of land in Vanuatu such that the recent government process to acquire the existing Artok lease interest was accompanied by a claim for compensation made on behalf of Tongoan people.

On Lelepa Island, Trudi Kalotiti is a principal weaver in the local Handicraft Revitalization Project run by the Vanuatu Cultural Centre. This is the latest in a long line of projects whose genesis was in the decision by the Vanuatu Cultural Centre in 1991 to establish a Women's Culture Project "designed to document and revive women's *kastom*" (Bolton 1999, 53). Lissant Bolton credited the establishment of the original project to pressure from women's organizations and then President of the National Council of Women Grace Mera Molisa, who claimed that in the national discourse about *kastom,* "women are missing. When men talk about *kastom* at this level they omit women, they pretend women don't have *kastom*.... If we make women's work of no importance *(samting nating)* then much will be lost" (1999, 183). Bolton concluded that "if national identity is founded on *kastom* then the assertion that women's knowledge and practice constitutes *kastom* grants them the right to operate in the new context of the nation" (1999, 53). Claims made about *kastom,* and who has *kastom* knowledge, are often starkly gendered. By contrast, Molisa understood that claims made in *kastom* operated as powerful statements of full citizenship and rights in the newly emerging nation-state.

In North Efate, weaving functions as claim to place. As an exceptionally skilled weaver, and despite being a *man-kam* (a person from another *ples*), Trudi has studied late-nineteenth-century photographs and is teaching other local Lelepa women how to weave *rong*. It is a careful reweaving, each basket representing a material claim to the temporal continuity of *kastom*. Quietly and subtly, through her personal proficiency, Trudi is making a claim to attachment to the landscape through the practice of weaving; she is making a claim to being a *woman-ples*.

North Efate: Place and People

Efate is the central island of the Y-shaped Vanuatu archipelago. It is the location of the national capital, Port Vila, and is around 770 square kilometers (297 square miles) in area. As discussed in the introduction, since 2000, Efate Island has witnessed a rapacious "land rush" of leasing, with much of the island's coastline now leased. Located an easy twenty-five-minute drive from Port Vila, the coastline of North Efate is covered in a dense patchwork of leases (see map 0.1).

North Efate is a regional area with a sociolinguistic and cultural boundary (map 2.1), as articulated by the people now living in Lelepa and Mangaliliu. It is a sociocultural space and not just a territory in that there are values attached to the place and relationships that bind it together. As the landscape most closely associated with the Lelepa versions of the Roi Mata cycle of stories, it is replete with sites of meaning.

The sociolinguistic region of North Efate stretches in geographical terms from the southernmost point of the coastline of Efate Island at Tuktuk Point to Udaone (Samoa Point) in the north. From a mountainous volcanic inland area, the landscape quickly descends the steep escarpments, crosses the shore past coral reefs, and plunges into the deep waters of Havannah Harbour. The geology of North Efate is dominated by limestone and raised coral reefs. Across from the mainland coastal area is Lelepa Island, accessed by boat from the Lelepa landing. Farther to the south is the smaller, uninhabited Artok Island.

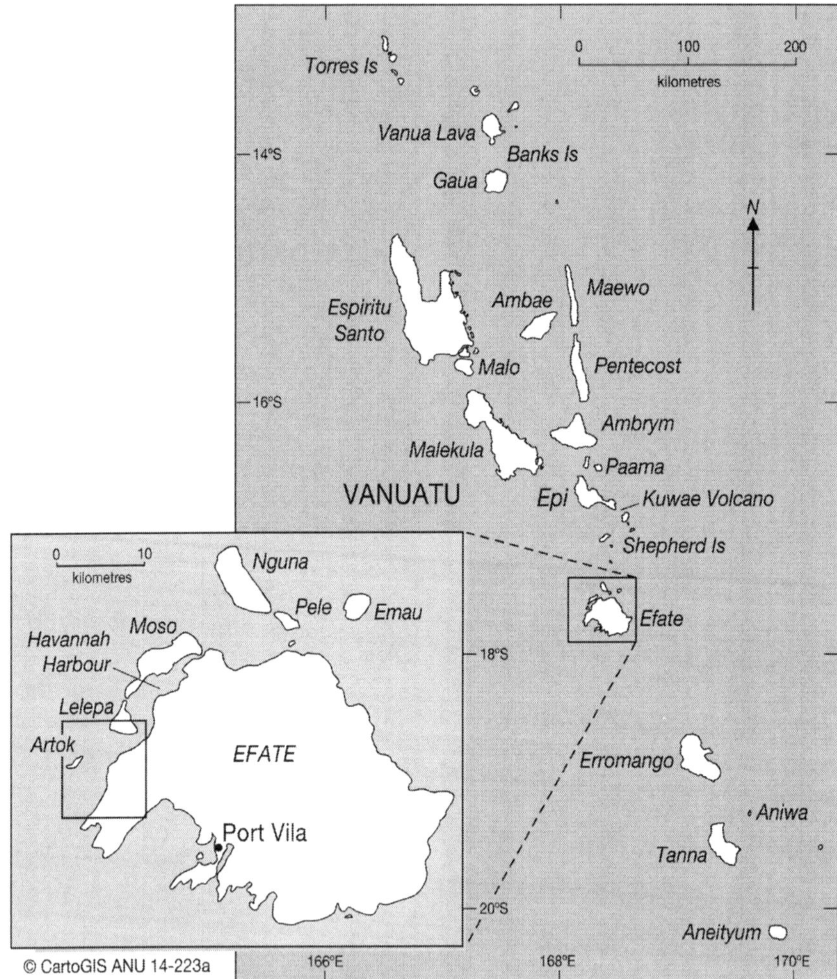

MAP 2.1. Location of the North Efate region in the Vanuatu archipelago. Courtesy of CartoGIS ANU 14-223a, The Australian National University.

Volcanic soils ensure that a band of rich agricultural land stretches from the coast to the base of the escarpment, which, along with rich marine resources, provides the subsistence livelihood for much of the region's population. Unfortunately, much of the area of rich agricultural land adjacent to Havannah Harbour is leased.

Two key *kastom* sites in the North Efate landscape are the old *kastom* village of Mangaas (the residence of Roi Mata) and Feles Cave (the place of Roi Mata's death) on Lelepa Island (map 2.2). Together these sites make up Chief Roi Mata's Domain World Heritage site, which was inscribed by the United

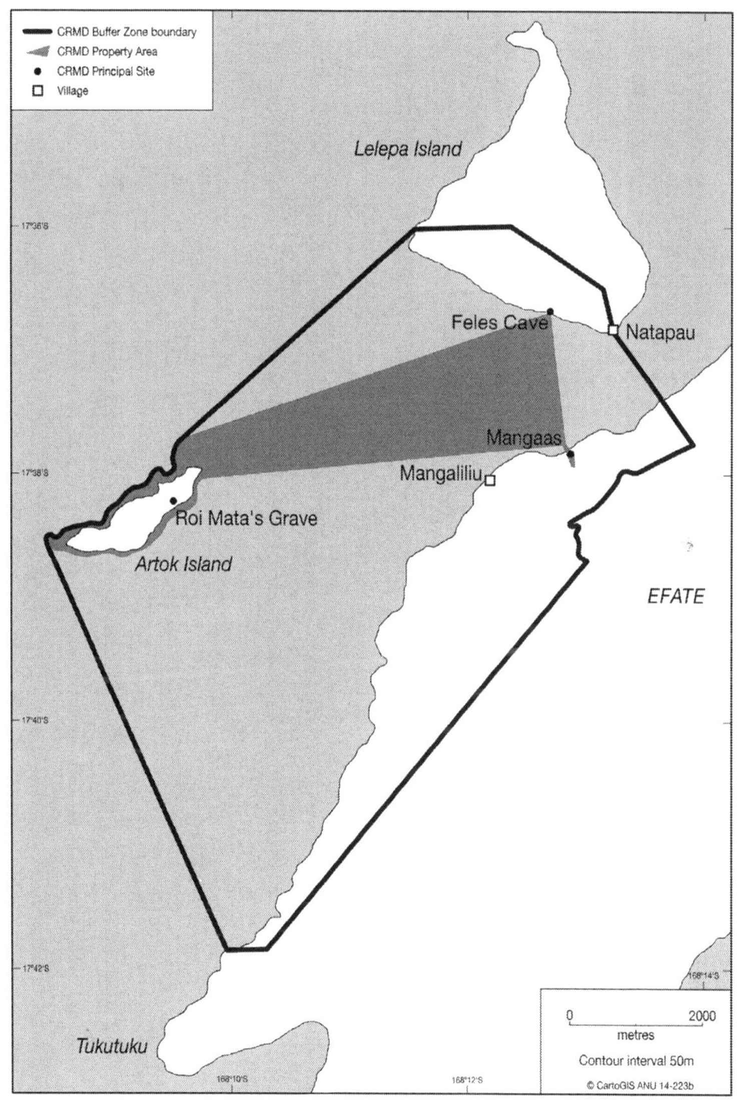

MAP 2.2. The boundaries marking the core area and buffer zone of Chief Roi Mata's Domain World Heritage site, North Efate, Vanuatu. Courtesy of CartoGIS, ANU 14-223b, The Australian National University.

Nations Educational, Scientific and Cultural Organization in 2008 as an example of a continuing cultural landscape governed by chiefs (UNESCO 2008).

The other important locations are the villages of Mangaliliu located on the mainland coast, and Natapau located on Lelepa Island. The population of the North Efate area lives mostly in the village of Mangaliliu and on Lelepa

Island, although increasingly housing is also located along the ring road that circles the island and cuts along the coastline. The 2020 census records the population of North Efate as 3,550 people, with slightly more women (1,800) than men (1,759) (VNSO 2020, 23). In the villages of Mangaliliu and Lelepa there are numerous locales: churches, small stores operating as extensions to houses, houses for mamas, community halls that also function as chiefly *fareas* (houses), schools, and *nakamals* (seat of customary governance). Of the population of North Efate, 63 percent is aged under twenty-nine years, suggesting a very significant youth base (VNSO 2016, 47, 98).

Lelepa people across North Efate remain largely dependent on subsistence farming and fishing for their livelihoods, with only 13 percent of the adult population reporting that they are employed (VNSO 2016, 138). The 2020 census similarly suggests that of 2,087 adults available to work, only 29.5 percent participated in the formal labor force by participating in paid employment to some degree in the week of the census (VNSO 2020, 199). People living in the North Efate region regularly participate in waged employment in Port Vila. Previous surveys suggest, however, that employment opportunities in the waged economy are starkly gendered, with men forming the overwhelming majority (almost 80 percent) of "employed" people on Lelepa Island (VNSO 2009, 218). These gendered opportunities are also visible in terms of various seasonal employer schemes: in 2016, of the 135 Lelepa people from North Efate who had participated in the schemes, 117 (or 74 percent) were men (VNSO 2016, 146).

Most Lelepa adults list their educational level as having completed primary school (86 percent), 13 percent state that they have completed secondary education, and less than 1 percent list their educational achievement level as tertiary (VNSO 2016, 128). However, these educational statistics relate to people living in North Efate. If Lelepa Islanders living in Port Vila were taken into account, the numbers finishing secondary education and gaining entrance into university would certainly be higher. Similarly, Lelepa Islanders employed in senior government positions often live in Port Vila.

In terms of religion, in 2009 the population of Lelepa Island overwhelmingly identified as Presbyterian (90 percent), with less than 1 percent of people identifying their religion as Seventh-day Adventist (VNSO 2009, 35). However, the long-held influence of the Presbyterian Church may be waning, with the 2020 census data for North Efate recording that of the population of 3,333 adults, just under half (1,551, or 46 percent) identified as Presbyterian, with Seventh-day Adventist (373), Assemblies of God (302), and Neil Thomas Ministry (301) as the next largest congregations (VNSO 2020, 52). Census data on marital status indicated that only 40 percent of couples were what is termed "legally married" in a church, while the majority of couples participated in *kastom* weddings or lived together. Divorce is widely understood to be condemned by the church, and no Lelepa Islanders reported being divorced. The long history of the Presbyterian Church in the region, as well as the English-speaking Natapau Primary School, may be why many Lelepa Islanders (87 percent) have a basic level of English language proficiency compared to the fewer than 1 percent who can read basic French (VNSO 2009, 46, 99). However, the presence of a French-speaking primary school in Mangaliliu means that there is a significantly larger French-speaking population there. In 2009, most households on Lelepa Island (75 percent) reported the Lelepa language as their main language. In 2020 across North Efate, 92 percent of adults reported that they could read and write in English, while only 27 percent of adults reported they could read and write in French (VNSO 2020, 170, 172).

Contemporary North Efate, although generally thought of as a "rural" locale located on land held under customary tenure, is more appropriately understood as a peri-urban area. Rawlings argued of Pango Village that "town and village exist side by side, and it is within this context that urbanization occurs. Urban space can be accessed without relinquishing one's place" (1999a, 76). Similarly, Lelepa people move to and from Port Vila in a way that renders the landscape of North Efate almost an expansion of the peri-urban space. Starting in the early morning (around 5:30 am), a small cavalcade of trucks and buses leaves Mangaliliu to take people to work and school in Port Vila, returning throughout the day and at the end of the day. From Lelepa Island people take a ten-minute boat ride to Lelepa landing on the mainland of Efate Island before either taking an organized bus or truck or hailing a truck that is traveling around the ring road into Port Vila.

Weaving Place from Multiple Strands

Place is not inert; it operates as a locus of individual agency and social practices. Competing narratives of place are layered onto the landscape of North Efate. Margaret Rodman remarked that "places, like voices, are local and multiple. A place has a unique reality, one in which meaning is shared with other people and places. The links in these chains of experiences are forged of culture and history" (1992, 643). Meanings map landscapes and construct place in particular ways. Landscape here is used to describe not only the contours of the physical landscape but also as a particular "seeing of space" recognizing that space is replete with local meanings and voices (Blomley 1998). As Epeli Hau'ofa reminded us, "We cannot read our histories without knowing how to read our landscapes (and seascapes)" (2008, 73). Place is the source of knowledge and practice in which landscape functions as a mnemonic device; "stories are written into the landscape because of their association with particular places" (Bolton 1999, 46). Memories and stories also function as claims to place.

Meaning is woven around the place of North Efate in multiple ways, both material and spiritual; place is lived, it is spoken of in *kastom* narratives, it is crafted in textiles and slit gongs, and it is sung and danced. Locally privileged *kastom* meanings center on three principal narratives: (1) the idiom of land as a *saloa;* (2) stories attached to the ancestral figure of Roi Mata and *naflak* kinship structure; and (3) the spirits and ancestors who inhabit the land. These narratives trace meanings onto the landscape and allow for continuities across time. Together these three narratives bind people to place, weaving *kastom* claims to particular areas of customary land and to chiefly authority over the land.

Land as a *Saloa*

Carved as a large wooden plate (figures 2.1 and 2.2), the *saloa* is an important metaphorical and spiritual idiom for the relationships of Lelepa people to place. As the culturally expert Vanuatu Cultural Centre field-worker *(filwoka),* Lelepa woman Leisara Kalotiti explained that a *saloa* represents how "every member of the family eats off the land. Every person has an opportunity to

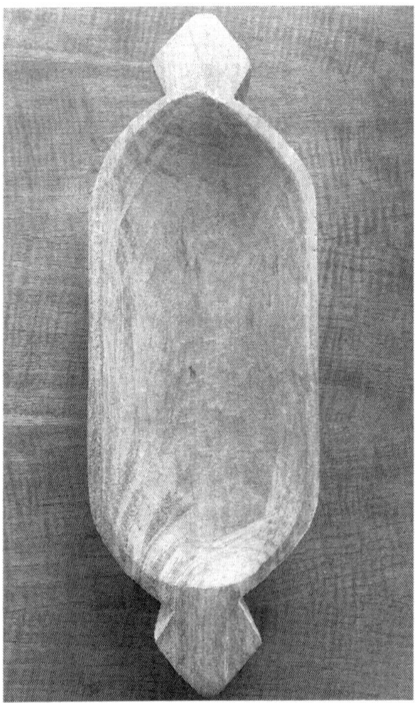

FIGURE 2.1. Inside of a carved *saloa* plate, Canberra, 2 February 2016. Photo by author.

FIGURE 2.2. Reverse side of a carved *saloa* plate decorated with the image of a chief and pig's tusks, Canberra, 2 February 2016. Photo by author.

make a garden and grow food." She added, "Our ancestors taught us that land is a *saloa.* If I go and garden on a piece of land that belongs to a male ancestor, I can eat out of the garden. When I have finished, or when I'm dead, another family can grow a garden and eat of the land also. Our ancestors said land is a *saloa* that all different members of the family can eat out of.... The land continues for all time" (interview, May 2011). In its material form, a *saloa* exists as a shared resource. Land and people exist, and are conceived of, as a unified whole (Rodman 1987, 33). People are embedded and sustained by land as a *saloa* and, in turn, have responsibilities to the landscape and the ancestral beings that inhabit it.

Local oral histories discuss the importance of the *saloa. Kastom* narratives center on the ancestral figure of Roi Mata and his brothers, Roi Mantay and Roi Muru, as they journey across the landscape of North Efate. In one story, the wooden *saloa* plate takes an embodied form representing the close association between material objects and ancestral power in the landscape. The story describes the journey of Roi Mantay, who having drunk kava, finds that it has left a bitter taste in his mouth. As he travels across the coastal landscape with his *atafi kutu* (assistant chief "mosquito"), he searches for coconuts to wash away the taste. As the two men travel, they stop at important *kastom* places and collect material objects for their trip, and "at Creek Ay, *saloa,* the wooden dish, explains that he will take care of the grated coconut" (Guiart 2013, 41). The idea of land as a *saloa* has also been used as a basis for asserting land claims in tribunal hearings. In a 2003 North Efate land tribunal decision, the tribunal of chiefs declared that in *kastom,* land is understood to be a "*kastom* dish a *Silowa* where the perpetual ownership of the land is held under a chiefly title where the chief owns the land on behalf of his people" (*Peter Taurakoto, Chief Arier Kaltang v Chief Nearutalo Napalaunaot,* North West Efate Area Customary Land Tribunal, Land Appeal Case 1 of 2003). *Silowa* is the South Efate spelling of *saloa*). These multiple narrative accounts demonstrate some of the ways that a *saloa* is locally understood as the idiom for place. Together they offer insights into Lelepa people's conceptions of land as it informs *kastom* as the ways of *ples.*

Chief Roi Mata and the Meaning of *Naflak*

Divine narratives of place describe the actions and movements of ancestral figures within the landscape of North Efate. Suspended over and embedded in the landscape is the powerful ancestral figure of Chief Roi Mata. Considered to have lived around AD 1600, Roi Mata has been described as the paramount chief of all Efate chiefs who developed the *naflak* totemic systems in use throughout central Vanuatu and who is now buried on Artok Island (Guiart 1964, 97; 2013, 39). The Roi Mata *kastom* story cycles involve narratives of Roi Mata alongside his brothers, Roi Muru and Roi Mantay. Most famous of all the stories is the account of how Roi Mata created a *natamwate* (feast) proclaiming various individuals as belonging to the *naflak* systems on Efate, thereby ending the Great Efate War.

By this account, Roi Mata sees that there is war all about him and decides that men die every day. Wondering how to find a solution to the problem, he decides to give a big peace feast—*natamwate*—to which people come without their weapons. He sends out the invitations all over Efate, Nguna, and Emau asking the people to come to Tukutuku on a certain day the following year. Each man is to bring a gift, a thing different from those chosen by his neighbors, including even his own wife. Everyone comes on the appointed day. Roi Mata receives each man and his present, depositing the latter onto one of a long row of heaps, with a different heap for each kind of offering. When all the people invited have arrived, Roi Mata says: "I have given this feast to teach you how to be friends. Everyone who has brought yams is from now on a yam; everyone who has brought taro is a taro; and so on. If a man henceforth falls into trouble, let him go and see his friends of the same category in another village, where he will find help and refuge instead of being killed. There will thus be protection for every man in every place" (Guiart 1964, 97). Roi Mata retains enormous cultural significance in local histories both within North Efate and across the central islands of Vanuatu.

In contemporary Efate, *kastom naflak* identities continue to bind people to specific places and to kinship relationships between each other. Termed *namatrau* by Guiart, it is better understood by Lelepa people as a *naflak* system of *nakainanga* matriclan totems in the Lelepa language, with each totem representing a large matriclan group. Each *naflak* reflects a natural species such as an octopus or coconut. Historically, the *naflak* tribes that Lelepa people belonged to included the yam, *nawi;* coconut, *nanu;* arrowroot, *makaru;* sugarcane, *karam;* breadfruit, *napetaw;* taro, *natale;* octopus, *wita taw* (red octopus) and *wita loa* (black octopus); shellfish, *kay;* clamshell, *karaw;* stone, *vatu;* tree, *nefao* (Guiart 1964, 100–101). According to Lelepa people the list developed by Guiart misses other *nawi naflaks* like *nawi mako, nawi malo,* and *nawi tu'r.* Most *naflak* groups are represented among the contemporary Lelepa population. However, there are some *naflak* groups with few or no members, so people—including the wives of Lelepa men who come from other islands—are being strategically adopted into them.

Naflak in the Lelepa language comes from *na-flak,* where *flak* means "being pregnant." Tribes are birthed from the womb. Leisara elucidated: "Women birthed the *naflak.* When children are born, they follow the *naflak* of their mother" (interview, Sept 2010). Lelepa people continue to describe their genealogies with reference to the female ancestors who birthed their *naflak.* The role of women as the "mothers of the tribe" creates an emplaced narrative of women in the landscape of North Efate. This understanding posits women as central to the continuance of the *naflak* as the mediums between people and place.

Following matrilineal descent, children are members of the same *naflak* as their mother, and a man will hold the same *naflak* as his sister's children. *Namatrau* groupings continue to define large family relationships, and members of the matriclan often share responsibilities for the support of other members during *kastom* activities, including weddings, adoptions, and funeral ceremonies. Chief Mormor, one of the central advocates for *naflak* identity, explained, "The meaning of *naflak* is that in the *taem bifo* there were tribal wars. Then there was peace because Roi Mata set up the *naflak* system. So I am octopus, another man is coconut, so now we can know each other. Everyone who is coconut will know everyone else who is coconut. If a coconut has some business to make, he will say 'I have got *naflak* family who can help me.' For me, I am *weita,* so all *naflak weita* must come and help me. This is the meaning of *naflak*" (interview, Nov 2014). In spite of Mormor's advocacy, the influence of *namatrau* groups in organizing *kastom* activities is waning. For example, weddings were previously organized by *naflak* matriclan groups working to prepare pandanus textiles for gift exchange and large communal meals attended by several hundred people. Now, weddings are increasingly organized by family groupings in accordance with direct kinship obligations, which do not necessarily correspond with *namatrau* groupings.

As a kinship structure, the *naflak* system continues to define eligible marriage partners for Lelepa people. As Richard Matanik explained, "When it comes to marriage, *naflak* is alive today. I am *naflak weita.* That means that I cannot marry *weita;* I must marry another *naflak.* I married a woman from the *nanu naflak,* but I could have married a woman from the *vatu* or *malu naflak*" (interview, Nov 2014). Guiart wrote that "sexual intercourse with a member of the same totem was punishable by death, the corpse of either culprit being left in the bush to rot" (1964, 98). *Naflak* identity also denotes who is able to dig a grave. This task must be performed by someone who is not of the same *naflak* as the deceased person. The *tabu* (prohibition or ban) against marriage or having sexual relations with someone of the same *naflak* was, until recently, still enforced. However, in August 2015, one couple from the same *naflak (nanu)* was married by the Seventh-day Adventist Church on Lelepa Island. This marriage has been widely condemned by other *naflak nanu* members and has been the source of much community contestation. Paradoxically, the wedding was presided over by Chief Mormor, who himself bases his chiefly authority on *naflak* claims.

The Sacred Power of Place

Chiefly power in North Efate—termed *natkar*—is a claim to sacred power embedded in a specific place and with authority over a particular area of land. Sacred power in the landscape of North Efate takes two broad forms. First, there is ancestral sacred power associated with place per se. Second, there is the power associated with place, of which one kind is *nakaemas* (sorcery), historically harnessed by powerful men as part of a chiefly hierarchy. While historically both forms of power have operated as social sanctions, contemporary narratives of *nakaemas* increasingly distinguish between the power of place that attacks those who have not adhered to the correct practices in *kastom* and accusations or threats of *nakaemas* by an individual associated with a land dispute (McDonnell 2015).

Roi Mata's own place of residence was in the village located at Mangaas. After the burial of Roi Mata on Artok Island, the island became *tabu*. This means it is dangerous for a person to spend a night on the island and "fatal to touch the grave"; marine resources from the fringing reef surrounding the island should also remain protected by *tabu* (Garanger 1982, 56; Guiart 2013, 39). Thus, the following words are repeated in the traditional funeral chant: *"Retoka fanua tabu i nae nae"* (The sacred land of Retoka is *tabu* and a source of danger) (Garanger 1982, 56). Since the burial of Roi Mata, no one has held his chiefly title, which would be tantamount to claiming supreme chiefly authority over Efate Island. Guiart wrote that the mana of the Roi Mata title is too high, meaning that the title is held waiting for the return of Roi Mata. He noted that the last candidate for the title was "Billy Kaloat Nawota, brother of Kalosale Masaloa, who left for Queensland and died shortly after his return" (Guiart 2013, 39). There are, however, Lelepa men who claim a special affinity with the title and who dream of visitations from Roi Mata. Many Lelepa people state that the archaeological digging by Garanger and others at the Roi Mata gravesite has altered the sacred power *(natkar)* of place. For Lelepa people, this explains why the burial precinct, which was previously kept clear of weeds and fallen leaves by the *natkar* of Roi Mata, has since become overgrown. The effect of these perceived changes in the sacredness of the burial site may partly explain why the *tabu* associated with collecting fish, marine life, and wood from Artok Island is no longer strictly observed.

In the landscape of North Efate, key locations represent different places of encounter with the ancestral beings and spiritual forms that animate place: there are sites that represent the spiritual journey taken by the dead to the ancestors; places for the living to communicate with ancestors; and places for the living to harness sacred power. For Lelepa and Ngunese people, Tuktuk Point marks the junction in the journey after death to the spirit world. Working on the adjacent Nguna Island in the 1970s, Ellen Facey wrote similarly that Ngunese people believed that after death their "spirit journeyed under the sea to Point Tukituki" (1981, 305). As well as physical locations that mark pathways to the spiritual realm, in the contemporary landscape of North Efate, specific places are identified with certain activities or phenomena: changing weather; calling on ancestral power for support in war, fighting, or disputes; good fortune and other benefits; and collecting luck for fishing. Increasingly ceremonies are held at Mangaas in the compound of Roi Mata to ask for ancestral help, protection, power, and guidance. There is also a location that is widely understood as being the place where a person (overwhelmingly thought of as a man) can go to summon and harness sacred power.

Rocks and trees are animated, and the land is embodied with spirits and ancestors. The *natkar* of chiefs is linked to particular places such that a chiefly titleholder can travel to specific *tabu* places in his domain so as to call on the power of his ancestors *(natamate)*. In the landscape of North Efate, spirits inhabit the landscape, living in trees, in waterfalls, in the bush, and, in particular, in large *nambanga* trees. As one Lelepa chief explained, "If you sing to the spirits in *tabu* places, they will join with you and come and help you. They are good spirits [who] will help all *man-Lelepa*" (interview, Nov 2014). Across Vanuatu, the material world is inhabited by spiritual and ancestral beings: "both human-made objects—houses, canoes, carvings, textiles—and the natural environment—hills, animals, rocks, waterfalls—do not merely represent but are in fact the repositories or embodiment of what in English are sometimes described by terms such as 'ghosts' or 'spirits' " (Taylor 2016, 149). In Vanuatu, the diurnal (and nocturnal) presence of visiting ancestors and spiritual beings personifies place.

Parts of the coastline of Havannah Harbour inhabited by *sengalengale* (little people), who interfere with washing, knock over objects, and steal food from houses and gardens. In contemporary Lelepa narratives, these people are an unseen presence in the landscape. By contrast, Garanger reported that "a Lelepa man assured me that when he was a youth he had been attacked by one of these *sengalengale* in Creek Ai valley—this was a very small woman with extraordinary long nails and very large ears, her body covered in hair" (1982, 22). Similar accounts exist across Vanuatu and indeed across Melanesia. Bolton referred to these "little people" as *levsepsep* and compared them to the *mawe* "invisible people" of Ambae (1999, 45).

Lelepa people observe that *sengalengale* have become increasingly angry as their place has been developed for residential subdivisions or hotels along the coastline of Havannah Harbour. A Lelepa chief described how the disturbance of place through local "development" can have profound implications.

> They [*sengalengale*] belong to the *ples;* when the *ples* is disturbed they become angry. Men can die because you have destroyed their *ples* because they have power. The power they have is very strong. This is like the power of a *tabu* stone where if you destroy the stone you will become sick.
>
> There was a time on Lelepa when people destroyed a *tabu* stone that was used to call the wind. For the men who broke the stone, a big wind came and dragged their houses into the ocean. This kind of thing reminds us that *ples i kat powa* [the place has power]. (Richard Matanik, interview, Aug 2012)

Ples in this context is embodied by the ancestral figures of the historical or recent past and by spiritual beings and devilish figures that inhabit the landscape. *Sengalengale* are the personification of *ples;* they are *ples* embodied, and they become increasingly angry as their place is destroyed. It is this personification of place that enables the land to have agency—agency that can be either benign or vengeful.

Chiefly *Natkar*: Harnessing Sacred Power

Historically in North Efate, there was a finely calibrated balance between the practice of sacred power and the authority of men within the chiefly structure who were able to control the use of that power. Hierarchical chiefly structures consisted of a chief, or *nawota* in the Lelepa language, supported by a number of other men who also held titled positions. Each *nawota* had an *atafi,* an assistant chief whose role as the chief's spokesman was to ensure that the chief's proclamations were followed. These titles are still retained for many of the remaining dominions in North Efate. A *nawota* was also supported by a *munawae* (sorcerer), a *tasinga* (the ear of the chief), a *mau* (the workman of the chief), and a *namataisu* (chief's carver).[1] The role of the *munawae,* or sacred man, was "to perform extraordinary feats by virtue of his ritual knowledge and personal relationship to the world of spirits and gods." All chiefly dominions included spirits who dwelt in "particular caves, a hole in a rock or a tree, or in the sea"; the *munawae* was responsible for going to the place of the spirit and leaving a food offering so as to guarantee a plentiful harvest or success in warfare (Facey 1981, 305).

Recognition of chiefly *natkar* authority came from the close relationship between a *nawota* and his *munawae* (Capell 1938; Facey 1981, 310). For example, the holder of the Roi Mata chiefly title had a *munawae* whose title was Marikurai (Guiart 1964). The contemporaneous habitation of a place by the living and the dead meant that the role of the *munawae* was to save people from unexplained sickness and to protect them from being taken by ancestors, *natensa* (bad spirits), or *nakaemas.* Unexplained sicknesses were understood to have been sent by the ancestors, and "thus sacred men visited them in spirit and would find the sick person's spirit bound by the ancestors. He [the sick man] would die unless he admitted the misdeed of which they accused him and rectified the situation" (Facey 1981, 305). In this sense, *munawae* act as mediums between ancestral beings and contemporary inhabitants of a landscape.

Chiefly Authority over Land and People

In pre-Christian times, chiefly titles were attached to dominion over a specific area of land. This dominion gave the chiefly titleholder the authority to grant use and access rights to other members of the tribal group (Guiart 2013, 46–51). In return for granting access to the land, each chief would receive an annual payment of homage—a *nasautonga*. For instance, Roi Mata as a paramount chief would receive an annual *nasautonga* from the lower class of *naflak* chiefs whose dominions were located along coastal Efate from Udaone (Samoa Point) to Tukutuku (the region now defined as North Efate). This is similar to the chiefly title structure and land allocations on parts of Epi Island (see discussion in Arutangai 1987, 264). Historically, the duties of the chief involved ensuring the welfare of the tribal group as well as "war-making; peace-making; resource management by putting *tabus* on certain crops or areas to ensure a sufficiency, especially for feasts to propitiate the spirits, as well as appropriate allotment throughout the dominion of gardening space for every-day needs" (Facey 1981, 301). Each chief had absolute power over everything in this dominion, including the people who lived under his jurisdiction; he could order the murder of a subject (Facey 1981, 301; Capell 1938).

Dominions were inhabited by villages with smaller groups of houses for extended families termed *farea* (Facey 1981, 298; Guiart 2013, 46–51). A *farea* was a matrilineal but patrilocal family group consisting of generations of men living in the same locale and bringing wives to live in their area (Rawlings 1999a, 81). Each dominion also had a *mwalala* (dancing ground), edged with elaborately carved slit gongs representing the images of dead chiefs, where dancing, pig sacrifices, and chiefly investiture took place (Facey 1981, 298).

Inheritance of chiefly titles was organized based on matrilineal principles. Under the *naflak* system, chiefly titles transferred from a chief to his sister's sons. Guiart explained the passing on of a chiefly title as follows: "The main title of a *farea,* that of local group chief is passed on by matrilineal descent; as far as possible preference would be given to a son of one of the dead chief's sisters, at least if he was already within the *farea* or the same *mwalala*" (2009, 4). Chiefly titles, both historically and in contemporary practice, are mapped against dominions, with each dominion corresponding to a particular family grouping, or *naflak*. Historically each *naflak* had its own leadership, referred to as *masei,* meaning star (Layard ca 1915). Matrilineal principles of heredity ordered access to power and titles, which involved rights to govern over areas of land and to collect *nausautonga* (annual payments of homage) from subordinates in the hierarchy (Facey 1981, 301). Roi Mata received *nausautonga* from all chiefs with corresponding domains located around the coastline of North Efate, including Udaone, Fatenlengi, Fatakau, Mangaliliu, Pwauluku, Tuktuk, and Siviri (Guiart 2013, 39–40).

Transformation: The Mission Project in North Efate

Pre-Christian settlements in North Efate appear to have been coherent social groups organized mainly around matrilineal principles and presided over by a chiefly titleholder. Contemporary oral histories continue to trace the influence of Christianity as a point of dissonance in the transmission of chiefly structures and of claims to chiefly authority with reference to sacred *powa* (power). As one Lelepa chief explained, "Every chief had many *tabu* places of their own. When the missionaries came, they said to the chiefs, 'You cannot use these *tabu* places.' Then the chiefs didn't use the *tabu* places. The *kastom* stories for these places were lost, and the ways of harnessing power from the *ples*. Now some men are learning about some of these places from out of a book from José Garanger and Guiart. But who will show us these places, and how will we access the power?" (interview, May 2018). Christianity, it appears, created ruptures in the practice of *kastom* as the ways of place.

Dramatic political and social transformations accompanied the mission project in North Efate due to the movement of people to the coast, the destruction of sacred objects, and missionary interventions in *kastom* practice (Rawlings 1999a, 80). The mission project began in 1846 in North Efate with Samoan teachers being stationed at what is now known as "Samoa Point," before quickly dying from malaria (Miller 2001, 59). The early evangelist project in Vanuatu was considered extremely dangerous following the murder of missionary John Williams in Erromango on 20 November 1839 (Miller 2001, 38–39). In 1853, the London Missionary Society ship returned and placed two Rarotongan teachers and their wives on Lelepa Island at the "invitations from two of the Lelepa chiefs, one of whom was Marifatu" (Miller 2001, 60; see also Latai 2016). According to local accounts, just "nineteen days later the teachers and their wives were murdered and eaten," and the son of one of the couples was later drowned by locals (Miller 2001, 61). Missionary records suggest that Chief Marifatu later offered the Reverend Daniel Macdonald, a Presbyterian missionary based at Havannah Harbour from 1872 to 1902, three pigs as compensation payment for the death of the teachers. Macdonald was outraged: "Three pigs are no equivalent for the five men they tomahawked and ate." Macdonald then used British "war boats" to try to intimidate Marifatu, but when he landed on Lelepa Island with Captain Carey, Martifatu was "nowhere to be found" (Macdonald, quoted in Miller 2001, 110–111).

The murder by Lelepa Islanders of the Rarotongan teachers and their wives was followed by the first of many documented epidemics in which 150 people, out of a population of around a thousand on Lelepa Island, died (Miller 2001, 61). In local oral histories, this epidemic continues to be understood as a form of divine punishment for the death of the Rarotongan missionaries. From this event onward, Macdonald and other missionaries continued to document the significant decline in the local population due to epidemics. For example, Macdonald reported that in the one-year period between 1889 and 1890 alone, the population declined by fifty people (Miller 1987, 98–99). In 1883, Macdonald wrote that "an epidemic of dysentery occurred in a part of the district during the year which completely depopulated one heathen village, and broke up one Christian village, whose teacher died, and whose remaining people moved to the neighbouring village of Seviri [Siviri]" (Macdonald 1893, 15). Early Polynesian evangelists were followed in July 1870 by the Reverend Peter Milne, who settled on Nguna Island, where he lived until his death in 1924. In 1872, Macdonald settled at Havannah Harbour, where he lived for twenty years (Miller 2001, 126).

The early mission project heralded permanent population movements from Efate Island's interior to its coast and outer islands. In the 1800s, the population was located in the interior of Efate Island—in villages on the plateau above the escarpment named Imtang, Worantubou, Boufa, and Ravenga. John Ephinstone Erskine noted that "the population appears to be considerable, but to be divided into tribes of between three or four hundred persons" (1853, 333, quoted in Rawlings 1999a, 80). Later accounts from 1889 suggest that depopulation caused the movement and amalgamation of the population of sixteen settled areas into smaller settlement areas in the following locations: on Lelepa Island at Natapau and Leosa; on Moso Island at Moso and Siwa; at the mission station at Samoa Point (Udaone); and, finally, at Siviri (Miller 1987, 81). These shifts were in part due to the depopulation caused by early mass epidemics, but they may also have been a response to the successful proselytizing of early, mainly Polynesian, missionaries and associated conversions to Christianity. Oral histories that I have collected from Lelepa people, and that Facey collected among Nguna Pele people, also suggest that people may have relocated to seek refuge from the violent localized warfare that was still occurring across Efate Island (Facey 1981, 308).

Movements of populations from the interior to the coast were often accompanied by the burning of old villages and the destruction of sacred objects. Milne regularly oversaw the destruction of *napeas* (slit gongs) in abandoned interior villages. As he wrote, "The voices of chiefs and the images of dead chiefs, the slit drums, had [all] been burnt, and, in many instances, sacred stones and conch shells had been delivered up to Milne by chiefs or their sacred men" (Facey 1981, 304; see also Miller 2001, 134). As well as destroying sacred objects, local missionaries regarded the practice of *nakaemas* as immoral. Missionaries regularly imposed fines on their congregations for the "sins" they committed, including the practice of polygamy, bridewealth, kava consumption, and *nakaemas* (Milne, quoted in Miller 2001, 101).

Chiefly Conversions: The Story of Chief Marifatu

Across Melanesia, missionaries appear to have skillfully appropriated chiefly authority in order to ensure the successful large-scale conversion of populations to Christianity (White 1992, 81). Missionary journals are replete with triumphant accounts of the conversion of powerful chiefs, who are soon followed in their newfound faith by their people. For instance, on Nguna Island, Milne recounted that the conversions of chiefs Mariwota of Tikilasoa, Matakoale of Tanaropo, and Maripongi of Tanomeila were, in each case, the turning point in the conversions of the population (Miller 2001, 127, 134).

Facey wrote that after Matakoale's conversion he renounced his ten wives, keeping only one; worked with Milne to burn *napeas;* and gave many of his sacred objects to Milne (1981, 308). By carefully juxtaposing these historical missionary accounts with local histories, we can explore the central agency of chiefs in their responses to the mission encounter.

The history of Chief Marifatu provides a central account of local Indigenous agency in response to the mission project in North Efate. Local histories describe Chief Marifatu as the central figure in the initial opposition, and subsequent conversion, to Christianity. These accounts provide insights into the mission project so as to breathe life into and offer critical engagement with archival material that is dominated by missionary accounts from the time. Local histories allow us to read historical missionary accounts against the grain; they reposition Indigenous agency in ways that illustrate the woven histories of *ples.*

* * *

As the sun sets, I sit on a wooden platform built to catch the prevailing "sweet winds" that come off the salt water on the coast of Lelepa Island. I am with a group of Lelepa chiefs and men, wise in the ways of *ples,* drinking kava from coconut shells. At my instigation, discussions begin to circle around the early missionary period in North Efate. These discussions are etched with the shame of the deaths of early Rarotongan missionaries, a continual source of sadness for the contemporary Christian population. Matanik offers a slow, thoughtful narrative of the life of Marifatu; as he speaks, other men offer quiet comments of agreement or add details to the story. There is a slow cadence to the story until Matanik becomes louder and passionate describing Marifatu as a heroic figure:

> Marifatu was a good leader. He was a man who had been taken by the missionaries overseas to an LMS [London Missionary Society] missionary school and then was brought back to Lelepa Island. . . . He was not happy that the missionaries didn't want people to live following *kastom* and that they should only follow Christianity. . . . He said to the missionaries, "*Bifo,* we lived, we prayed, we had good lives, and you came to try and change us. Why would we want to change?"
>
> Marifatu was the leader who gave the order for Lelepa people to kill the missionaries because he knew that the missionaries who came were diseased.
>
> Many Lelepa people had died of diseases. Chief Marifatu said that it was the white people who had come with the diseases that had killed Lelepa people. That's why he gave the order that Lelepa men needed to kill the missionaries and their child. They were drowned behind Lelepa Island where there is a stone called *lakantamas.* They drowned the missionary, his wife, and his child. (interview, Nov 2014)

The careful narrative account repositions Marifatu in the context of the independence narratives of the two pillars of identity for ni-Vanuatu: church and *kastom*. Marifatu is represented as a prescient visionary—a leader who understood the dangers of missionaries and their capacity to transform *kastom* and to carry disease and death. By this account, the missionary project of conversion is brought into sharp relief against local histories that describe the dramatic social and spiritual upheavals associated with the missionaries and the attempts by local leaders to navigate the uncharted waters of Christianity. In this account, the deaths of the Rarotongan missionaries are made understandable, representing not a violent opposition to Christianity but rather an attempt to manage the deaths resulting from epidemics.

Missionary accounts from the time suggest that Chief Marifatu regularly challenged the spiritual authority of the missionaries. Macdonald records a translated version of one of Marifatu's speeches: "Marifatu . . . jumped up in a rage, shouting and flourishing his spear. Immediately the drums and dancing ceased, and Marifatu made a speech inciting the assembled savages to massacre the Mission party. . . . 'Who,' said Marifatu, 'are these missionaries? What are they *taboo* too? I tomahawked some of them years ago and nothing ever happened to me' " (Macdonald 1898, 23–25).

For almost fifty years, Lelepa people held steadfast in their opposition to the Christian mission, with the population on Lelepa Island, although the largest in the region, being "the last to give up heathenism and embrace Christianity about 1898." The turning point in Lelepa people's acceptance of the Christian faith was the conversion of Chief Marifatu (Miller 1987, 98; 2001, 105). On conversion, the authority of "head chiefs" was skillfully appropriated by the church, and these important chiefs were often appointed to senior roles in the church, with Marifatu elected as deacon toward the end of the century.

The Missionary Legacy: Ordaining Chiefs

Commitment by local populations and chiefs to Christianity, together with the involvement of missionaries in ordaining chiefs, heralded a significant transformation in the passing on of chiefly titles. Chief Mormor posited missionary influence in the North Efate region as the point of departure from *naflak* (matrilineal) descent structures toward *blad laen* (patrilineal) descent: "Land belongs to *naflaks* only. I must look after the boundary of the land of the *nawita* tribe because I am the chief of the *naflak* line. The *blad laen* system is something that came from outside; it belongs to the missionaries; it does not belong to us" (interview, Nov 2014). Mormor's comments detail not only the missionary involvement in changes to descent structures related to chiefly titles over dominions but also how these changes created transformations in landholding arrangements.

In North Efate, missionaries were involved in the suppression of matrilineal chiefly descent and kinship relations. Facey wrote of the missionary-influenced transformation in chiefly descent principles: "The position of matrilineal principle had been seriously altered by the change of hereditary succession through males, that is, chiefly titles passed from father to son instead of 'mother's brother' to 'sister's sons' " (1981, 304). Guiart commented that Milne was reasonably successful in the "suppression of matrilineal tradition, considered as being most heathen and unwholesome, [and] as contrary to the scriptures" (2013, 21).

Historical records illustrate the role played by missionaries in anointing chiefs. A key event was the investiture, by Milne, of twelve new Christian chiefs in North Efate in 1900. Milne presided over the ceremony during which Bible readings were conducted and chiefs were asked to declare their love of God, after which time the gathering said, "God save the chiefs." Taripoaliu, as the son of Matakoale, the famed chiefly teacher of the church, was named "head chief... over Nguna, Pele, Kalkula and part of Efate around Siviri" (Don 1927, 270). Milne went on to state that "he is the first head chief ever made on Nguna, and the honour was conferred because of his outstanding character and ability... nowadays the chief is chosen by popular election" (quoted in Don 1927, 270–271). This description by Milne of the process of "electing" a "head chief" as a patrilineal successor marks a complete departure from previously existing *naflak* matrilineal descent arrangements, thereby documenting a historical moment of profound cultural, social, and political transformation.

Writing on chiefly transformation of the *naflak* system in Pango, Rawlings suggested that in 1909 a new chief of Pango—Chief Kalpram—was installed by the Reverend James Mackenzie in large part because he was literate in English and the South Efate languages—a talent highly prized among Presbyterian missionaries who wanted to halt French influence in the area (Rawlings 1999a, 82; Miller 1987, 39–40). Writing a few months after the installation of Chief Kalpram, Mackenzie stated, "I suppose that during all these years I have installed over a dozen [chiefs] at different villages" (quoted in Miller 2001, 40). While this appears almost as an offhand comment, the enduring implications of each of these missionary decisions continue to play out in the contemporary politics of chiefly title claims across Efate Island and other parts of Vanuatu.

On Efate Island, *naflak* matrilineal descent structures gave way to missionary values "which emphasised patrilineal rights of succession, new codes of education, the acquisition of English language, a commitment to Christianity and the ability of a chiefly candidate to use these skills to negotiate relationships with foreign powers" (Rawlings 1999a, 82). Chiefs increasingly became viewed as men who mediated relationships between the village and the apparatus of church and colonial state.

Conclusion: Continuing Narratives of Place

Standing in the museum entrance in the Vanuatu Cultural Centre, I have just finished a long presentation, alongside Lelepa chiefs, of our efforts to create community leases to protect the customary *naflak* land against leasing by investors. The presentation is over, and the chiefs and I are quietly talking to a range of people who have come up to speak to us following the presentation. A French anthropologist pushes his way to the front of the group to speak to me. He says in a loud voice, "This work is irrelevant. I don't know why you bother working with these people on Efate; they have lost their *kastom* and don't know anything about land" (journal entry, June 2012). Indigenous people living on Efate Island have not "lost their *kastom*" as critics sometimes claim. Adopting a decolonial methodology that privileges Lelepa people's deep ontological conceptions of place allows me to write back against these claims.

As discussed in this chapter, contemporary North Efate narratives of place are fixed around three principal themes: (1) the idiom of the *saloa* as a wooden plate that everyone can eat from—customary land that sustains people in their relationship to place; (2) the ancestral figure of Roi Mata and the continuance of the *naflak* system; and (3) the sacred power of place that is manifest in the spirits and ancestors who inhabit the landscape and is the basis for chiefly *natkar* and authority. These contemporary meanings of place have survived the ravages of colonization and the dramatic political and social transformations that heralded the arrival of Christianity in North Efate: namely, the movement of people to the coast, the destruction of sacred objects, and missionary interventions in *kastom* practice. Local Lelepa chiefs described the transformations of *kastom* associated with chiefly ordination by missionaries:

> The missionaries changed our chiefs. If you look carefully at Lelepa, you can see Christianity has changed chiefs. Christianity changed the way of *kastom*. It was no longer the same as *bifo* with chiefs ordaining chiefs; it was a missionary that ordained a paramount chief of Lelepa, Chief Lapsale.
>
> Sometimes this [chiefly ordination] was just missionaries deciding; sometimes it was chiefs with the missionaries. All missionaries just looked at was who understood Christianity. Chiefs would look at *blad laen*, or sometimes *naflak*. The missionary would do the ordination, but the chiefs and the people would need to consider what line the man had who wanted to be ordained. (interview with Lelepa chiefs and elders, Nov 2014)

This account highlights the dramatic influence missionaries had on the recognition of the principles of matrilineal descent and associated chiefly authority and dominion over land. Missionary-anointed chiefs represented alternate claims to authority and legitimacy beyond the sacred power historically associated with *nawota*. The process of matrilineal chiefly succession was radically altered by missionaries on Efate Island, representing a transformation in localized power and authority to a small, select group of men and their sons. As we have seen, succession of chiefly titles not only dictates authority over a people but also signifies authority over landscapes.

In spite of the transformations associated with Christianity and the colonial-period land rush, the practice of exploring understandings of *kastom* as the ways of place illustrates how *kastom hemi laef yet*—*kastom* continues to animate the day-to-day lives of people in North Efate. Like the weaving of a *rong*—of deftly plaiting black fibers against white—and like Lelepa people themselves, we must acknowledge the historical legacies associated with cultural transformation while also celebrating the flexible and fluid practice of *kastom. Kastom hemi laef yet;* for Lelepa people, the ways of place endure.

Chapter 3
Performing Property, Throwing Silver Dollars

Across Oceania, colonization by European powers was made by reference to the doctrine of discovery, treaty making, or the legal fiction of terra nullius, the idea that the land was literally empty of people. In the New Hebrides, by contrast, property claims gave rise to sovereign claims between the two rival powers, Britain and France. While colonialism in the New Hebrides took a particularly unique form—that of a joint condominium between Britain and France—in practice, like comparable processes across Oceania and in Australia, Aotearoa New Zealand, and North America, it centered on the appropriation of land.

Colonial land transactions can be interpreted with reference to the "performance of property," a term I use to acknowledge that law is at its core a cultural product imbued with authority (Derrida 1990, 941; see also McDonnell 2013). Power dynamics inform the processes of colonization such that the performance of property becomes the authorizing discourse of the newly imposed colonial legal system over the existing Indigenous one. Seeing title making as performance renders the exercise of colonial power and authority visible in a way that is palpable and embodied (Peters 2008, 180). It allows us to observe the ways that bodies, space, and property are mutually imbricated (Banivanua Mar and Edmonds 2010, 3), with settlers emplaced and Indigenous people displaced from the landscapes. Performances of colonial land dealings were gendered and raced (Butler 1990b), performed exclusively by men: Australian and French agents as purchasers of land titles and Indigenous men supposedly involved in selling land, although often with little comprehension of the meaning of these transactions in colonial law. Colonial performances of property provide important precursors to understanding contemporary land dealings in Vanuatu and allow for reflection on the enduring legacy of property and the way that colonial land transactions are echoed in contemporary land dealings.

In this chapter, I suggest that, like Patrick Wolfe's concept of settler colonialism as a structure (2006, 388), property may also operate as an enduring colonial structure rather than a specific temporal event. Consideration of the legal processes associated with the commodification of land by colonial powers is important because the continuing, obdurate impacts of these transformations on the material landscape, as well as on aspects of identity and agency, endure in contemporary postcolonial realities. Surveyed lease title boundaries, once documented in colonial survey maps, are difficult to erase and regularly become the contemporary basis for the re-leasing of landscapes. In post-independence Vanuatu, original condominium survey maps are regularly used to mark boundaries of titles over customary land, allowing convenience and ease for those investors involved in contemporary lease making with chiefs. These continuities provide the impetus for writing against the silences of the past, and their ongoing impact in the present, by carefully documenting the often unequal and violent nature of lease making at the colonial frontier, as informed by the imposed cultural logic of property. These continuities show how dispossession of Indigenous groups is an ongoing process, even in postcolonial, independent, self-determining Pacific states. It points to the disquieting truth that colonial logics endure even in self-governing Indigenous states—including the capital-centric logic of the ownership model of property.

The ownership model of property continues in legal systems across supposedly postcolonial Oceanic states, meaning that the sites around which wealth and power coalesce show continuities with earlier colonial arrangements. I explore, in this and the following chapter, how many of the foundational legal arrangements for dispossession, namely the Torrens Title property systems, have remained in place across Pacific countries after independence. This suggests the deep paradox central to the creation of many independent Oceanic states: that while the political claims of independence were founded on the return of alienated lands to Indigenous peoples, post-independence legal arrangements in these same states allowed for the continuance of property arrangements such that many Indigenous groups have been dispossessed again—their lands recolonized by foreign interests.

Silver Dollars: Property as the Basis of Colonization

Like other colonial frontiers, early encounters between foreigners and locals in North Efate were often marred by extreme violence. An account written by Presbyterian missionary the Reverend John Geddie details one incident that suggests the brutal scale of this violence. In his diary from 1848, Geddie wrote of his first approach to what would later be named Havannah Harbour:

> A more spacious and splendid harbor I never saw. In all directions the scenery around is picturesque and lovely. . . .
>
> . . . About midday we came to anchor off a village. . . . No canoes came off for a long time. At last, after many signals, one canoe ventures within speaking reach. As soon as the natives learnt that Mose and Sualo were on board their fear was gone and several other canoes came off. The shyness of the poor natives may be

> accounted for. It was this very place that, a few years before, the crews of three sandal wood traders, after shooting about one hundred of the natives, had smothered as many more by the fire at the mouth of the cave in which they had taken refuge. Humanity shudders to think of such fiendish deeds. The natives of this place pleaded with the teachers who visited them, that they might also have teachers, supposing that their presence might prevent foreigners from firing on them.

By this account, hundreds of people died at the hands of sandalwood traders, and some of them may even have taken shelter in the same resting place as Chief Roi Mata.[1]

In this early colonial period from the mid-1800s onward, Havannah Harbour was the hub of British interest in the archipelago. The coastal landscape of North Efate was subjected to lease making and appropriation, while the adjacent deep harbor hosted the boats that were engaged in the early labor trade out of the archipelago to Australia. At the same time, the first colonized land on Efate Island was settled by Englishman Captain Donald Macleod, who in 1870 began one of the first cotton plantations in the archipelago (Miller 1981, 90). By 1873, eleven cotton plantations were located on land adjacent to Havannah Harbour (Morrell 1960, 180).

Across the archipelago, missionaries had petitioned various British officials, entreating them to act against the abuses of the labor trade from the 1860s onward. In 1868, Geddie presented a petition signed by eight Presbyterian missionaries to the governor of New South Wales, the Earl of Belmore. Having outlined their evidence relating to the practices of ships involved in the labor trade, the petition finishes with the following words: "We have no hesitation in denouncing the trade in human beings, as at present carried on amongst these islands, as in violation of the natural rights of man, as calculated to be injurious to the social, moral and spiritual interests of the natives... as in short a revival of the slave trade" (Geddie 1868). This petition indicates the detrimental moral and spiritual effects of the labor trade, in addition to referencing the supposedly established British position of ending the slave trade among the missionaries at least, if not among the local British plantation owners or Australian recruiters.

With its deep waters, Havannah Harbour became the central meeting place for ships involved in the labor trade. The reestablishment of a Presbyterian Mission in 1872 by the Reverend Daniel Macdonald and his wife prompted renewed contestation between local missionaries and both labor traders and plantation owners. Macdonald argued that the labor trade was being sanctioned by British colonial powers who supported the traders with gunboats, noting, "This labor traffic is worse since the gun-boats of 1872 were sent than before. The effect of these gun-boats is to protect traders... [from] savages and to countenance them in every enormity and outrage" (Macdonald 1878, 28). Macdonald also reported numerous problems with the men on trading ships, their "desire for local women," and their sale of alcohol to locals

(Macdonald 1875). Many of these missionary protests pivoted around notions of race, "savagery," and sexuality.

As well as challenging the labor trade, missionaries contested the legality of many of the colonial lease transactions made between Indigenous people and European planters or colonial agents. The Reverend Peter Milne repeatedly challenged land dealing by Donald Macleod over Kakula Island, describing in detail the unfair nature of the transaction:

> Macleod paid for the island with silver dollars. The man had been drunk and did not know what he was doing when he had allegedly agreed to sell Kakula island. . . . Milne took the people with him by boat to Havannah Harbour where they talked to Captain Macleod on his ship and urged him to take back the money and leave the land to the people. Macleod refused. The patient vendor then pushed the silver dollars into Macleod's pocket and scrambled down into Milne's boat. Macleod pulled out the silver dollars and threw them back. They missed the boat and flew into the Harbour.
>
> "You've thrown away *your* money!" shouted the excited North Efate man. They returned to their villages believing that Kakula was still theirs. (quoted in Miller 1981, 127)

This experience of transacting Kakula is echoed in many land dealings that were entered into between locals and planters and commercial operators across the archipelago during the early colonial period.

The title over Kakula illustrates how transactions over land in the early colonial period were legally recognized as legitimate if they were in the appropriate legal form, regardless of the ethics of a transaction, including whether the transaction was understood or voluntarily entered into in any meaningful sense. Assertions of claims to territory were largely between European colonial powers rather than any designated set of acts of relations between Europeans and "natives." Wolfe wrote that in these processes of territorial claims, the rights accorded to natives reflected the balance "between European powers in any given theatre of colonial settlement" (Wolfe 2006, 390). In the New Hebrides, rival claims by Britain and France to the territory meant that by a strangely circular logic the performance of property itself became the legal claim made by European powers. The story of colonialism in the New Hebrides is uniquely entwined with rival claims made to territorial annexation as property.

Colonial property law willfully assumed both parties were equal. Writing on land transactions in "Frontier" North America, Stuart Banner commented that these transactions took place along a continuum, at one end contracts between more or less equal parties, as occurred at the beginning of land sales between "Indians" and "whites," and at the other end "conquest," in which negotiations between parties were demonstrably unequal. Even at this point of conquest the performance of property is still legitimated. However, Banner explained that "by the late nineteenth century, there was little pretense that land cessations were voluntary in any meaningful sense of the word, even as they retained the form of negotiated treaties" (2009, 4). Wolfe wrote that the legal right of preemption gave the discovering European power a sovereign monopoly in conducting land transactions with natives, with the result that the territorial frontier became established through "greed-crazed investors who had no intention of allowing the formalities of federal law to impede their access to the riches available in, under, and on Indian soil" (2006, 391).

Property law became the mechanism that was used to give effect to the processes of colonialism, to make legitimate and create a legally acceptable basis for the dispossession of Indigenous people from land. Imposed ideas of property provided the authorizing narrative for colonization, rendering the annexation of land from Indigenous people legally legitimate in the terms of the laws of the colonial powers. Land transactions in the correct legal form met the requirements of property, providing an argument against claims of injustice, effectively working to legitimate the dispossession of Indigenous people (Banner 2005, 2009; Merry 1999).

Like those of the North American frontier, land dealings in the colonial period in the New Hebrides occurred along a continuum from contract to conquest, albeit between rival colonial powers, neither of whom had an absolute sovereign claim over the archipelago. Milne's historical accounts of the Reverend William Watt's negotiations over a parcel of land on Nguna Island in North Efate in 1870 show the schism in cultural logic that often informed land dealings between missionaries and locals. There are missionary accounts of negotiations with Chief Mariwota of Tikilasoa during which a "deed of sale" was drawn up describing the boundaries of the land and was signed by three separate landowners in exchange for calico, beads, knives, scissors, and a small chest. While the missionaries were "pleased with the ease with which they acquired the land on Nguna and carefully drafted a document to avoid future problems regarding ownership," they did not realize that the land they were allocated was the home of the devil spirit Taloa. Accordingly, all the Ngunese avoided the missionary "lest they should share in the fate they considered certain to overtake him" (Don 1927, 90). A similar situation occurred with the siting of the Erakor Mission in the 1860s on a small island in the bay named Erakor Island, on haunted land (Presbyterian Mission New Hebrides 1864).

Missionaries, engaged in performing property to create title deeds over land, were often unaware of the *kastom* resonances of the landscape for local people—in some cases to their own detriment in terms of attracting a congregation. For ni-Vanuatu, there was probably little to be lost in a transaction over land that had no productive value because of the spiritual and metaphysical beings that inhabited the landscape. Many of the transactions at the beginning of the colonial project to develop the New Hebrides—envisaged in both spiritual and economic terms—are marked by this complete miscomprehension between supposed "buyers" and "sellers" around the nature of the transaction. The transactions demonstrate competing cultural logics and the way in which the performance of property was a central tool used to impose European colonial meanings of land to give effect to colonization.

Property Cloaked in the Flag of Empire

The fair, legitimate, and voluntary nature of early British and French colonial land dealings was often an artifice, as pointed out by contemporary commentators. Australian journalist Julian Thomas, traveling in 1887, wrote of the land titles created in the New Hebrides and subsequently registered by the British colonial administration in Fiji that "the British flag was being used to cover transactions with the natives which would not be acknowledged in any other part of the world." In his letter, Thomas "strongly questioned the legality of these extensive land purchases for the purpose of speculation" (J Thomas 1887). This image of the British flag being used to cloak the true nature of land transactions is evocative, reflecting the role played by colonial governments in legitimating the land rush through their legal and administrative processes and through use of colonial force.

As large-scale colonial land rushes were taking place in the 1880s in the New Hebrides, both Great Britain and France agreed to naval patrols by gunboats to "protect the lives and *property* of their nationals [emphasis added]" (Van Trease 1987, xi). This was the same property that had only recently been created under dubious "legal" means. Colonial gunboats were not just in the New Hebrides to *protect* property; rather, the threat of force was implicit in the *creation* of this form of "protection." Howard Van Trease noted that "the Governor of New Caledonia ordered the captains of French warships operating in Vanuatu waters to certify the dates of the purchases, thus giving them official Government recognition" (1987, 27). This act of recognition, backed by the force of warships, gave otherwise ambiguous legal documents legal effect. The British employed a similar strategy in 1881, with the British high commissioner for the Western Pacific issuing a notice requiring that land grants be registered in Australia and Fiji. A French naval officer observed in 1898 that the forceful eviction of people from land often led to "a thousand annoyances... which cannot end without the intervention of a man-of-war by regular acts of war" (Leouve 1898). To make this process easier, "a British warship was permanently stationed in the New Hebrides to administer the legislation, and its officers intervened in the making of grants of land to British subjects and supervised the drafting of the contracts of sale" (O'Connell 1968, 73). Ultimately the legality of many of these deeds remained contentious and became central to the ongoing struggles between the colonial powers and the major work of the Condominium Joint Court when it began dealing with land claims in 1927 (Van Trease 1987, 63).

The conquest-driven nature of colonial land transactions is best illustrated by the operations of the French Compagnie Calédonienne des Nouvelles-Hebrides (CCNH). The CCNH, spurred on by the colonial aspirations of the French Government, began by purchasing existing land titles, including those of Macleod in Havannah Harbour, and then in 1882 moved on to purchasing land directly from local inhabitants. Together, CCNH agents purchased an extraordinary 95,460 hectares (235,887 acres) of land, approximately 8 percent of the total landmass of Vanuatu on the islands of Malekula, Efate, and Epi, over a two-month period. Van Trease described the processes used by the company agents on board the ship *Caledonienne* as follows: "Unsuspecting islanders were enticed aboard with promises of trade goods or liquor, then persuaded to affix their marks on pieces of paper transferring vast amounts of the coastline, designating the hills as back boundaries" (1987, 26–27).

Similar leasing practices, although on a much smaller scale, were replicated by the Australian-based South Sea Speculation Company. Company agents traveled aboard the *Fairy Queen* purchasing vast areas of land (Van Trease 1987, 27). This company was followed by the Australasian New Hebrides Company, established to trade and acquire land in the New Hebrides "by purchase, barter, lease, license, reclamation or otherwise" (Articles of the Australian Association of the New Hebrides Company 1889). This ominous-sounding article within the company's registration documents seems to signal that agents should attain Indigenous land by any means, regardless of legal process.

Commentary at the time questioned the legitimacy of many of these early colonial leases. Writing in 1871 after a trip to Tanna, Geddie stated that "the natives on the west side of Tanna have sold much of their land to white men. . . . It is very doubtful if these land transactions were properly understood by the natives, and they will in no distant time be a fruitful source of trouble" (cited in Thompson 1970, 29). Similarly, Captain Cyprian Bridge wrote in 1882, after an investigation into land sales between Indigenous inhabitants and settlers, that while these transactions were "reasonably fair," "there has been difficulty in getting the natives to understand the real nature of an out-and-out sale of land and its alienation in perpetuity." While Bridge may have determined that these transactions were fair, many missionaries and other commentators at the time continued to question their legitimacy. Ultimately, the legitimacy of lease titles became a central issue in subsequent negotiations around the joint British–French condominium administration.

Conflict over Land Titles in Havannah Harbour

An example of the conflict that arose between missionaries and local French plantation owners, tenants of the CCNH, over both title making and the dispossession of the local populations took place in Havannah Harbour from the mid-1880s onward. In Havannah Harbour, missionaries voiced concern that the French annexations would impact the land held by Presbyterian missionaries as reserves for "natives" and that French aggression meant that people could no longer access gardens and were, according to Macdonald (1887), at risk of "starvation." Historical accounts suggest that the aggressive and rapacious purchase by the CCNH of both former British plantations around Havannah Harbour as well as additional areas of "native land" in North Efate forced people off their land and led to the movement of settlements from the inland area to Lelepa and Moso Islands (Miller 1987, 81). The mission station at Udaone on the northern side of Samoa Point became a major resettlement site for displaced locals. In 1882, concerned by the large-scale dispossession of Indigenous people, Macdonald organized for the mission-held title over a large area of Havannah Harbour and Samoa Point to function as a reserve for natives. Under this arrangement, the "natives of Udaone, Suwa, Moso, Siviri etc., by a document witnessed by Lieutenant-Commander King, of H.M.S 'Sandfly', gave their land properties in trust to the New Hebrides Synod on behalf of themselves and their heirs forever, to prevent the said lands becoming alienated by them by force or fraud.... The same lands ceded to the mission have ever been since and are still in the occupation of the said natives or their descendants, who have thereon cultivated their plantation patches, providing themselves with the necessities of life from the fruits of the soil" (Macdonald 1887).

The creation of a large mission reserve was contested by the CCNH, who claimed to have secured a title over a portion of the same land by Deed of Sale. The company claimed it held a Deed of Sale made by J C Dagget, an American who claimed to have purchased the land from "Tekau" or "Tokie," a native of Vate, in 1871. In response, Macdonald repeatedly challenged the legal validity of this French claim: "Upon examination I pronounced this alleged title to be legally worthless, and utterly refused to recognise it, and the natives unanimously protested as before, that they have never sold this land to anyone" (1887).

From 1886, French planters and the CCNH's property interests were supported by a French military post located in Havannah Harbour and by the regular patrolling of French gunboats. In correspondence, Macdonald repeatedly raised his concerns with the British Resident about the aggression of the local French planters and troops toward local people, but with little success (Macdonald 1887). Local missionaries opposed French colonial expansion with vigor, writing to both the Australian Government and to Queen Victoria citing the "grief and alarm [caused by] the landing of French troops and the establishment and continued occupation of military posts at Havannah Harbour, Efate" (Federal Committee of Presbyterian Missions 1886). Missionaries also wrote to the Australian Government warning that "the French had landed soldiers and formed military posts at Mallicolo [Malekula] and Havannah Harbour... [as a] violation of treaties, ensuring the neutrality of the islands and protecting British interests" (Jubilee History of Presbyterian

Church Victoria 1888). Correspondence between the British and French governments finally led to the withdrawal of French troops from Havannah Harbour in 1888 (Miller 1987, 86). The land issues remained unresolved, and Macdonald and others continued for many years to correspond on the matter with the prime minister of Australia, among others (Macdonald 1906). Lawyers for the Presbyterian Church also continued to write to the CCNH as late as 1906 claiming title to the Havannah Harbour land, stating that the CCNH had "acted wrongfully in seizing the land and destroying the property of the natives" (Davis and Campbell Solicitors 1906). At this point, the land was determined to be "under dispute" and became one of the many matters to be later considered by the joint court.

The "Pandemonic" Condominium Establishes Torrens Title

A major source of tension for the condominium administration was the different approach to land dealings, with predominantly French settlers involved in a large-scale land rush across the islands of the New Hebrides from the late 1800s and through much of the 1900s. French colonial rule, for the most part, consciously enabled this land rush, while the British were ineffectual in persuading the French to halt the large-scale leasing of land in transactions that occurred mostly without the knowledge of the Indigenous population (Van Trease 1987). In 1878, "Notes" were exchanged between Britain and France in which they agreed to maintain the independence of what became known as the "New Hebrides." This position subsequently changed in 1906 when "the condominium" was established to reflect the interests of British and French missionaries and settlers (O'Connell 1968, 73). Under the condominium, the British and French jointly ruled over the country, with representatives from both foreign powers making up the condominium, which established joint laws and met as a joint court over certain matters (O'Connell 1968; Rodman 2001). Each country retained jurisdiction over its own citizens and maintained a separate administrative structure, which led to duplication in many governmental functions and the creation of geographical enclaves of either French or British administrative control.

Land was central to the initial condominium agreement, with the British ceding to French pressure to create a legal mechanism to confirm existing French land claims (Van Trease 1987, xii). In the convention, signed between Britain and France in 1906, the joint court was established to deal with land disputes in accordance with the Torrens Title system of land registration, whereby existing European title interests were indefeasible once registered unless successfully challenged (Van Trease 1984, 20).

The Torrens Title system of land registration originated in South Australia in the 1850s and is itself a product of colonial knowledge exported from the colonial administration in Australia to Vanuatu, as well as to Fiji, Papua New

Guinea, and Solomon Islands. Under Torrens Title, a change in the ownership of land was completed by transfer of registered title deeds, and all titles were guaranteed by the colonial administration. Challenging these property interests involved producing legal documentation, something unlikely to be possessed by Indigenous groups who were largely unaware of court proceedings in relation to deeds over their land, which was often "illegally sold or . . . the boundaries were incorrect." In the history of the joint court, only a single "native caveat" against the registration of a title was successful, suggesting the profound indifference of the condominium administration to examining the claims of Indigenous groups over areas of land (Van Trease 1984, 24).

In many cases, the joint court process took several decades before assessing the validity of registration, by which time many of the original inhabitants who may have been able to give evidence about the original land transactions had died. Further, Article 22 of the 1906 Convention stated that all titles registered in Suva or Noumea before 1 January 1896 were valid and could not be legally challenged, as they were made "in good faith," meaning that "even if the deeds presented to the Court . . . were incorrect, or in some way fraudulent, they could not be challenged" (Van Trease 1984, 20–21, 23–24). In an efficacious legal sleight of hand, titles, made in dubious circumstances in the large-scale speculative land rush that took place before 1896, were rendered "property" by agreement between one colonial power and another. By the time the joint court had completed its work on determining rival European disputes over claims to titles on Efate Island, over three-quarters of the island had been alienated. By 1980, the joint court had made over 1,400 judgments amounting to 241,678 hectares (597,199 acres) of land or leases across almost 20 percent of the total land area of Vanuatu. Of these titles, the overwhelming majority, representing 12.2 percent of the landmass, was held by French interests, 3.1 percent was held by British interests, 5 percent was held in native reserves or by Indigenous people, and 0.5 percent was held as state land (Van Trease 1984, 21–22). Toward the end of the condominium period, large-scale leasing by largely foreign expatriate interests, particularly where it resulted in the dispossession of Indigenous people, created growing concern among ni-Vanuatu and generated increasing national support for independence.

Independence and the Establishment of Custom Landowners

Independence leaders began to discuss the need for land reform so as to create better recognition for Indigenous rights. In his book, *Land and Politics in New Hebrides,* Barak Sope wrote: "Revised land laws are needed, taking full account of New Hebridean ideas and not concentrating on French and British land laws alone. . . . If New Hebridean ideas are ignored, the British and French will never succeed in imposing a new tenure system upon the indigenous masses. European laws can in no way obviate the deep-rooted emotions and social contracts that tie the indigenous person to his land" (Sope 1974, 5).

Across Melanesia, state sovereignty was expressed in opposition to colonization as the reclaiming of Indigenous claims to land. These nationalist narratives were employed to garner the support of citizens in the newly created states. The early symbolism of Vanuatu's statehood—the flag, the name of the state, the motto of the new state, and the words of the national anthem—attests to the importance of *kastom* and place in the nation-building project. Land and citizenship issues were entwined in the drafting of the Vanuatu Constitution, which involved lengthy debates around the rights of citizens with respect to land. While the British colonial administration argued for the recognition of citizenship based on birth in the state, ni-Vanuatu leaders remained concerned that this would give "expatriates, settlers and planters automatic citizenship upon independence which they could then use to preserve their land holdings" (Rawlings 2012, 66). These issues were resolved in the final drafting of the constitution by the provision that expatriates and settlers could acquire "naturalised citizenship" after ten years of residence (Rawlings 2012, 66; see also the Vanuatu Constitution, Article 12). A clear distinction is made in the constitution between Indigenous and non-Indigenous citizens; only Indigenous citizens can own land.

The constitution allocates exclusive rights of possession to Indigenous citizens to land. Article 73 states that "all land in the Republic of Vanuatu belongs to the indigenous custom owners and their descendants." This is further qualified by Article 75, which states that "only indigenous citizens of Vanuatu who have acquired their land in accordance with a recognised system of land tenure shall have perpetual ownership of their land." By this definition, all Indigenous citizens are "custom landowners" (or the condensed version, "custom owners"). Colin Filer similarly argued that under the Papua New Guinea Constitution, Indigenous citizens become custom landowners defined through clan structures (2012, 602). In Vanuatu, the concept of Indigenous citizen "custom landowners" is entrenched in discussions of land rights. Here the concept of citizen custom landowners resonates closely with the idea that all Indigenous people are *"man ples,"* the Indigenous identity that represents the symbiotic attachment of person and place. In this formulation, to be without land is irreconcilable with concepts of Indigeneity—my land, my life.

The constitution also establishes a central role for the state in protecting the landholdings of Indigenous citizens. Drafted in recognition of the large-scale alienation of customary land associated with the colonial period, Article 79(1) was designed to provide additional state protection to Indigenous citizens engaged in land transactions with either "naturalised citizens" or other foreigners: "Notwithstanding Articles 73, 74 and 75 land transactions between an indigenous citizen and either a non-indigenous citizen or a non-citizen shall only be permitted with the consent of the Government." The second section of Article 79 stipulates that state consent to a land transaction shall be given unless the transaction is prejudicial to the interests of:

(a) the customary owner or owners of the land;
(b) the indigenous citizen where he is not a custom owner;
(c) the community in whose locality the land is situated; or
(d) the Republic of Vanuatu.

Here Article 79(2)(b) appears to contradict earlier articles by separating the category of "custom owner" from that of "indigenous citizen." This framing seems to introduce the idea of autochthony—that is, being the first inhabitants of a place—as the basis of claims to custom landownership. Confusingly, customary land rights are defined in the Vanuatu Constitution as *both* communal (Article 73) *and* individual (Article 79(1)). Elsewhere, the constitution identifies land rights as being individual and gendered male. If it is the case that land rights are both communal and individual, then there are no indications about how to resolve obvious tensions between individual and group-based decisions over land, or how this "communal" group should be constituted. The gendered language used in the drafting of Article 79 also appears to enfranchise men as individual Indigenous citizens with claims to protection by the state, while at the same time disenfranchising women by omission.

Constitutional arrangements also define how "custom" is recognized within the legal system of Vanuatu. While numerous articles within the constitution allow for customary law to be regarded as a source of law (Articles 47 and 95), before the land reforms of 2014, this situation did not give rise to strong, effective legal pluralism largely because the legislature and judiciary failed to provide guidance as to how this recognition could occur (Forsyth 2009, 139–174). Recognition of "custom" within the legal system has been tempered by the continuation of the previous Anglo-common legal system in the post-independence period. This follows global trends in which many postcolonial legal institutional arrangements were informed by colonial legacies (Merry and Brenneis 2003; Forsyth 2009). Filer argued that the legal recognition of "custom" in Pacific legal systems is fraught because custom "was actually born *out* of the armpit of Australian colonial law" (2007, 137–138). Leaving aside discussion of the authenticity of "custom" as the basis of recognition, Filer's conception of "custom" is of a concept that is not distinct from law but rather is a description of a set of social relations altered by legal arrangements and capitalism (Filer 2007, 137). However, Filer's emphasis on custom as a relational process evolving out of law places too much emphasis on legal processes ("the armpit") as distinct from localized contextual negotiations around the meanings of custom.

Law in Vanuatu has historically been characterized by a plurality of institutions rather than deep legal pluralism that would allow full recognition of customary institutions and the role of "chiefs" in governing and lawmaking (Merry 1988, 870; see also Forsyth 2009; F von Benda-Beckmann 2002). Vanuatu's legal system before 2014 was defined by institutional pluralism, with numerous state and customary institutions determining land claims. Historically all state institutions were involved in determining land matters, including all courts in Vanuatu and the Vanuatu ombudsman, who investigates breaches of the "Leadership Code" in the constitution and, in particular, abuse of ministerial powers over land. This included the highest court—the Court of Appeal—constituted by judges from neighboring countries in the South Pacific, as well as from the Vanuatu Supreme Court. The next level in the court hierarchy—the Vanuatu Supreme Court—comprised four judges (one located in Santo and the others in Port Vila). Below the Supreme Court was the Magistrates' Court made up of ni-Vanuatu magistrates located in Port Vila, Luganville, and Malakula. Under the Magistrates' Court were the Island Courts (which still have some limited jurisdiction over preexisting land cases but have been largely replaced by the arrangements included in the Custom Land Management Act [No 33 of 2013]).

Numerous customary institutions and chiefly structures also make land-based determinations, including: the Malvatumauri (National Council of Chiefs), although the Malvatumauri is also afforded some state recognition; the Island Councils of Chiefs; the chiefly *nakamal* (chief's house); and local individual chiefly determinations. State and customary institutions are not, of course, as distinct as just described. For example, chiefs often preside in Island Court matters, and court judges may be involved in local *nakamal* determinations as members of a customary group. In this way, the general descriptors of "formal," "customary," and "law" appear "inadequate to describe the overlapping, contested and dynamic social fields" of these institutional arrangements (Fitzpatrick 2005, 457). In Vanuatu, overlapping normative orders have also historically caused problems of legal institutional "forum shopping" between various institutions (Forsyth 2009, 197; see also K von Benda-Beckmann 1981). However, the capacity for forum shopping is limited to certain wealthier sections of the population. Urban-based formal state courts remain comparatively more expensive and inaccessible to the largely rural population of Vanuatu and, in particular, to rural women and youth.

In 1999, the Vanuatu Supreme Court chief justice declared that due to the immense backlog of existing land cases, the state courts would no longer accept any new land cases (Simo and Van Trease 2011, 8). This decision led to the creation of the Customary Land Tribunal Act in 2001, which attempted to provide an alternative mechanism, outside of the formal state-based court system, for the resolution of land disputes in accordance with customary law. Customary land tribunals allowed for land determinations to be made by chiefs and other elders who were expert in "custom" at a village, local, area, or island level in accordance with customary law. Under the Act, land tribunals of chiefs and "elders" must resolve disputes and determine the rights of parties "according to custom" (Customary Land Tribunal Act, Section 28).

Customary land tribunals began operating in Vanuatu in 2003. Between 2003 and 2011, a total of 133 decisions were recorded as being made by customary land tribunals, with approximately half (47.4 percent) being resolved at the local village level (Simo and Van Trease 2011, 11). While customary land tribunals did not operate on all major islands in Vanuatu, there were land tribunals operating in Santo, Malo, Ambae, Malekula, Efate, and Tanna. Three reviews of customary land tribunals were conducted during their period of operation. These reviews found a major problem with the operation of land tribunals: matters that went through layers of the tribunal could then be appealed through the court system, allowing for forum shopping by claimants hoping for judgments in their favor. Problems with forum shopping gave rise to the impression that the claimant with the "deepest pockets" would have the resources to repeatedly appeal to win the case. Since 2003, the operation of Customary Land Tribunals has been reviewed on three occasions: in 2004 by Joel Simo; in 2005 by a New Zealand Agency for International Development–sponsored team including Simo, Professor Don Patterson, Geoff Mavromatis, Josepha Kanawi, and Alicta Vuti; and, most recently, in 2011 by Simo and Van Trease.

Ultimately the Customary Land Tribunal Act offered only limited recognition for customary law within the state system, with land disputes repeatedly appealed to the formal state courts. This situation has been characterized as "weak" legal pluralism because the state is still central to the source of law in this system and to other supposedly preexisting customary institutions (Griffiths 1986, 5). Formal state-based legal arrangements ideologically shaped the way land claims were recognized in the customary land tribunal system; claims were often framed in terms of chiefly titles and custom landownership rights rather than the *kastom* management practices relating to the use of and access to land. The result of this weak legal pluralism was that resolving land matters involved a dystopian matrix in which claims of landownership informed by "custom" were often determined in the formal state legal system.

"The Register Is Everything": How Property Enables Dispossession

Despite the constitutional recognition afforded to custom owners, soon after independence the legal arrangements in Vanuatu were again dominated by an imported Anglo-Australian model of property rights. Independence did not create a radical overhaul of the legal cartography with respect to land. Writing on colonial legal arrangements in Fiji and Hawai'i, Sally Merry and Donald Brenneis commented, "It is noteworthy that postcolonial states do not walk away from the law of the colonial era. These colonial legacies of institutions and practices provide a matrix in which consciousness, identity, and life chances take shape. They provide discursive resources central to the notion of sovereignty, to the claiming of position and power in a postcolonial world, as they did in the colonial one" (2003, 25–26). Colonial legal institutions are often maintained by postcolonial states because of their perceived importance to state formation. Before the land reforms of 2014, land law in Vanuatu retained foundational contradictions around the nature of landownership between the constitution, which recognizes land held in perpetuity by Indigenous people, and land legislation, which privileges indefeasible property rights. The Vanuatu Constitution and subsidiary legislation entrench the Western legal concept of property as *the* basis for asserting relationships to land. Constitutional articles manufacture prescriptive identities for people engaged in land transactions; land becomes "property" owned by a "custom landowner."

The idea of land as property is implicitly constructivist. Joel Simo wrote: "Not only do Melanesian beliefs affirm the sanctity of land, but they also totally contradict the imported notion of 'ownership' of land. Land is held rather than owned by the people, who are entrusted by their society to be the custodians of the land in the interests of their children and future generations" (2010, 40). Writing about Vanuatu's land-law arrangements, Simo challenged the way property enables dispossession by allowing landscapes managed by Indigenous people to be reimagined as a commodity able to be purchased.

Property is best understood as a series of relations among social actors to an object of value. The assertion of property has three central claims: first, the idea that there is a social unit—in Oceania this typically takes the form of a landowner or landowning group, often legally structured as a corporation, trust, or incorporated land group—that holds the property rights; second, that property has value that is linked to commodification and the market; and finally, that there is a hierarchy of differential rights of various social units to property (von Benda-Beckmann, von Benda-Beckmann, and Wiber 2006, 10). These broad tenets of property take a particular form in the ownership property model that has evolved in the Western legal tradition. This ownership model has the following principles: (1) it assumes a possessive individual or corporation acting as an individual (Foster 2007), identifiable by formal title and motivated by self-interested behavior; (2) the owner retains all rights of enjoyment (termed "exclusive possession"), including the power to exclude others; (3) the owner's interests are set against the interest of others; and (4) property is regarded as essentially private property, which privileges the interests of those who have private property against those who do not (Blomley 2005, 126; 2013, 26). The view of property as an absolute right is a trope that conceals the negotiations that take place internal to property. Property, expressed as a relation of ownership, is just one model of property, whereas the term "property" has been expressed in a variety of ways in different societies, across time, and history (Blomley 2013). In spite of the plurality of potential arrangements with respect to property, the ownership model of property continues to "exert a powerful imaginative hold, shaping our understandings of the possibilities of social life, the ethics of human relations and the ordering of economic life" (Blomley 2005, 125). The model posits the individual owner as universal, when there is in actuality a plurality of social institutional arrangements that could constitute property both in Western legal regimes and in a Pacific context. The privileging of the ownership property model in Vanuatu, and elsewhere in the Pacific, is indicative of the dominance of formal state legal institutions in making land determinations over customary institutions.

The ownership model of property is firmly entrenched across various countries and cultural contexts because of its performative basis; it functions as a persuasive statement of claims to others (Blomley 2013; Rose 1994). Across Oceania, property is performed as surveying, mapmaking, fence building, real estate advertisements, and the ceremonial ritual of lease making and registration. Acts of property reshape the landscape to accord with the meaning of property, but property does not preexist these performances (Blomley 2013, 33). Colonial performances of lease making create entrenched understandings of property and form an interpretive, repeated scheme of meanings. The cultural power of the ownership model of property is that it has enabled the reimagining and reinvention of both landscapes and relationships to land in Vanuatu. Place becomes property and Indigenous people become "landowners."

Possession is often termed to be the origin of property (Rose 1994). Dispossession of Indigenous people requires not only the creation of property but also the act of possession. A claim of title is a claim of possession against the world. In Vanuatu, in both the colonial and postcolonial periods, speculative land rushes have created titles, and yet the land has not always been possessed. Historically Anglo-Australian law has interpreted acts of possession in terms of the elements of "capital-centric" production, denying possessory rights to Aboriginal Australians through the doctrine of terra nullius. "Capital-centric" is a reference to the important work of J K Gibson-Graham (1996), which challenges this discourse and argues for an alternative vision of the economy that includes nonmarket and noncapitalist activities. As discussed, terra nullius is the Latin expression that means literally "the land belonging to no one"—the legal fiction that was used to erroneously describe how the continent now known as "Australia" was supposedly not under the sovereignty of any state. Even where property rights to land were recognized by colonial powers as being held by Indigenous people—such as in Hawai'i or Aotearoa New Zealand, where the cultivated landscape was recognized as being held under a form of possession—land was reconfigured as property and made alienable. The colonial violence of Indigenous dispossession offers a prescient reminder that establishing property rights in land has had profound implications for Indigenous societies. The effect of creating property relations by commodifying land can be interpreted through its impact on social relations and also through the ongoing violence of dispossession.

Vanuatu's adoption of the ownership property model has radically reconfigured the complex tapestry of customary social relationships held in relation to place into a property right held by an individual custom landowner. Given the vortex of constitutionally undefined customary arrangements over land, legislation plays a pivotal role in allocating rights, managing land dealings, and administering procedural arrangements with respect to land leasing. Exploring contemporary land legislation is necessary when considering the mechanistic nature of law in transforming customary landscapes into property.

The Anglo-Australian ownership model of property continues to dominate the administration of land in Vanuatu, as evident in the continuance of the Torrens Title system of registration. Torrens Title registration was retained in Vanuatu and elsewhere in the Pacific despite dramatic differences between Anglo-Australian and ni-Vanuatu conceptions of property. Introduced just three years after Vanuatu's independence, the principles of Torrens Title registration provided the foundations of land administration in the *Land Leases Act* (Cap 163), thereby allowing the registration of customary land. The effect of Torrens Title registration is to create an indefeasible title to land, a form of property rights that is literally "unable to be defeated," except on the very limited grounds of fraud or mistake (*Land Leases Act,* Part IV). The impact of Torrens Title registration has had particular legal implications for the constitutional rights of custom landowners in Vanuatu in the period of the land rush.

Courts in Vanuatu have repeatedly stated that in interpreting competing claims over an area of land, "the register is everything" (*Ratua Development Ltd v Ndai* [2007] VUCA 23; Civil Appeal Case 32 of 2007, 30 Nov 2007). In a Vanuatu Court of Appeal Case, *Ratua Development Ltd v Ndai,* the court held that the custom owners of an area of leased land did not constitute an "interest in land" and therefore their claim that a lease should be defeated on grounds of fraud or mistake could not apply. As an aside, in 2013 I redrafted this section of the act and changed the definition such that "persons of interest" now included custom owners. This formed a small component of the land reforms passed by Parliament and subsequently gazetted in 2014. Following the principles of Torrens Title, land legislation prior to 2014 was designed to protect registered lease interests almost regardless of the circumstances of land transactions. The formal state system remained largely unconcerned about the nature of the lease negotiation and whether the people who hold customary rights had been involved in, or benefited from, the registration of their customary land. Property interests prevailed over any assessment of custom landownership. In this way, the post-independence land rush demonstrates a continuity with the colonial period land rush. Large areas of land were again leased, following independence, by individual men signing away customary land previously belonging to groups of people with interwoven rights of use and access. A property transaction once registered becomes indefeasible.

The effect of Torrens Title registration in Vanuatu is to create a repository of property interests almost regardless of preexisting customary landholding arrangements or the unequal and unfair conduct of land transactions. The effect of registration is to "protect persons dealing in registered interests in land" regardless of "the circumstances in or the consideration for which such proprietor or any previous proprietor was registered" (see *Land Leases Act*, Section 23 and, in particular, Section 23(1)(a)). Furthermore, the director of lands is also exonerated from any facts relating to a registered interest. Registered interests in property are backed by the force of the state, often working against the interests of the broader custom-owner group.

The effect of Torrens Title registration was that it became something of a defensive shield operating for property interests in land, almost regardless of the circumstances in which the leases were negotiated in terms of consent or fairness. In a continuity from colonial lease making, the effect of registration is to privilege the performance of property over the context of who was actually involved in making the lease or the equity of the transaction. This is the instrumentality of property law. The effect is to detach land from customary systems of management to legally dispossess custom owners of their rights.

Title Making and the Transformations to Place

Like earlier joint court processes, court proceedings in contemporary Vanuatu often involve the tabling of colonial leases to make a determination of custom landownership over an area of customary land. Accordingly, these original title documents are increasingly viewed as politically sensitive, often concealed as secret documents by people who are hoping to prove or disprove land claims based on colonial title deeds.

These documents provide important historical insights into the processes by which the ownership model of property has instrumentally refashioned ideas of place as well as materially altered Indigenous landscapes. Historical documents of land titles over the Mangaliliu Plantation illustrate significant transformations in customary relationships to land in North Efate over the last century.

Historically all land in North Efate, including coastal estates, was managed under particular *naflak* chiefly dominions, as discussed in earlier chapters. In contemporary North Efate, chiefly titles continue to denote dominion over a particular area of land and group of people belonging to a specific *naflak*. For example, the area of Creek Ai is located under the chiefly title of Arier *(naflak nanu);* Tuktuk Point and surrounding land is located under the chiefly title of Mwasepongi; Farea Mangatoon is held under the chiefly title of Tongolemanu *(naflak vatu);* and Mangaraoau is held under the chiefly title of Mormor *(wita).* For reasons detailed in this book, the practice of descent of chiefly titles is changing. Increasingly, land leasing is exacerbating conflict over both chiefly titles and the areas of land over which chiefly titles confer dominion.

In the 1986 Vanuatu Supreme Court case *Taurakoto v Mormor* ([1986] VUSC 7[2]) relating to the settlement of Mangaliliu Village, the court reviewed a series of colonial land title documents. The first was a title over "Mangaliliu Plantation" dating from 1899. I have not included an image of the actual title instrument because of local political sensitivities surrounding the transaction. However, in *Taurakoto v Mormor,* the chief justice stated: "The Appellants supported their claim to be true custom owners of Lots 104 and 3078 by introducing for example a deed; dated 1899 made between the Chiefs of Lelepa and the Australian New Hebrides Company, showing that Lot 103 was sold by them for the benefit of the Community of Lelepa Island and that the money obtained therefrom was divided among the Community. The signatories to the deed show that broad representation of the Community signed it."

Rather than following chiefly dominion rights and naming a specific chief, this title describes the customary land along the coastline of Havannah Harbour as a shared resource, a *saloa,* belonging to the people of Lelepa Island. The land transaction over Mangaliliu Plantation was made between the Australian New Hebrides Company, which purchased the title, and Paramount Chief Natematesaru of Lelepa Island and numerous other chiefs, many of whom placed their fingerprints on the title deed as a demonstration of their consent to the transaction.

This 1899 title deed makes explicit the motivations of the chiefs in leasing the land "for the benefit of the community," with the money from the sale of the land going to the Lelepa community. The lease instrument indicates that, historically, mainland Efate Island was regarded as a shared resource for all Lelepa Island people, the coastline being recognized as a place where people were allocated gardening rights. In this way, the title document describes Mangaliliu customary land as a communal asset—*saloa*—even at the same moment as it was being commodified and sold as property.

A subsequent title over an adjacent area of coastal land, dated 1918, indicates rights belonging to the paramount chief to sell customary land located on the coastline of Efate Island. A second title, over another coastal area of North Efate, dated 12 July 1918, is between at least three Lelepa chiefs (as lessors) and Mr Jeannin and Kabbar (as lessees). The Christian names of the chiefs are included next to their signatures. This title document similarly suggests that customary land was viewed as a shared resource held by the Lelepa people, as represented by their chiefs. However, in this lease instrument, only a small number of fingerprints indicate the consent of Lelepa chiefs.

The 1918 title instrument is cosigned by Mr Seagoe as "Acting Native Advocate." His signature is placed next to a legal attestation that states, "I certify that I was present at Leleppa on the 12th July, 1918, and attended a meeting held by the above natives, when the terms of this document were agreed to. I affirm and sincerely believe that all the natives concerned were in complete agreement to its terms and unanimous in the execution thereof." However, despite this attestation, only three of the thirty-one named chiefs appear to have consented to this agreement—a seemingly small number for such a large group of men. There is also no reference in the title document to the paramount chief of Lelepa, suggesting that his authority with respect to land transactions was no longer acknowledged, as compared to the previous lease dated twenty years earlier.

The passage of time precludes us from properly understanding the nature of many colonial land transactions. However, independence leaders such as Ifiran Barak Sope have argued that the sale of land was not possible under pre-independence customary tenure arrangements (1974, 7). Claiming lease signatories as the prior "custom landowners" for an area of land is deeply problematic, particularly given that these early lease dealings occurred at a time when ideas of "ownership" of landscapes as property were even less appropriate.

Land titling offers a window into the colonial project, including the power dynamics created, the resources allocated, and, above all, the way land was alienated. The land transactions of the colonial period provide an important historical reference point for consideration of contemporary leasing. They illustrate how the dispossession of Indigenous inhabitants is legitimated by claims to property rights. Colonial land transactions imposed the cultural logic of property, thereby radically altering ideas of place. Havannah Harbour, as a major port for the labor trade, became one of the first sites of settlement in the colonial frontier. While agents engaged in land transactions with "natives" purported that their titles should confer property rights, missionaries and other contemporary commentators claimed that the British flag was being used to cloak the nature of these property transactions. Each new land title furthered the process of colonial state formation in the New Hebrides, a haphazard process eventually resulting in the "pandemonic" condominium arrangement.

Independence did not bring with it an untethering from the colonial ties of property. Despite the rights allocated for custom owners in the constitution, the effect of Torrens Title registration was to truncate existing customary ties and landholding claims. Court processes in Vanuatu regularly involve the examination of earlier title documents, but with little attention to the veracity of the documents or the context of previous colonial land negotiations. Where original lease negotiations were inequitable, these inequities have been erased by the passage of time and further obfuscated by the legal form and assumption that title making takes place between equal parties. By tendering lease instruments as the basis for contemporary land claims, rival claimants may also conceal the agency of ancestors—male chiefs who may have signed against rivals or as representatives of a larger group.

Conclusion: The Enduring Effect of Silver Dollars

Exactly one hundred years after the original exchange over Kakula Island between Macleod and an unnamed "North Efate man" that so incensed Milne, the Island Court sat down to determine the custom ownership over the island. The ni-Vanuatu magistrate and three custom advisers heard evidence in court from a range of disputing family groups. The evidence during the case states that the island was uninhabited at the time of the original land title. During the hearing of the case, the Maserei family made a claim over the island. The basis for this claim was the original sale of the land. The account of the evidence in the court case reads: "Chief Maserei was the man who sold Kakula to a white man name MacLoud [*sic*] on behalf of SFNH [Société Française des Nouvelles-Hébrides] company in 1884."

The identity of the unknown man was claimed. The circular logic of property means that the family claimed ownership based on past land sales. It is the previous commodification of place that gives rise to contemporary custom-ownership rights. The final judgment of the Island Court appears to follow this logic, at least in part. The Island Court has found that the Maserei family are the custom owners of Kakula Island but that this ownership is shared with three other family groups who all lived on the coastline of Efate Island. Nowhere in the judgment does the nature of the original transaction over the island become part of the evidence. No one asked whether Chief Maserei agreed to sell the island and understood the nature of the land title, whether there could possibly be consent if he really was drunk, or whether the land title should stand given that the silver dollars were thrown into the depths of Havannah Harbour. These are the questions that pierce the historical silences, that call into question the basis of the original colonial leases and, more broadly, the processes of colonization. Without careful attention, the performance of property may be repeated, with parties who were formerly dispossessed in colonial times being dispossessed again as contemporary land claims are based on colonial lease instruments.

* * *

Years after the Island Court decision, in 2019 I am walking the length and breadth of Kakula Island. Trespass signs dot the island protecting the property interests of the locally based expatriate owner. As a result, the reef around the island is crawling with sea cucumber and large crabs, rarely fished by locals. We walk around inspecting the debris from the tourist infrastructure, damaged during the most recent cyclone, that is scattered across the sand beaches on the island. My guide from the nearby Pele Island, who himself claims ownership over Kakula, begins his own account of the early colonial lease transaction:

> The name of the man they sold the land to was Macleod. His ship was anchored in Havannah; he came off the ship and bought the land from one man with a fingerprint. After the man went and saw the missionary and showed him the money, he didn't know what the money was for. The missionary said to him this was a purchase over Kakula but that the transaction wasn't proper. Then the missionary and the man went in a rowboat to the ship; they rowed out into Havannah Harbour. The missionary gave Macleod back the money. He placed it on top of the ship because Macleod refused to accept the money back.
>
> Macleod collected the coins, but the missionary and the man pushed off from the ship and began to row away. Macleod was angry; he didn't want the money back. He threw the money at the rowboat, but he missed the boat, and so the coins drowned in the salt water of Havannah Harbour. Even though the money drowned in the salt water, the title over the land stayed. (pers comm, Feb 2019)

Here then is an account that allows us to focus on the performance of property in its palpable, bodily form. In this account, we begin to hear the motivations of the various actors and how missionary Milne worked to personally challenge Macleod. Milne also wrote letters to various officials and engaged the services of the legal teams of the Presbyterian Church. Macleod became angry and belligerent in response to direct challenges to his lease transaction. He was clearly prepared to push his claim, although no money had actually been received. This remains the account of an altercation between two white men. The local man is largely rendered silent, removed from the performance of property in part because this is a cultural logic that has already excluded him. Over one hundred years later, even after independence, Kakula Island remains leased. Warned off by trespass signs, locals are largely displaced from the landscape that they continue to sing and tell the stories of. As described by the man from Pele Island, they remain acutely conscious of the history of land sales and their enduring impact on the lived landscape.

While the silver dollars drowned in salt water, the performance of property endures.

Chapter 4
Custom Landownership a Frankenstein Corpse?

We sit on the edge of Lelepa Island on a bare wooden platform structured under two shade trees in one of my favorite spots. As the afternoon lengthens, our conversation circles around the practices of leasing land, even more poignant as we look out across the water to the mainland at the ever-growing patches of cleared land, as well as the foreign-owned buildings, resorts, and jetties that jut out from the green coastline of Havannah Harbour. It is almost time for kava, but not quite; the sun is still above the horizon. The chair of the Council of Chiefs, Pierre Makmar, a brilliant and erudite philosopher who is expert in *kastom,* begins a complex exposition around the effect of landownership on ideas of *ples:*

PIERRE MAKMAR: The words "custom owner" are different from landholder. Landholder holds the land, that is all. The words "custom landowner" are confusing. They are wrong when you think about *ples.* You hold land in *kastom; kastom* is what gives you the rights to hold land. This is something that should be under *kastom*. . . . In *kastom* the most important thing is *ples.* The idea of *ples* does not match with the idea of a "landowner." Now landowner means you have the right to sell the land.

RICHARD MATANIK: Yes. It should not mean that you are the landowner and that you have the right to sell the land. It should mean you live on the land, you eat out of the *ples,* sleep there, make a house. (interview, March 2012)

* * *

Customary tenure arrangements are fluid and flexible. Customary use rights to land in Vanuatu—as much as they are able to be generalized—form a complex woven mat of interconnected relationships to landscapes through overlapping access and use rights. Authority within landscapes is often tied to claims of rights to allocate access and use rights to others. Customary use and access rights include rights to build a house, to garden, or to make collections of food and plants for other uses, as a *saloa,* a shared resource that sustains people. The concept of *ples* has an even deeper meaning, referring to the spiritual connections to land, the bodily manifestation of land as identity. As Pierre Makmar described so powerfully, this understanding of being a *man-ples* who belongs to the land is ruptured by the concept of custom landownership.

Custom landownership is an oxymoron, as eloquently described in the foundational tensions alluded to by Pierre Makmar. Here he holds in tension the idea of *ples* as foundational to *kastom,* artfully contrasting the role of holding the land with the imposed concept of "custom landownership" that provides "a right to sell the land" as commodified property. Landownership based on "custom" creates a legal nomenclature that at once looks like offering a model of recognition for the "other" emplaced Indigenous identity while at the same time destabilizing the foundation of that identity, reconfiguring Indigenous relationships to land by asserting that place must be commodified and "owned."

Writing on land dispossession, Tania Li asked that we view capitalism not as a singular global force but rather as a series of localized entanglements held in tension with concepts of "Indigeneity" and "dispossession" (2010, 410). In Oceania, this tension takes a particular legal form, as the concept of Indigeneity as being bound to land is recognized in property law as "landownership." Late capitalism in Melanesia demonstrates the potency of "development" projects that involve resource extraction, logging, land deals, and the imagined speculative riches of carbon farming (REDD+ programs) in reorienting the language of Indigenous identity. The identity of landownership centers on a foundational contradiction between the rights established in the *kastom* system—based on reciprocal and relational models of sociality and personhood representing overlapping claims to place—and those afforded in property as individualized rights over land.

A large and growing body of scholarship focuses on the idea of the "landowner" as an identity that has a powerful valence in claims made over resource extraction—in mining, gas pipeline, logging, and land leasing processes—across Melanesia (Filer 1997, 2006, 2007; Golub 2007, 2014; Jacka 2015; Stead 2017). Landowners have become a central element of the political discourse in Papua New Guinea, Solomon Islands, Vanuatu, and Timor-Leste around law, customary land, and resource extraction. Across Melanesia, men who can claim rights as landowners often have greater material wealth relative to other members of the broader customary group due to their access to compensation or royalty payments for resource extraction projects, logging, or land deals. This increased wealth and status enables landowners to become socially and politically powerful.

Large-scale resource development in Papua New Guinea has created what Colin Filer described as an "ideology of land ownership" through which custom landownership is equated with Indigeneity, thereby allowing landowners to become the established beneficiaries (1997; 2006, 68). Filer argued that the ideology of landownership informs the property-based, transactional nature of resource extraction in which compensation is paid by investors to the supposed "customary owners of natural capital" (2006, 78). Landowner is a category that has "emerged from and become solidified by resource extraction policies and practices," in particular the need for mining, gas pipeline, and logging companies to have a functional legal entity to whom they can pay benefits (Wardlow 2019, 54). In Papua New Guinea, landownership forms the basis for compensation claims by Indigenous people for benefits from forestry and resource extraction projects. Establishing landowner rights often involves the creation of "clans," and, in particular, patriclans, through the Land Groups Incorporation Act 1974 so as to access royalty streams from mining, oil, gas, logging, oil palm, and other exploration projects.

In contrast with Papua New Guinea, the identity of a landowner in Vanuatu is attached to property claims over land. Rather than landownership being associated with the royalty streams that are coupled with resource extraction, in Vanuatu claims relate to specific parcels of land and to the benefits that flow from leasing land. The identity of a landowner is mobilized in Vanuatu to establish the property rights associated with exclusive possession. These include the individualized rights to lease land and to access the benefits or rental streams associated with leasing land. In Vanuatu, custom landownership represents a claim of Indigeneity, as established by the constitution. As elsewhere in Melanesia, claims of landownership are a permanent fixture in dialogues around land in Vanuatu, in both formal court and customary settings. Ideas of landownership intersect with local leadership and authority in profound ways that influence land transactions throughout the archipelago.

Across Melanesia, negotiations over what is "customary" functions as a response to the expansion of state formation and Indigenous claims to resources. In this way, "customary law" and "customary social groups" can be understood as strategic responses from Indigenous people to the pressures placed on them by the state and investors (Weiner and Glaskin 2007, 7). In Vanuatu, assessment of *kastom* claims to landscapes is often regarded as immaterial to the legal identity associated with "customary landownership." Successive court cases offer examples of land being leased by powerful local men who do not have a rightful claim in *kastom* over land. For instance, in the Court of Appeal case *Kalotiti v Kaltapang,* two local men, Bruce Kalotiti and David Yam Kalmet, signed a lease over an area of land near Pango Point to a company who subsequently built the Breakas Beach Resort. Civil proceedings were brought in the Supreme Court by a large group of custom owners who claimed *kastom* rights over the land, requesting that their names be inserted as lessors and that an order be made that the VT 83 million premium payment for the lease be paid to them instead of Kalotiti and Kalmet (*Kalotiti v Kaltapang* [2007] VUCA 25[1]). Such cases illustrate that all that was required to create a lease instrument was the assertion of a "custom landowner," almost regardless of the truth of the circumstances. This is an example of what Benedicta Rousseau has called "the elision," the difference in meaning in legal interpretation between the English term "custom" and its supposedly synonymous term in Bislama, *kastom* (2008). This illustrates law's sleight of hand, its cultural power in purporting to recognize *kastom* interests in land while at the same time rendering these interests, legally and practically, unimportant.

In her poem "Custom," ni-Vanuatu feminist Grace Mera Molisa poignantly described the problematic process of translating *kastom* into "custom," the English word so central to Indigenous legal identity with respect to land—that of "custom landowner." Mera Molisa offered a prescient warning of the dangers for "women / the timid / the ignorant / the weak" involved in this process of translating. She wrote:

> Custom
> is an English word
> English
> a confluence
> of streams of words
> is a reservoir of every shade
> nuance and hue
> sharply
> contrasting
> Melanesia's
> limited vocabulary
> supplementing
> non-verbal
> communication.
>
> Inadvertently
> misappropriating
> "Custom"
> misapplied
> bastardised
> murdered
> a frankenstein
> corpse
> conveniently
> recalled
> to intimidate
> women
> the timid
> the ignorant
> the weak.
> *(Mera Molisa 1983, 24)*

As well as a response to state and investor pressure to "develop," landownership is socially transformative because it is increasingly understood as the basis for asserting claims to land even internal to the *kastom* system. In this process, *kastom* relationships to place, when translated in law, become bastardized as "custom landownership" of property. In this identity, custom and law are conceptually separate but are somehow conflated into the constructed identity of custom landowners such that "the result is a debate about customary law, customary land, and customary groups which articulates the ideology of landownership" (Filer 2006, 73). The ideology of custom landownership intersects with the agency of local men and elicits a new model of personhood—a possessive individual property owner. This is, as Mera Molisa wrote with such prescience, evidence of *kastom* "bastardised" through a legal identity predicated on "landownership," which creates political spaces in which particular men can exercise their authority by manipulating customary claims to land and chiefly authority.

State Formation and the Role of Chiefs

Chiefly authority is central to understanding the practical operation of "custom" in Vanuatu. Ideas of "custom" are central to claims of landownership as linked in the legal identity of a custom landowner. Defining "custom" in Vanuatu has, since independence, almost exclusively been the province of chiefs (Lindstrom 1997). While historically there has been little formal recognition of customary institutions by the state, in practice chiefs govern rural areas in Vanuatu. The role of customary institutions in establishing and enforcing local determinations suggests a significant disjuncture between the law as written and its practical operation. Serious criminal offenses are regularly dealt with by customary institutions that operate well beyond the ambit, or even the knowledge, of the state. The state remains removed from village decision-making, but it is strategically engaged at the behest of and for the political purposes of chiefs. Locally, chiefs provide the governance and operational "law" in rural areas in Vanuatu. At a national level, the processes of state formation in Vanuatu have created specific roles for chiefs as the authors and arbiters of "custom." Interpretations of "custom" must be understood as part of the dialogue in the political struggle between individuals over chiefly authority, as chiefly authority operates as providing a major claim to personal power.

Chiefs have long been central to processes of state formation in Vanuatu in ways that are similar to Fiji but that remain distinct from other Melanesian countries. Colonial administration of the archipelago depended heavily on the role of local "chiefs." The term "chief," which began as a colonial imposition, has now been adopted and adapted into localized models of leadership and "custom" authority, prompting Lamont Lindstrom to comment that "today's *kastom* chiefs, although undoubtedly *kastom*, are not simply customary" (1997, 212). As already discussed, when missionaries arrived in North Efate, there was an established hierarchical system with a *nawota* holding paramount authority over land and people within a particular dominion. This "chiefly" leadership model, as understood by early missionaries in central Vanuatu, became the basis for a model of localized leadership established by Presbyterian missionaries and, following the church, colonial authorities across the archipelago. Missionaries and colonial authorities actively created "chiefs" throughout Vanuatu as an effective form of "indirect rule" to manage dealings with outsiders such as colonial agents, land speculators, and traders (Forsyth 2009, 69; Lindstrom 1997, 212; MacClancy 1983, 20; White 1992, 74). In the condominium system, "chiefs were created to represent and negotiate on behalf of their community with outsiders, with people who stood outside the indigenous system of interaction altogether" (Bolton 1998, 184). Chiefs became the mediums between existing ideas of Indigenous emplaced identity and authority and the agenda of colonial powers informed by the global politics of empire building. This role of the chiefs as "brokers" between the rural constituency and the state continued in the postcolonial era.

Chiefs became a central pillar in postcolonial state formation. Establishing *kastom* as a central concern of the newly independent state of Vanuatu also meant acknowledging chiefs as the "spokesmen" of *kastom,* for they were exclusively men. These processes of state formation resulted in chiefs being increasingly conflated with custom. At independence, the valorization of *kastom* resulted in the constitutional role of the newly formed Malvatumauri (National Council of Chiefs), which was established as a key institution of state alongside Parliament, the Executive, the President, and the Judiciary. Drawing on the account of Chief Willie Bongmatur Maldo, the first president of the Malvatumauri, Lissant Bolton described how in the period before independence the processes of electing chiefs to participate in the Representative Assembly, the body designed to negotiate dealings with the then condominium government, resulted in lengthy meetings to try to define what a chief was between alternative claims to heredity, grade taking, Christianity, and claims based on *kastom* knowledge. These electoral processes also effectively politicized chiefs (Bolton 1998,185). This idea of "electing" chiefs to represent "custom" has been maintained, and the Malvatumauri comprises "custom chiefs" from every major island across Vanuatu. They are elected for four-year terms and meet as a council once a year (Vanuatu Constitution, Chapter 5; National Council of Chiefs [Organisation] Act 2006 [Cap 183]).

At independence, chiefs were recognized as the key arbiters of *kastom* within the newly defined structures of the state. Article 30(2) of the constitution, prior to redrafting in 2014, described the functions of the Malvatumauri as being the provision of advice to Parliament on "any question, particularly any question relating to tradition and custom, in connection with any bill before Parliament." This role is further expanded on in Article 76, which details a specific requirement that Parliament consult with the Malvatumauri before implementing national land laws. However, in practice, these mandated roles were never given effect, and Parliament habitually passed land legislation without consulting the Malvatumauri.

The personification of "custom" resides in the social and political life of Vanuatu chiefs. Twenty years after independence, Bolton commented that the "conflation between chiefs and *kastom*... is so taken for granted in Vanuatu today that it is hard to unpick" (1998, 180; White 1992, 75). Since independence, chiefs have been handed jurisdiction over an increasing number of legislative, judicial, and law-enforcement functions in rural and urban areas, many of which derive from the idea of chiefs as the arbiters of "custom." However, the increasing recognition of chiefs within the architecture of the state has prompted questions about the identity of contemporary chiefs and whether current chiefs embody the proper values of *kastom*.

Attempts to Pass Jurisdiction to Chiefs

In 2006, Parliament passed the National Council of Chiefs (Organisation) Act, which discusses the operation of the National Council of Chiefs at the apex of a hierarchical structure that flows down to the Island and Urban Council of Chiefs. The act lists the functions of the National Council of Chiefs as those conferred on it by Article 30 of the constitution. It also has the responsibility to keep and maintain a proper register of chiefs and provide advice on matters relating to custom. This prompted the question of which chiefs should be included in the register. In 2012, the Malvatumauri produced a survey for all members of the National Council to fill in, which included questions such as who they governed and whether they were elected chiefs or *kastom* chiefs (Chief Kalkot Mormor, interview, May 2012). With this survey, the Malvatumauri has continued its efforts to render coherent the largely irreconcilable ideas of governance and chiefly jurisdiction inherent in alternative colonial, state, and *kastom* pathways for "chiefly" status across the archipelago. This has created a conundrum of how to institutionalize and recognize models of chiefly leadership that operate from various personal and political claims to authority (White 1992, 95). Efforts to formalize claims to chieftainship will inevitably result in disputes, with a large number of chiefly disputes currently before the courts in Vanuatu.

Passing state jurisdiction to chiefs through legislation also risks codifying customary practices and the traditional authority of leaders. Under the National Council of Chiefs (Organisation) Act, chiefs are formally elected to the national, island, and urban councils of chiefs rather than chosen following customary practices. The role of the island and urban councils of chiefs is to: resolve disputes; set the amount of money for bridewealth; promote the use of custom and culture; promote peace, stability, and harmony; and encourage sustainable social and economic development (s 13). These last two functions seem remarkably similar to those expected of the national government, which is perhaps a recognition that chiefs, rather than the state, govern vast areas of Vanuatu. The powers conferred on chiefs to undertake these functions are drafted as "all powers deemed necessary" (s 4), which seems to suggest that chiefly jurisdiction operates unless it is superseded by that of the state. In practice, there is very little oversight of the act, and the "functions" outlined as being performed by chiefs receive no resourcing from the state. This suggests limited formal recognition of the role of chiefs by the state but a tacit acceptance of their role in governing rural areas (Forsyth 2009, 207–208).

The postcolonial state seems to have adopted many of the governing structures long associated with the colonial models of "indirect rule" that increasingly position chiefs within the local and national structures of the state. The state's tacit acceptance of the role of chiefs offers them the ability to perform the role of broker, mediating between the village and state, nongovernment, civil society, and donor organizations and programs. Lindstrom argued that the title of "chief" can operate both to "serve ambitious individuals who scheme to claim it... and the state, which, by recognizing and admitting *jifs* [chiefs] into government councils, puts to work able ambitious local leaders within national political structures" (1997, 212). Chiefs serve the state as "middlemen and brokers" operating both as "spokesmen" communicating the needs of rural villages to state agencies and increasingly as village-based leaders implementing government policy within the village (Rodman and Counts 1983, 1; Philibert 1982). This persistent role of "broker" is also evident in contemporary land transactions in which chiefs facilitate customary land leasing with investors from outside the village.

Contested Claims of Authority and Landownership: *Taurakoto v Mormor*

Claims in custom often provide the basis for asserting chiefly authority over land. Across Vanuatu, chiefs are understood to be the representatives of larger groups of landowners, regardless of whether they have any clear customary claim over the land. It is regularly assumed that chiefs hold a form of customary authority over the allocation of land rights, which can make conducting land transactions more efficient than dealing with large, unruly groups of landowners with overlapping claims. Increasingly on Efate Island, legal challenges with respect to who holds a chiefly title are equated with claims to landownership. Property and authority function as alternate yet entwined claims to personal power. In this way, claiming chiefly status involves both a claim to rights over land as well as the claim to authority to govern over a territory. An example of how these claims are used to assert authority over landscapes can be seen in the Vanuatu Supreme Court decision *Taurakoto v Mormor* ([1986] VUSC 7[2]).

The *Taurakoto v Mormor* case involved contested claims over a series of titles held over the former French coconut plantation at Mangaliliu. The respondents to the 1986 case were the recent settlers of the Mangaliliu plantation area—Chief Kalaure Mormor, supported by his brother, the paramount chief of Lelepa Island, Chief William Kalsong Natamatewia. This settlement of Mangaliliu was opposed by a group of Lelepa chiefs led by Peter Taurakoto. *Taurakoto v Mormor* is a pivotal case in considering Lelepa people's claims both to rights over land as well as to the authority to govern the landscape of North Efate. The case highlights: first, alternate claims to rights over land based on patrilineal or matrilineal descent structures; second, transformations in local customary landholding arrangements and ideas of *ples;* and third, claims to chiefly authority as the basis of landownership rights, the condensation of chieftainship with landownership. During the case, Chief Mormor claimed custom landownership rights over Mangaliliu based on three alternate claims: (1) matrilineal descent rights from a female ancestor; (2) claims to authority over the dominion of *naflak nawita;* and (3) rights as the "paramount chief" of Mangaliliu in which chiefly authority is identified with landownership over Mangaliliu.

The history of the case begins with the 1985 Council of Chiefs' decision to evict Chief Mormor from Lelepa Island for numerous serious breaches of *kastom.* Following this decision, Chief Mormor and his brother, then Paramount Chief Natamatewia, resettled at Mangaliliu community on 6 August 1985, leaving Lelepa Island without a resident paramount chief to govern other Lelepa Island chiefs. At this point, the population of Lelepa Island divided into two separate communities—one that remained on Lelepa Island and a second that relocated to the mainland of Efate Island at Mangaliliu. The formal settlement of Mangaliliu in 1985 by the brothers and their supporters created widespread tensions among the Lelepa population, with a substantial number of Lelepa chiefs, led by Peter Taurakoto, challenging Mormor's claims to being the custom owner of Mangaliliu; these challenges became the basis of the court case.

Since 1985, the population of Mangaliliu has grown into a substantial village. The *Taurakoto v Mormor* case remains politically sensitive, as it is the basis of the claim to the land rights of the former Chief Kalaure Mormor and his adopted son, the late Chief Kalkot Mormor. My adopted father, Chief Kalkot Mormor, died in Mangaliliu Village on 18 December 2015. I acknowledge my relationship to Chief Kalkot Mormor as his adopted daughter and the relational obligations that it brings. This account, however, is based on both the court case and discussions with a wide array of Lelepa men and women who have offered their perspectives.

Prior to their formal settlement of Mangaliliu, Chief Natamatewia and Chief Kalaure Mormor engaged in numerous acts of material possession of the landscape. For example, Chief Mormor entered into a road agreement for forestry development as an assertion of his claims. The brothers also engaged in erecting buildings and houses and establishing a commercial piggery on the land. During the court case, numerous Lelepa witnesses gave evidence that they moved to Mangaliliu to support Mormor's claims over the land. During and since the case, the two chiefs have strategically supported the settlement of hundreds of people, who have subsequently built houses and maintained gardens, to assert their land rights and authority over the landscape. In this way, and over time, the case remains entwined with the history of Mangaliliu Village and the rights of the current population of Mangaliliu to settle the area.

Alternate Claims to Place: Matrilineal and Patrilineal

Alternate claims over land represent rhetorical positions adopted in political contests of personal authority. The *Taurakoto v Mormor* case is one of many in North Efate that describes alternate claims to landownership based on matrilineal *naflak* and patrilineal *blad laen* rights. During the case, Mormor claimed land rights based on matrilineal descent, claiming he was descended from the female ancestor figure Turpet. In court, Mormor gave evidence on the matrilineal *naflak* system, stating that "land rights and totem rights *are the same thing.*"

Mormor's claims that matrilineal descent was the basis of land rights were challenged by the Taurakoto group comprising the majority of Lelepa Island chiefs, including many from the same family as Mormor. The Taurakoto group claimed that in *kastom* landownership is determined by patrilineal descent, arguing that "the people of Lelepa follow *only one custom* which is: *that rights of inheritance are through the male line* [emphasis added]." As a group, they produced oral accounts supporting the individual claim of George Kaltua Munelpa, who "following the male line is the true custom landowner of Mangaliliu Plantation." Munelpa himself stated before the court that "under custom, land rights are completely different from totem rights" and that "totem ownership has nothing to do with the ownership of land." Rather than supporting claims based on matrilineal *naflak* descent rights, the claim recognized as proper *kastom* by the majority of Lelepa chiefs was the claim of a possessive male individual custom landowner based on patrilineal *blad laen* descent rights.

Individualized Landownership

Today in North Efate, land rights along the coastline are almost universally described as rights of male individuals, heads of small family groups—termed *wan-wan* (one-one) rights belonging to an individual man. Claims of individual rights are based on the *kastom* of *laopeania,* meaning that any man who plants food or fruit trees on land that is not held under a chiefly title can claim rights to the land. As Richard Matanik explained to me in 2021, "All land belongs to the tribe, but *lao* means 'to plant,' *peania* means 'you own it.' So you plant a garden, then it belongs to you now. . . . When the Chief Natamatewia first sent Lelepa people, he asked them to plant gardens to block the plantation owners who were moving in and stealing the land. That was why the first men made gardens on the mainland. That is the meaning of *laopeania*."

These rights were described by a Lelepa chief as follows: "Where there is a piece of land covered in dark bush, if I go and clean it and make it into a garden, then I can claim the land as my own" (interview, June 2013). Similarly, Lelepa man John Kaloroa described land rights as acquired because a man's great-great-grandfather had worked the land (Arutangai 1987, 268).

Originally, chiefly allocated *laopeania* rights were given to Lelepa men so that they could garden around the coast of mainland Efate. In contemporary North Efate, many men claim *laopeania* rights over land allocated to their family by a former paramount chief of Lelepa Island or by another smaller dominion chief. In contemporary *kastom,* people name a patriarch in claiming rights over a particular area of coast, distinguishing between smaller plots of gardening land and larger areas of *naflak* tribal land:

> There is the land of the tribes, and then there is the land that during the time of warfare when all men were frightened of being killed our ancestors wanted to make sure that they were safe, so they made gardens close to each other, along the coastline. That way they could work in their gardens and if an enemy came, they would all be close to each other. That is why all men now own all small pieces of land along the coastline. Every place on the coastline is *laopeania.*
>
> With this gardening land when every man gets old, he can choose who he wants to pass the land to. He will pass it to his son, who can pass it to his children. Every small piece of land near the salt water is the same story. But the land of the tribes belongs to the tribes even today. (interview with Lelepa men, Nov 2014)

Originally allocated as large plots of coastal gardening land to a male head of a large family group, these rights have become increasingly individuated as, over four or five generations, they have been carved up and divided between sons, thereby becoming increasingly smaller plots of land. This passing of small plots of gardening land from father to son was also noted by Jean Guiart in the 1960s. Having written in detail about *naflak* groups, he concluded that land tenure is passed patrilineally: "A man receives from his father a share of patrilineally inherited land" to which he is able to add any plots that his wife may bring as "dowries" (Guiart 1964, 100).

In contemporary North Efate, people distinguish between large *naflak* dominion areas of land associated with chiefly titles, often locally termed "tribal land," and small coastal estates controlled by individual men. *Naflak* land is now delineated largely as areas of land held away from the coast toward the escarpment and on the plateau of Efate Island, with land held along the coast belonging to individual men representing small family groups.

Working in Pango, Gregory E Rawlings described a similar pattern around changing conceptions of place from *naflak* to *blad laen*. He detailed the findings of R J S Hutchinson—president of the Native Court held at Pango in 1970—who concluded a case using expert custom "assessors":

> The Assessors confirm that under native customs of Efate communally owned land was at one time virtually non-existent, but that since the arrival of the Missions and consequent establishment of villages some village housing areas were regarded as common land.... On the other hand on Efate up until three generations ago land in a village's land area (or "Namarakiana") were [*sic*] inherited matrilineally within the clan structure.... About 3 generations ago the custom of land inheritance changed and it became common for land to be passed from father to son in all the villages of Efate. (1970, 7, cited in Rawlings 1999a, 81)

Findings by this Pango Native Court have been reiterated in numerous more recent court cases on Efate Island.

Informed by the ideology of landownership, recent *laopeania* claims have become transformed into individualized custom-ownership rights. These individual landownership rights are asserted based on patrilineal descent expressed as claims that "my ancestor worked the land, the place here" or "this land is my ancestors' " (interviews with Lelepa chiefs and other men in Lelepa and Mangaliliu, June–July 2011). This ancestor is a patriarch, and these rights are passed following *blad laen*.

In deciding *Taurakoto v Mormor*, the Supreme Court justice made his determination based on evidence from his custom advisers that "patrilineal succession is followed in Lelepa Custom." Accordingly, the court found rights over the Mangaliliu Plantation were held by Munelpa. Over the last century, coastal land described in lease documents as a *saloa* belonging to the people of Lelepa, communally held for the benefit of all, has been transformed into rights held by individual men. As previously discussed, missionaries influenced both the matrilineal passing of chiefly titles, as well as the movement of people from the interior to the coast. The result is that in contemporary Efate, individualized plots of land have many of the hallmarks of property, and it is entirely predictable that the land rush on Efate Island has involved the leasing of many of these areas of coastal land.

In spite of the findings of the Supreme Court over ownership of Mangaliliu Plantation, claims of landownership as entwined with chiefly authority continue to remain unresolved and deeply contested. Chief Kalkot Mormor's claims over the landscape of Mangaliliu are based largely on the claims to authority of his uncle, Chief Kalaure Mormor. Chief Kalkot Mormor claimed descent rights to the chiefly title based on matrilineal principles and wrote that "my adoption resulted in the inheritance of the chiefly title and the promotion of *naflak* system" (Mormor 2005). He described in detail the process of his chiefly anointment as the nephew of the late Chief Kalaure Mormor: "Discussion about my inheritance of the chiefly title began in 1992. My dear uncle, the late Chief Mormor, had asked me to resign from my career as a teacher and keep close to him so as to replace him and take over his chiefly title as the new chief since he was a sick man. Sadly, he died on 31st of May 1993. The family met at the Tarei Centre for confirmation of who would be the next chief" (Mormor 2005, 3). The entwined claims of the former and current Chief Mormor are firmly entrenched in the matrilineal *naflak* descent system of landownership and chiefly authority. The court finding, in favor of a patrilineal descent model of landownership, functions as an ongoing challenge to the late Chief Mormor's matrilineal descent claim to Mangaliliu.

Chief Kalkot Mormor's narrative was one of chiefly authority over a village. He wrote that "I, Kalkot Kalotiti, became the new chief as the late Chief Kalaure Mormor has promised me to replace him in accordance with the Naflak System of owning the land of Mangaliliu. On 27 August 1993 I was ordained a custom chief at Mangaliliu by the Lelepa Paramount [Chief] Natamatewia and Chiefs' Council. I was the first chief to head a new village at Mangaliliu. This was the beginning of a new settlement at the coast" (Mormor 2005, 3).

For Kalkot Mormor, claims to chieftainship and landownership were embedded in the *naflak* system through which chiefly titles are passed following matrilineal descent from the titleholder to his sister's sons. Like his uncle, Kalkot Mormor claimed landownership based on *naflak* descent rights structured around the female ancestor Turpet. He claimed chiefly authority based on *naflak* principles of chiefly descent and on the proper processes of *kastom* chiefly anointment. Finally, equating chieftainship with landownership, Mormor claimed the status of a "paramount chief" with dominion over both Mangaliliu and surrounding areas of land, as well as the people who reside on the land.

Vaturisu Endorsement of Chieftainship as Landownership

Customary land claims are a process of constant negotiation, of narratives contested or congruent representing alternate claims to place. *Kastom* narratives of *ples* are political: the "rules of land tenure are one kind of strategic resource in interactions between people about access to land" (Rodman 1987, 32). Rules of land tenure are dynamic and contested, creating "breathing spaces" in *kastom* for the negotiation of competing rights and interests (Rodman 1995). On Efate Island, the countervailing narratives of matrilineal and patrilineal descent offer alternative ways through which people can assert connections to the landscape. Customary tenure arrangements represent what I have described as a complex, overlapping tapestry of rights, a mat woven from the "presence of simultaneous interests, dynamic layers of rights that co-exist with regard to a single land parcel" (Rodman 1987, 32). For many Lelepa people, *naflak* is an important source of identity relevant to the meaning of *ples* increasingly subsumed by, or juxtaposed against, patrilineal *blad laen* claims of custom ownership of the land.

Customary land law is processual, elicited over time across different people and contexts, and it is this flexibility and fluidity that can suffer in the process of codification, or even in attempts to document customary landholding arrangements (Ballard 2013, 52). Writing customary law can make rules fixed and unchanging. The process of writing customary law carries with it the danger of ossifying *kastom* or—echoing Mera Molisa—bastardizing *kastom* so that it operates against the interests of "women / the timid / the ignorant / the weak." This danger is evident in the Efate Vaturisu Council of Chiefs "Customary Land Laws," which endorse as "custom" the equation of chieftainship with landownership.

The decisions of Efate customary land tribunals and Efate Island Court suggest an increasing reliance on the statements of customary land law as written in the Efate Vaturisu Council of Chiefs "Customary Land Laws" (Vaturisu Council of Chiefs 2007). Finalized in 2007, these customary laws set out the role and functions of chiefs and detail the correct way of *owning* land held under customary tenure. The laws also circumscribe the meaning of *naflak* descent rights to land and chiefly titles. The Vaturisu customary laws are increasingly influential, and almost all decisions by island courts or customary land tribunals quote extensively from these customary laws as the guide to making a determination. The laws themselves were drafted by Chief Jimmy Meameadola from Moso Island, who himself is a regular judge on island land courts and customary land tribunals.

The introduction states that the laws were drafted in consultation with all members of the Vaturisu and under the guidance of its former president, Chief Kalkot Mormor (Vaturisu Council of Chiefs 2007). Chief Mormor himself described a process of drafting that involved extensive input by Jimmy Meameadola, with only limited input from the rest of the Vaturisu Council of Chiefs (interviews with Chief Mormor, May 2012 and Nov 2014). Chief Mormor suggested that the description of *naflak* represents a gross misinterpretation of the *kastom* of Efate Island (interviews with Chief Mormor, May 2012 and Nov 2014). The laws were apparently written to fulfill the requirement, as included in Chapter 5 of the constitution and in the National Council of Chiefs (Organisation) Act, that chiefs should manage all affairs related to "*kastom,* culture and tradition" (Vaturisu Council of Chiefs 2007, 3). This is the implication of affording chiefs' recognition in state institutions. Increasingly chiefs, and Vaturisu chiefs in particular, perform their roles as both authors of customary law and arbiters of custom within customary institutions and formal state-based legal arrangements. Power increasingly coalesces around a handful of powerful men in interpreting the meaning of *kastom.*

As in Vanuatu more broadly, landownership is a fixture in discussions of "customary tenure" in the Vaturisu "customary laws." Giving effect to chieftainship and landowner ideology, the Vaturisu define customary land as being land that is "owned" by chiefs, tribes, clans, or individuals through "kastom heritage or birth raet following the kastom of Efate" (Vaturisu Council of Chiefs 2007, 5). This conversion of *kastom* into "custom" is detailed by the Vaturisu's repeated use of the oxymoron of "custom ownership" rights to customary land. The Vaturisu define customary land rights on Efate Island almost exclusively as patrilineal *blad laen* rights. "If a custom owner is dead then the land must go to his son," thereby rendering descent rights relating to customary land as restricted lineally and gendered male (10). *Naflak* matrilineal rights, while being acknowledged as an aspect of *kastom* in some areas on Efate Island, are confined to a limited discussion of the rights of *naflak* chiefs over tribal land (13–14). The Vaturisu customary laws fail to acknowledge matrilineal land rights. This aspect of *kastom* and the legacy of Roi Mata in creating the *naflak* structure has somehow become obscured with statements that *blad laen* rights have existed "from time immemorial to today" (13–14).

The Vaturisu customary laws also describe the *"stret fasion blong onem wan kastomary graon"* (the proper way of owning customary land). In this discussion, the laws conflate the idea of chiefly titles and dominions with the ownership of customary land. All paramount chiefs are gendered male. Applying the twin ideologies of landownership with chieftainship, the laws state:

4.1. Following the proper way of all *kastom* chiefs from Efate and the offshore island, Paramount Chiefs have full customary custodial rights over all land inside the village boundary and he can allocate land to *wan-wan* (individual) custom owner.

4.2. The first allocation of land will go to all the small chiefs belonging to the Paramount Chief, meaning all members of his Chiefly Council.

4.3. The second allocation of land will go to each individual [*wan-wan*] head of a family that lives underneath the authority of the small chiefs (also defined as clans) for the place. The small chief can assist in this allocation. (Vaturisu Council of Chiefs 2007, 6; translated from Bislama to English by the author)

As the authors of customary tenure arrangements that are now relied on for the judgments of cases across Efate Island, the Vaturisu have, perhaps predictably, placed property rights of "ownership" and authority over customary landscapes with themselves, as self-declared paramount chiefs. Under these arrangements, the twin ideologies of landownership and chieftainship serve as the basis for claims in "custom" to ownership rights to lease customary land. Custom-ownership claims forge property rights symbolic of chiefly authority. In "custom," chiefly authority is increasingly equated to *ownership* over customary land.

Applying the ideologies of landownership and chieftainship, members of the Vaturisu have authored a set of arrangements that enable *them* to claim authority and property rights over vast areas of customary landscapes. This allocation of rights is both partial and political. With their self-authored customary laws, Vaturisu chiefs are enabled to judge the contested claims of fellow "paramount chiefs" over chiefly titles and thus, following the logic of the twin ideologies, property rights over the dominion held by a chief. Chiefly authority becomes property rights made manifest through the leasing of customary land.

Conclusion: Tearing the Fabric of Place

At independence, the nationalist political ideology associated with *kastom* worked to enfranchise chiefs in the processes of state formation. In contemporary Vanuatu, chiefs increasingly play a dual role—as an extension of the architecture of the state and as the "spokesmen" for villages in their dealings with state actors. Chiefs are increasingly involved in manipulating the "breathing space" between *kastom* and what is proclaimed as "custom." Each additional decision informed by the Vaturisu customary laws determines what *kastom* is and allocate rights to land accordingly. The effect of these customary laws is to circumscribe the multiplicity of local meanings and voices associated with place. This then is the danger associated with writing customary land laws: certain voices are privileged as the authors of "custom" while others are excluded in the description of claims associated with place. Writing *kastom* relations to land can potentially function as an act of dispossession, emplacing powerful men and their authority over landscapes and displacing the voices of other men, women, and young people.

Landownership is an entrenched category of identity with respect to land in Melanesia that functions not only as a legal identity but also enables the transformation of customary landscapes into commodified property. James Weiner and Katie Glaskin commented that legal mechanisms,

> Do not, as they purport, serve merely to identify and register already-existing customary indigenous landowning groups in these countries. Because the legislation is an integral part of the way in which indigenous people are defined and managed in relation to the State, it serves to elicit particular responses in landowner organisation and self-identification on the part of indigenous people. These pieces of legislation actively contour the indigenous social, territorial and political organisation at all levels in these nation-states—or at least in the way that indigenous people present them to the wider society. (2007, 3–4)

In considering the competing "custom" narratives associated with land, it is possible that Indigenous conceptions of personhood connected to *ples* may be radically altered and reconfigured by ideas of property as ownership. The identity of "customary landownership" requires the juxtaposition of *kastom* relationships to place with something largely outside of *kastom*—the ownership of land in an absolute sense.

The profound transformations to *ples* and identity associated with the idea of landownership are illustrated in the discussion by Lelepa people of the *Taurakoto v Mormor* court case. Locally, the original claims made by Chief Kalaure Mormor of authority over Mangaliliu remain deeply contested. One Lelepa chief reflected on the findings of the court case as representing both transformations in *kastom* ideas of place and transformations in ideas of chiefly authority. This discussion is juxtaposed against a narrative of the proper *kastom* practice as the ways of *ples* described temporally as the *kastom* as practiced *bifo:*

> Many men on Lelepa Island said at the time that the Mangaliliu Plantation land was for the community, but Chief Mormor with his brother William Kalsong Natamatewia said that the land belonged to the *wita* family alone. Then they moved onto the land and lived there. Other families were not happy, and so they took them to court. The court decided that one man was the custom owner.
>
> In *kastom,* chiefs should represent their tribes. Mangaliliu is *wita* land, along the coast. *Vatu* land is looked after by Chief Tuligmanu. The Mako family must look after *nawi* land.
>
> *Bifo* all chiefs held the land to look after on behalf of their people, all people of the tribe worked the land. Now this has changed. *Every chief says he is the chief of the land, as a custom owner* [emphasis added]. But it should not be that way. A chief should look after his people, and the people should work on the land.... If there is a problem among the people, the chief should solve it. A chief will say, "If you do not have food, I will give it to you. If you do not have land, I will give you land."
>
> *Bifo* all people worked on the land because land is a *saloa.* This was the way *bifo.* We say that *bifo* our ancestors were in the darkness and knew nothing, but *bifo* they had more *rispek.* When Christianity came, there was a cut to this way of life.
>
> Now we are in a new time of individuality [*evri man hemi tink tink long hem-wan*], we live in one small *nakamal.* When we were converted to Christianity, we learned many new things; now we have learned this new individual way also. This is what caused the change.
>
> If one chief decides to follow *kastom* and the proper way of handing over chiefly titles, then he should put the title back so that it follows the *naflak* line. (Lelepa chief, interview, Nov 2014)

This complex narrative clearly articulates the increasing individualization that informs both customary landholding arrangements and concepts of chiefly authority, placing these changes in the *longue durée* of the history of colonization and missionary activities. Transformations of landholding arrangements cut the woven mat, tearing at the fabric of *ples.* As land becomes commodified, chiefly authority becomes authority over property. The Lelepa chief described the newly individualized sensibility in which landownership is equated with chieftainship such that "*every chief says he is the chief of the land, as a custom owner* [emphasis added]." As ideas of *ples* have transformed, chiefly authority has merged with ideas of individual landownership such that an individual male chief can now assert land claims over vast areas of land. Gone are the ideas of place as a *saloa* and the proper function of a chief as caring for people. These ideas have been replaced by an assertion of individualized landownership, with rights to property often exercised by a chief.

This narrative account carefully maps the contours of dispossession and identity: the way landownership evokes individualization that is often claimed as chiefly rights over vast areas of land, the way land becomes property rather than place, and the impact that this has on the practice of *kastom* as the "ways of place." It is an account that echoes Mera Molisa's prophetic warning that custom landownership may increasingly be becoming a Frankenstein corpse.

Chapter 5
The Frontier of Desire

It is 2007. We have taken a break from working in Mparntwe (Alice Springs) and have come to visit friends in Vanuatu. Laurence has chosen to join one of our friends in a team running a race across the middle of the island. He has purchased some sneakers from a Chinese store in town and we are hoping they will hold together. While he runs, Will, aged eleven months, and I will join one of the first tours of the newly created Chief Roi Mata's Domain World Heritage site.

We meet the tour at the Vanuatu Cultural Centre. There are the usual delays, a short speech, then we head out of Port Vila. It is a long, dirt road and it is very slow going up some of the steep hills in our minibus packed full of people. It is around an hour later when we arrive in Mangaliliu.

We pile into boats and head over to Lelepa Island. As we head out onto the blue water I turn back and look at the mainland. The entire coast looks like a long strip of verdant green along the blue line of Havannah Harbour. It is green and blue as far as I can see.

* * *

It is 2019. I am in a truck with Matanik and Brigitte, traveling in a cavalcade of twelve utes and trucks full of Lelepa chiefs and other men, young and old. We have won a court case over two large areas of *naflak* customary land and have just finished walking the land for the first time since the judgment was handed down by the court. Everyone is elated. It is time to celebrate.

We jump back in our cavalcade of vehicles and head down the escarpment on the Efate ring road. Five minutes later we arrive at a newly cleared area of bush on the right side of the road, under the domain of Chief L. A huge circle of chiefs and men forms. Speeches are made and together we drink kava. Women wait under shelter with large platters of food.

But I wonder, why are we celebrating here on this new area of land? Why are we not celebrating somewhere closer to the water? And I realize it is because all the other areas of land along the harbor related to L's title have been leased. It is only this now. As Lelepa men say, *graon hemi finis* (the land is finished).

* * *

I begin with these two vignettes not to romanticize or revise, but to illustrate how the frontier of land transformation functions as a conceptual and real boundary. These accounts demonstrate in a visceral way the rapacious rush—the dramatic temporal scale—of the transformation of the material landscape. In just over ten years, the landscape of North Efate has been transformed from the green and blue of gardening land and adjacent coastal estates held under customary arrangements to walled gated communities for expatriates and tourism resorts. The frontier marks the changed meaning of land from narrated landscapes animated by ancestral beings, that are spoken, sung, and danced, into commodified property. In Vanuatu, as elsewhere, the frontier is mapped by spatial markers of possession: real estate signs, walls, gates, fences, and no trespassing signs. The enactment of property means that Indigenous inhabitants become trespassers in landscapes they have previously lived in, gardened, and fished for millennia.

Frontier narratives are often associated with speculation, to generate the "rush" component of resource demand (Tsing 2000). Tania Li wrote that this style of frontier culture emerges at the intersection of "global investors imagining . . . huge profits waiting to be made" as well as "visions of national territory as empty land" and "local imaginaries related to attracting investment, raising one's status in the national scheme of things (backwards places and people joining the march of modernity), and getting rich" (2012, 13). Many elements of this assemblage are present in what I term the "frontier of desire" for customary land, which emerges at the intersections of global capital, the idea of empty territory filled with foreign imaginings, and local demands for modernity and cash. The frontier of desire results from endless encounters and engagements with an "accelerating multitude of foreign desires and agendas" (Hviding 2003, 552). Building from this idea of the frontier of desire, in this chapter I pose a number of questions: What are the processes by which a named and narrated embodied landscape becomes refashioned as property available for purchase? Which narratives and images cultivate these foreign desires for Indigenous landscapes? At the frontier of desire, who are the actors—investors, middlemen, locals—who are engaged in purchasing and selling leases? Why are Indigenous people actively involved in the rush to lease the landscapes so central to place, identity, and *kastom*? Who wins and who loses in the rush to lease land? How does property enable processes of land transformation and commodification? These questions can only be addressed by deep ethnographic research undertaken over many years and complimented with detailed legal research into the actual lease instruments. In answering these questions, in this chapter and the ones that follow, I present a localized study of capitalist processes, one that offers insights into both actual lease making and documentation as well as the individuals involved in this convergence of desire. In this way, I offer insights into the frontiers of capitalism, particularly as they relate to the processes of dispossession.

Transacting customary land is an exchange that takes place at the frontier of desire—a foreign desire to possess land and a local desire to lease land for cash. Conceptually the frontier of desire functions to demonstrate how the meanings of land are dynamic and contested, as illustrated in the opening vignettes. Land is experienced and imagined in different ways creating a palimpsest of past meanings and social practices. Meanings are inscribed onto the landscape by both Indigenous people and foreigners who live and pass through it. Foreign desires are actively created and transposed onto the Pacific, animated by long-established narrative tropes that actively construct the landscape into an idealized utopian paradise (Alexeyeff and McDonnell 2018; McDonnell 2018). These tropes continue to inform foreign engagements with Pacific landscapes and the people who inhabit them. The allure of the North Efate landscape is informed by specific narratives: "survivors" seeking a "last frontier"; real estate investors wanting to purchase and sell "paradise"; and conservationists inscribing the landscape as "World Heritage." Together these foreign imaginings have cultivated a landscape saturated with desire—desire made manifest in the rush to lease land.

Leasing on the Frontier of North Efate

In material terms the land rush in North Efate represents a transformation of the physical landscape, from customary gardening land to residential subdivisions, tourist resorts, and restaurants. Locally, the "frontier" represents a "shock" and "disruption" to previous lives and livelihoods of Lelepa people (Tsing 2003, 2005). In material and cadastral terms, the frontier is represented by a growing patchwork of leases that covers the North Efate region (map 5.1). In the twenty years from 1980 to 2000 there were only three leases over customary land in North Efate: at Tukutuku Point, Leosa on Lelepa Island, and Artok Island (the burial site of Chief Roi Mata).

As with the broader national leasing data, the rush to lease land in North Efate occurred mainly in the decade after 2000. In North Efate between 2000 and 2015, 126 leases were registered over what was previously held as customary land. In researching land transactions, I obtained copies of most of these original leases of customary land. I then held long interviews, sometimes multiple interviews, with the landowners or landowning groups who had been involved in leasing the areas of land, as well as other chiefs, other men, women, and community members who also wanted to comment on acts of land leasing. These land-leasing processes have resulted in the recolonization of the landscape by foreigners. Between 2000 and 2003, twenty-eight leases were registered; after 2004 the real land rush occurred with the remaining ninety-eight leases being registered between 2004 and 2010, with thirty-one leases registered in 2005 alone.

Two factors made customary land in North Efate extremely attractive to investors from the year 2000 onward. First was the filming of the *Survivor* series. Second, North Efate's attractiveness as a real estate location was greatly enhanced by the completion of a tar-sealed ring road in April 2011, which

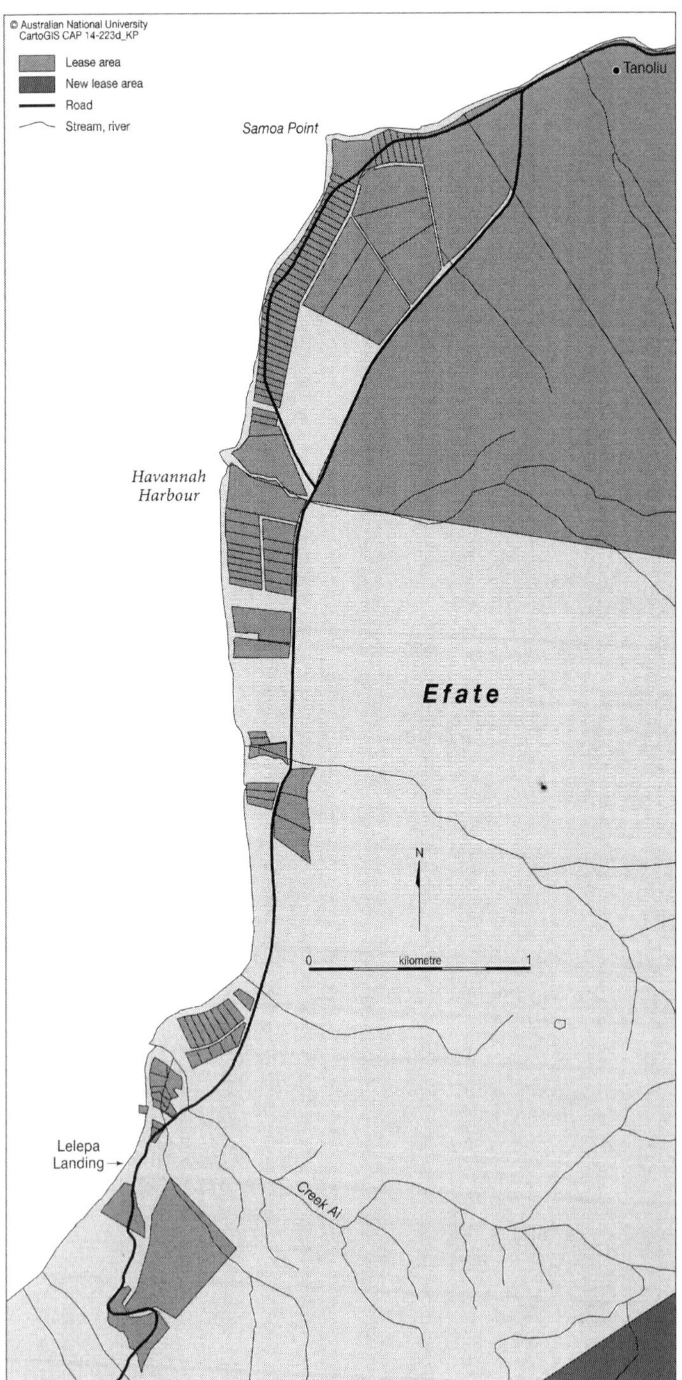

MAP 5.1. Lease data for the Havannah Harbour coastline, North Efate region, February 2015. Courtesy of CartoGIS CAP 14-223d_KP, The Australian National University.

changed traveling times from Port Vila from around one to two hours on sometimes impassable dirt roads, to around twenty-five minutes. The road was sponsored by the United States in a US$65.69 million project with the Vanuatu Government. Leasing spiked from 2005 to 2010 in anticipation of the completion of the ring road and the associated increases in value of customary land. These early purchases of customary land in North Efate amounted to speculative land investment with investors making substantial, windfall profits of between thirty and seventy times what was originally paid to local Indigenous landowners. Transactions involved investors cheaply purchasing seventy-five-year leases over customary land from local Indigenous landowners and then creating subdivisions on these areas of land, often by transferring existing agricultural leases to subdivisions. In the final transactions, investors then on sell individual small plots of subdivided land as residential "beachfront" estates. Much of the customary land purchased by investors in North Efate follows this transaction process in that customary land has been subdivided and resold as small blocks of coastal beachfront estates for expatriate housing purchased mainly by Australians, New Zealanders, French, and, more recently, the occasional Chinese resident. Almost half of all leases in the North Efate area (sixty-three) are for residential housing. Of the remaining nonresidential leases, fifty-three (or almost 40 percent) are for commercial developments including tourism operations, restaurants, and other businesses. Developments in the region include Vanuatu's only five-star resort, "The Havannah," as well as numerous smaller resorts and a scattering of restaurants. Of all these businesses, only one, "Havannah Eco Lodge," is owned by a Lelepa man, Gideon Manelpa. Of the remaining leases, eight (6 percent of all leases) are for agricultural purposes, two leases are for industrial purposes, and the remaining lease is a special-purpose lease for the Natapau Primary School on Lelepa Island.

Existing patterns of customary land management are reflected to some extent in the leasing data. *Laopeania* "gardening" land, held by individual men as family representatives around the coastline, were the first parcels to be leased (see map 5.1). This is in part a response to investor demand for coastal estate located close to the Efate ring road, but it is also a reflection of the pragmatic reality that it is easier to negotiate lease arrangements with an individual man rather than a group. The pattern of leasing shows a large number of relatively smaller-sized leased areas around the coastline of Havannah Harbour. These leases represent purchases of large areas of customary land that were then subdivided into smaller plots. Most leases in the region hug the coastline of Havannah Harbour, but in 2012, two large leases over tribal *naflak* land were "grabbed" by the Monvoisin family and their partner Ludovic Bolliet and signed off by then Minister of Lands Steven Kalsakau. The subsequent seven-year court case to overturn these leases on the grounds that they had been issued based on fraud and mistake, and bring the land back under customary control, was the cause of much celebration for Lelepa people, as detailed in the opening vignette.[1]

Adjacent to the ring road, much of the coastline of North Efate is now leased, meaning that Lelepa people are restricted in their access to much of the coastal estate. Leasing of coastal land has also reduced accessible gardening land for Lelepa people, and many community members acknowledge the potential for food security issues in the future, given the rapidly growing population of North Efate. Lelepa peoples' experience of Tropical Cyclone Pam in 2015—a Category 5 cyclone that destroyed food crops—has further reignited local discussion of food security issues and access to gardening land, as well as highlighting the politics of relief distribution at a local village level and between communities (McDonnell 2020). Issues associated with reduced access to food are particularly significant, given that for many people low levels of formal education mean their main livelihood opportunities are based on subsistence farming and fishing, as well as seasonal worker schemes.

North Efate as a *Survivor* Playground

The story of this land rush in North Efate is entangled with the filming of the *Survivor* reality television series. In the mid- to late-2000s, North Efate hosted the filming of three versions of the *Survivor* series: the American *Survivor: Vanuatu—Island of Fire,* the Australian *Celebrity Survivor,* and the French *Koh Lanta.* The best known of these was the American *Survivor: Vanuatu,* the ninth edition of Mark Burnett's reality television season, which was filmed on location from 28 June to 5 August 2004 (Burnett, Parsons, and Probst 2004). The season was filmed over fifteen episodes and shown in America from 16 September to 12 December 2004. Exploration of the *Survivor* "playground" allows consideration of how North Efate is represented to foreigners—either as contestants in the reality television series, or, subsequently, as purchasers of real estate.

The *Survivor* narrative involves a group of "adventurers" traveling from the "civilized" world to unexplored territory (Delisle 2003, 45–46). The first episode of the *Vanuatu* series opens with imagery of the host, Jeff Probst, "conquering" Yasur Volcano (which is on Tanna Island). As the camera pans across Mele Cascades waterfall (back on Efate), Probst's voice-over begins: "We are . . . in the nation of Vanuatu in the South Pacific. It is a land with a fascinating history of cannibalism, where rituals like sorcery and black magic are still a part of daily life."

As "adventurers," the competitors (and audience) have landed in an exotic landscape captured by the alterative narratives of colonial encounters. On the one hand, the game is portrayed as a kind of Treasure Island with money to be won. On the other, the host introduces the idea of dangers lurking for the competitors—a "Heart of Darkness" narrative, complete with cannibalism and black magic.

A particular manufactured, picturesque aesthetic is required for the backdrop to the *Survivor* series: the landscape is rendered empty, supposedly uninhabited by Indigenous people. In the opening scenes of the first episode of the *Vanuatu* series, the camera follows the edge of Efate Island and zooms down to a yacht, with the competitors aboard, heading across the waters of Havannah Harbour before panning across vast areas of Efate and Tanna islands. These shots have been carefully manipulated so that the landscape is rendered terra nullius; only the host and the contestants remain visible in an otherwise empty, uninhabited landscape. Competitors—who are termed "castaways" in the promotional material for the show—and the armchair tourists, who make up the audience, "seek unspoiled beaches or primitive habitations as signifiers of other, exotic locales" (Delisle 2003, 43; see also Burnett, Parsons, and Probst 2004). This anachronistic Pacific backdrop allows the competitors and the viewers to imagine that they have "returned to a primitive, untouched world" (Delisle 2003, 47).

Toward the end of the opening sequence of *Survivor: Vanuatu,* the yacht with competitors on board lets down its anchor. At the same time, a flotilla of canoes enters the water from the mainland, Efate Island, near Mangaliliu Village. Painted and costumed for television in pseudo-custom designs from across Vanuatu, the Lelepa men cry out as they paddle toward the yacht. On board the yacht, the *Survivor* competitors look nervous. Finally, the *Survivor* host is lifted from a canoe and onto the yacht. With the host's appearance, the competitors look relieved—they have been saved from an encounter with the "natives." Once on board, the host begins his scripted narrative: "The game is about to begin, but before it does, you have to be *granted access to the land.* So, you are going to take part in a tribal ritual. It is a rite of passage and an invitation to *stay on the land*. . . . Chief Mormor is going to preside over all of this; he is a real chief [emphasis added]." Like the first explorers who arrived on ships, the competitors must be granted access to the land by a chief.

As the contestants land on the beach, a group of Lelepa men run at them with spears. In his later commentary, one contestant, John, stated, "There were a bunch of tribesmen running with spears. My first reaction was 'What is going on? What? Are we supposed to defend ourselves?' " This first episode of the television series is titled "They Came at Us with Spears," and it is clear with whom the audience is supposed to identify in this "Us" and "Others" description. The staged performance of this opening sequence is a reenacted moment of "first contact" that is only plausible if the landscape seems to be inhabited by "savages." According to the internal logic of the series, it is a landscape in need of discovery. In a later part of the opening sequence, Chief Kalkot Mormor grunts and mimes the act of kava drinking to the male competitors. In reality, Chief Mormor speaks excellent English but cannot, of course, do so with the contestants, as this would vitiate the trope of "savagery." The opening scenes finish with Chief Mormor killing a pig in front of the competitors, who are visibly shocked: it is their "first contact" with the "culture" of the "savages."

In the landscape of North Efate, the "access to land" granted to *Survivor* has been difficult to contain. The *Survivor* television series lent the landscape international recognition. Locally, the main beach areas from the American show, located along the coastline toward Tuktuk Point opposite Artok Island, became known as "*Survivor* men's" and "*Survivor* women's" beaches—a renaming of the landscape in reference to the American series. At the completion of the American *Survivor,* investors vied for local men to sell them customary land at the location of the "*Survivor* beaches." As one Lelepa man described, "After *Survivor* went on the TV people came for the land. *Survivor* advertised our land, then everyone wanted to buy the land" (interview, Nov 2014). In their narratives of leasing, Lelepa men identified the filming of the *Survivor* series as the beginning of the rapacious land rush.

The filming of the *Survivor* series created investor interest in customary land and simultaneously the "vision" among local men of the cash money that could be made from leasing land. The influence that the *Survivor* series had on the leasing of customary land, was described by a group of Lelepa men as follows: "There were only a small number of leases, Tuktuk and Leosa. Only a few men had leases on their land... *Survivor* made the land sales. When the land sales on the *Survivor* beaches started then after that all men had the vision of land sales. Many custom owners went to find investors in town. Many investors came to find custom owners to sell them *Survivor* beach land. There were many real estate agents too who said, 'I have got money to buy your land and investors who are interested, if you are interested in selling'" (interview, May 2011). The *Survivor* series enabled the reenvisioning of the landscape in North Efate, from a landscape held under customary tenure to a landscape commodified as property and turned into cash.

Paradise Commodified: Real Dream Estate

The filming of the *Survivor* television series and the subsequent land rush illustrate how long-established tropes—paradisiacal empty landscapes and anachronistic time, as well as the threatened darkness and menace of "savagery"—continue to inform how foreigners engage with landscapes in the Pacific. These narrative tropes create a cultural loop. An imagined landscape becomes a site of desire; the desirability of the landscape creates the commodification of customary land, and the foreign buyer purchases customary land to replicate and experience "paradise." In Vanuatu, tourism and real estate are entwined, with both sectors creating emotional images in the minds of foreigners that are projected onto physical places "in ways that successfully respond to, and rekindle, the imaginary" (Kahn 2003, 307).

The way paradise tropes inform the geographical imaginary of the Pacific is evident in the popular tourist day trip around Efate Island. Real estate billboards that line the ring road celebrate the imaginary of the Pacific as paradise by advertising land for sale as "Paradise Found." This is a destination so utopian it exists only in dreams furnished by a company called "Real Dream Estate" (figures 5.1 and 5.2).

The "Paradise Found" real estate advertisement is designed in the style of a mid-twentieth-century adventure book cover, creating a cultural arc back to earlier fictional representations of the Pacific in popular "pulp fiction." The imagery is the iconic motif of paradise: A young "native" girl dances under a large full moon, her breast clearly outlined, as lagoon waters appear to lap gently and palm trees sway.

These real estate billboards are the stuff of carefully contrived fantasy, the allure of a place replete with foreign visions. Farther along the road, a second Real Dream Estate sign is a reproduced copy of Paul Gauguin's 1892 painting, *Arearea* (Joyousness) (figure 5.3). Here the real estate company has chosen Gauguin's image of Tahitian women as an entry point for the cultivation of foreign desire, in which bodies and landscapes become merged. Miriam Kahn wrote that in Tahiti no one has played a more powerful role than Gauguin in creating an enduring vision of the people and the landscape (2003). It is these powerful and potent images that are now used to sell customary land in Vanuatu. On this real estate sign, two women sit under a palm tree; the woman in the foreground looks coyly at the viewer with curiosity. The women

FIGURE 5.1. Close-up image of "Paradise Found" real estate sign in the style of a pulp fiction adventure book, 22 September 2014. Photo by author.

FIGURE 5.2. "Paradise Found" real estate sign located near Eton Beach, Efate Island, 22 September 2014. Photo by author.

FIGURE 5.3. Gauguin's *Arearea* (Joyousness) painting inspired this Real Dream Estate sign located near Eton Beach, Efate Island, 22 September 2014. Photo by author.

in the image are bare from the shoulders up, illustrating clothing never worn by ni-Vanuatu women. The image represents an imagined "native" femininity and a contrived vision of paradise inhabited by Gauguin's fetishized Tahitian women. Like the landscapes illustrated by early expedition artists, these real estate signs are peopled with alluring "dusky maidens" (Tamaira 2010). These real estate images rearticulate the long-established cultural motifs associated with Pacific landscapes, evoking both heterosexual masculine desire and an established cultural authenticity through which foreign ideas are transposed onto customary land in Vanuatu.

That these real estate images reproduce existing cultural images is essential to establishing an "authentic" claim to paradise within the mind of foreign viewers. Early imaginings of Tahiti have been central to establishing these enduring cultural motifs; the "myth of Tahiti is like a pebble that centuries ago was tossed into the water, rippling far and wide, lapping at distant shores, and piquing imaginations around the world" (Kahn 2003, 309). In the shifting iconography of paradise, the carefully curated images of "Tahiti"—itself an artifice—are now used to advertise the sale of customary land in Vanuatu. These advertisements reveal that it is not the actual landscape that foreigners purchase but rather the allegorical layering of cultural motifs that create the landscape as a site of desire. Gauguin's images have come to represent a generalized iconic reenvisioning of the Pacific, regardless of how far away Vanuatu is from Tahiti or France. Foreign dreams are transposed onto Pacific landscapes in ways that demonstrate little consciousness of local realities. The imagery of real estate advertisements and tourism marketing is designed to conceal the social tensions associated with land leasing, as well as the conquest inherent in customary land transactions, whereby investors take the lion's share of profits (McDonnell 2015).

Paradise as Property

Across the Pacific, real estate advertisements function to commodify paradise as "property." The idea of property established by Pacific real estate advertisements allows a particular voyeuristic envisaging of landscapes that both distance and objectify, thus enabling commoditization (Rose 1994, 271). Visual representations such as maps, real estate advertisements, and tourism campaigns allow for the creation of land as property, removed from the socially embedded landscapes of Indigenous people. Visual representations construct places in the mind of the viewer. Real estate advertisements, like those of reality television and tourism, carefully manufacture an aesthetic based on the terra nullius trope. In this way they create a landscape empty of local people, awaiting possession. Representations of landscapes in real estate advertisements include images of landscapes either unpeopled or peopled by a single white person. These representations function as a visual reduction of the landscape. They render the landscape flat with a single meaning: property.

Images produced in real estate and tourism create visual references to "paradise" and "virgin," uninhabited landscapes, visually displacing Indigenous inhabitants and effectively obscuring the tensions associated with contemporary land dealings and tourism. This reenvisioning of customary landscapes as real estate creates an ahistorical and atemporal experience of land, existing only at the moment of the gaze. The visual representations of the land echo the "act of imagination" central to property—that it is possible to buy an exclusive right to possession (Rose 1994, 271–272). On Efate Island, the concocted amnesia of untouched landscapes displaces historical understandings of the landscape as previously leased and used for large-scale copra plantations, ignoring the thousands of years of gardening that have taken place in the landscape, and, most importantly, omitting the fact that Indigenous occupation dates from at least three thousand years ago (Bedford, Siméoni, and Lebot 2017). Mimicking colonial acts of "discovery," the planting of the colonizer's flag morphs into the erecting of a real estate billboard, with "first contact" occurring at the moment a foreign gaze rests on the real estate sign. Fantasized ideas of paradise provide a form of visual colonization by allowing the viewer to overlook the actual historical, cultural, and social realities associated with the place.

Visual representations offer an illusion of paradise, entreating the viewer to purchase the imaginative narratives associated with descriptions of landscapes. Reproduced "touristic" images of the Pacific are "unimaginatively similar" and function as commodified constructions of place (Kahn 2000, 16). In Vanuatu, curated images for real estate are largely interchangeable with each other and those in brochures for tourist destinations; they foreground white sandy beaches, crystal blue water, and abundant palm trees. Across Vanuatu, real estate advertisements repeat—almost continuously—the same visual metaphor of an empty "virgin" landscape ready to be colonized. Tourism effortlessly glides into land purchasing, and real estate advertisements read like a utopian vision of an "unspoiled landscape" empty of people—a "land time forgot."

Real estate and tourism advertisements describing Vanuatu as paradise also promote what the French call a financial paradise *(paradis fiscal)* (Van Fossen 2012, 4). On the *Destination Vanuatu* website is written, "It is rare to find the combination of a fiscal and tropical paradise which exists in Vanuatu" (PG IT Consulting and MMA Consulting 2017). Flows of funds in and out of offshore financial sectors are easily laundered through the purchase of land in Vanuatu, and the sectors are interlinked. Greg Rawlings wrote, "When islands and their enclaves promote themselves as tax havens, they in a sense attract new kinds of 'beachcombers'—bankers, investors, financiers, expatriates—who temporarily colonise their shores" (1999b, 48; 2002). In this context, Vanuatu becomes a destination framed by the colonial imaginings of a treasure trove with land deals ripe for plunder and supplies of cheap Black labor. Land transactions financed through these offshore accounts are at the frontier between the global forces of capital, the emplaced local, and the idealized fiscal paradise.

Paradise as a Playground for White People

The idea of repossession allows us to consider the agency of Indigenous people in employing the narratives and visual tropes attached to Pacific landscapes. However, it is also apparent that images of "the Pacific" offer foreign audiences a series of seemingly interchangeable, romanticized locations that supposedly exist beyond the demands of the industrialized capitalist complex. Representations of the Pacific in reality television, real estate advertisements, and tourism campaigns offer access to a commodified, reenvisioned paradise that is overwhelmingly represented as a playground for white people. White, bikini-clad women are a regular motif in real estate and tourism images across the Pacific, serving as a reminder of who is defining this paradise (figure 5.4). The gaze, in continuity with earlier representations of the Pacific, remains profoundly male. Images of a bikini-clad white woman lying on a beach against a Pacific backdrop are so often repeated that they establish their own internal authenticity or culturally ingrained sense of the familiar (Kahn 2014, 161). The images themselves are reproduced en masse and made available for purchase from international photography firms such as Getty Images. More often than not, they are the fabric from which marketing campaigns are stitched.

The allure of Pacific landscapes is attached to desire for the women who inhabit these otherwise empty, contrived scenes. That the female figure is white repeats long-established practices of transposing sexual desire for particular types of women into Pacific scenery. In his production of postcards and

FIGURE 5.4. Couple playing in water for the Vanuatu "Discover What Matters" tourism campaign, 2014. Photo © David Kirkland, reproduced courtesy of Vanuatu Tourism Office.

calendar images of Tahiti and Tahitian women, photographer Tera Sylvain mainly employed non-Tahitian women, crowning their heads with flowers or placing a hibiscus flower behind an ear to create a local flavor (Kahn 2014). Much like Gauguin before him, Sylvain recognized that "men who visit Tahiti want a woman they already possess in their head or in their libido" (Kahn 2014, 157). Foreign male tourists or real estate purchasers seek a playmate in their Pacific landscape.

Images of white, bikini-clad women lying on beaches or playing in Pacific locales are highly provocative, given the history of the bikini. No doubt few tourists are aware that the bathing suit was named after Bikini Atoll, which, from 1946 to 1958, was the site of the testing of twenty-three nuclear bombs that resulted in severe and enduring health and ecological consequences for Marshall Islanders. Teresia Teaiwa wrote that, given the history of the garment, the bikini "is testament to the recurring tourist trivialization of Pacific Islanders' experience and existence." She argued that the naming of the garment as a "bikini" plays into coded references of Islanders as "exotic," drawing references to the scantily clad "dusky maidens" of earlier colonial representations. Given the contemporary juxtaposition of the bikini with a repeatedly bombed and irradiated Bikini Atoll, Teaiwa stated: "By drawing attention to a sexualized and supposedly depoliticized female body, the bikini distracts from the colonial and highly political origins of its name. The sexist dynamic the bikini performs—objectification through excessive visibility—inverts the colonial dynamics that have occurred during nuclear testing in the Pacific, objectification by rendering invisible" (Teaiwa 1994, 87, 93, 94). Building on the brilliant work of Teaiwa and expanding from the specific horrors of Bikini Atoll to other visual images of Pacific places, it becomes obvious that tropical scenes that center on a white woman in a bikini work to effectively displace Pacific bodies from the landscape.

Images of white women located in Eden-like scenes are such established motifs that they encourage an intimacy of the viewer with Pacific landscapes. Adria Imada made this point as she described the use of hula girl imagery to create an "imagined intimacy" with Hawai'i (2011). These are not simply images of sex, sand, and sea; they are images that flatten the landscape by obscuring other histories of people and place. By centering on white, female, and scantily clad bodies, the visual images enable foreign claims to possession, whether through tourism or real estate. Kanaka Maoli scholar Haunani-Kay Trask wrote that the foreign imagined female native of Hawai'i comes out of the "depths of Western sexual sickness" (1991, 23). She argued that, like Vanuatu, the projected imagining of Hawai'i has profound implications for the Indigenous inhabitants of the place:

> Today, glass and steel shopping malls with layered parking lots stretch over what was once the most ingeniously irrigated taro lands, feeding millions of Hawaiians over thousands of years. Large bays, delicately ringed long ago with well-stocked fishponds, are now heavily silted and cluttered with jet skis, windsurfers, and sailboats. Multi-storey hotels disgorge over six million tourists a year onto stunningly beautiful (and easily polluted) beaches, closing off access to locals... exclusive housing and beach areas remind the Native Hawaiian who owns Hawai'i: the foreign, colonial country called the United States of America. (Trask 1991, 23)

The process of dispossession of Indigenous inhabitants from the landscape begins with the act of reimagining place as empty or as a romantic playground.

"The Pacific" represented in real estate and tourism campaigns functions as a backdrop; Oceanic landscapes become romantic playgrounds for white, heterosexual couples. If and when a man is included in the scene, it is a white man joining his lover. Aside from the white people who inhabit the landscapes of real estate and tourism images, an occasional local—a smiling child or group of smiling children—may compose the scene, creating the visual motif that the Pacific is a welcoming place where people are happy and friendly (Kahn 2014, 154; Taylor 2017). The final image from a Vanuatu Tourism campaign, "Discover What Matters," shows a white couple smiling and embracing while swimming. In this image, the Vanuatu landscape is represented by ubiquitous blue waters, suggesting that, in reality, the image could have been shot almost anywhere. "What matters" is that the landscape provides a backdrop for romance and fun. The subject of the image is the white, heterosexual couple; it is *their* paradise.

A Convergence of Desire: "Landowners," Investors, and Middlemen

Along the frontier of desire, various points of convergence occur between the desires and expectations of foreigners to possess a "slice of paradise" and the desires of local men to lease customary land to secure large cash payments. Contemporary leasing in North Efate involves transactions between a powerful local man, often a chief, or a small number of men and a speculative land investor. Powerful Lelepa men have been instrumentally involved in seizing the opportunities offered by *Survivor* tourism and land sales. During filming, the American *Survivor* crew was hosted by Lelepa man Manelpa on customary land located on the edge of Havannah Harbour. As the land rush began, Manelpa was one of the first men involved in leasing another plot of customary land located near *Survivor* beach. Using the money earned from leasing his customary land, as well as from hosting the American *Survivor* crew, Manelpa built a tourism business on his Havannah Harbour land. In yet another twist to the story, the material used in the *Survivor* television series is now physically embedded in Manelpa's tourism business. Close to the water in the main *farea*-style café built by Manelpa, the rock carved by one of the "tribes" during the filming of the *Survivor* series is prominently displayed on the base of the bar, its central location signaling the primary importance of the *Survivor* series in enabling the reenvisioning of the customary landscape for a tourism business. The rock also provides a central motif for tourists visiting Havannah Harbour in search of a "*Survivor*" experience.

On the other side of the transaction, speculative land investors are mostly resident expatriate or "naturalized citizen" investors or their middlemen. Middlemen are indeed always men. Many investors are naturalized citizens—a particular form of citizenship defined in the Vanuatu Constitution (Chapter 3, Article 12). They are often members of long-term resident families that have a long, intergenerational history in Vanuatu. Accordingly, as a group of investors they are extremely culturally and legally expert at pursuing land deals. Many investors have long-term business interests in Vanuatu that offer employment opportunities for ni-Vanuatu. All investors have long-term relationships with local ni-Vanuatu employees and friends, and with numerous chiefs located in villages throughout Vanuatu.

In the twenty years after independence, the patterns of wholesale leasing of customary land to naturalized citizen investors were already established. Data collated for rural leasing in Efate from 1980 until the year 2000 shows that overwhelmingly the largest grants of customary land were made to politically influential investors. These included a lease of 2,077 hectares and 62 acres (totaling 5,194 acres) in 1980 at independence to the Russet family; 765 hectares and 70 acres (totaling 1,160 acres) to Gilbert Dinh Van Than in 1986 and a further 342 hectares (845 acres) in 1989 to Simone Dinh Van Than; and grants of 242 hectares (598 acres) to Harry Kalpram and Jean Ferrari in 1994 and 1997, respectively (Farran 2002, np). Many of these individual investors or family groups continue to be major players in the speculative land market.

Speculative land investors purchase land as part of a broader portfolio of local business or offshore financial sector interests. In Vanuatu, developer and building interests are overwhelmingly dominated by members of the local families who, while originally of European or Vietnamese descent, have since had long-term, intergenerational histories in Vanuatu. Many of these families predate Vanuatu's independence and their members consider themselves to be white "ni-Vanuatu." Other real estate investors have more recently arrived, drawn to Vanuatu by the promise of its tax haven.

In North Efate, the major naturalized citizen investors include: American Robert Bohn, director of the Vanuatu-based European Bank and the offshore Vanuatu Financial Centre whose wharf development is a major case study; the French Monvoisin family and Bolliet, who were implicated in two fraudulent ministerial land dealings described earlier in this chapter; Australian Andrew Munroe, director of TransPacific Property Consultants; Vietnamese-descended Alain Lew, owner of Port Vila Hardware and former chairman of the Board of Airports Vanuatu Ltd; and French David Russet, agriculturalist, subdivision developer, and owner of the Tana-Russet shopping complex. Finally, the Dinh family, descended from Vietnamese laborers, are major investors in North Efate and are prominent businesspeople, owning over ten companies that dominate many of the major commercial activities in Vanuatu. The Dinh family has a chain of supermarkets and a commercial building company and employs over five hundred people in Vanuatu (Garae 2013). Both Gilbert Dinh Van Than and Bohn have been extremely influential in politics in Vanuatu, and Bohn is a former member of Parliament. Some of these investors engage directly in land transactions, but many employ middlemen to act on their behalf.

Relationships between speculative land investors and chiefs and other local men are mostly informal, involving a series of payments to ensure that they act in the interests of investors. In practice this means that chiefs either sign lease agreements, acting as the supposed "custom owner" of an area of land, or exert pressure on the actual custom owners to lease their land. The role of chiefs in land negotiations often involves use of their personal authority either to influence land dealings or to act as the representative "spokesman" on behalf of custom owners.

Middlemen often facilitate relationships with local chiefs allowing investors the benefit of remaining anonymous and removed from leases, which are often negotiated in dubious circumstances—such as when landowners are drunk. Middlemen are from outside the local area and are often expert in managing the legal processes of registration through the administrative bureaucracy of the Department of Lands. For example, one middleman previously worked as a government employee in the Customary Land Tribunal

Office. Similarly, Levi Tarosa was formerly a senior lands officer and also held the position of valuer general before becoming a self-proclaimed "doctor for land" adept at facilitating land deals (G Ligo 2012a, 2012b). Relationships between investors and middlemen sometimes take the form of formal legal contracts, whereby middlemen lease the customary land directly and then sell the lease to an investor. This enables investors to avoid the tensions often associated with the initial leasing of customary land as well as providing them with an already registered legal interest.

Many registered titles over customary land are held by either a limited liability company or a trust. These legal arrangements are a means of transferring assets and avoiding tax.[2] The major property developer in the North Efate region is TransPacific Property Consultants Limited that operates under the control of Directors Andrew Munroe and Laurence Harrison. In 2015 TransPacific held twenty-five leases in North Efate. Like other property developers, TransPacific is a corporate web involving a large number of other established legal entities. Munroe is also the principal partner of Moores Rowland, an offshore financial service provider based in Vanuatu, which provides a range of offshore company, finance, and trust services. Tracing connections between companies in Vanuatu is exceedingly difficult. After extensive research, it is clear that TransPacific holds a number of leases across various islands in Vanuatu as speculative land investments through a web of legal entities including: Tope Estate Limited (which holds leases in Tope Estate located next to Mangaliliu community); Endeavour Investments Limited (with a lease in Malekula at Norsop Beach); Cybernautic Limited; Ocean Breeze Estate Limited (with a commercial lease title in Pango created in 2006); Crystal Limited (with a rural-commercial lease created in 2007); Jopepa Limited (with an agricultural lease located at Tisman Bay, Malekula created in 2006); Sunshine Beach Development Limited (with a commercial and tourism lease over Malelvon Island, Port Olry, Santo created in 2008); and Nambawan Properties Limited (with an agricultural lease signed by the minister of lands as lessor over Rentabao created in 1989).

Aside from TransPacific, the next major developers in the North Efate region are Black Magic Development Limited and Black Magic Holdings Limited, two companies that together hold twenty-four leases over customary land. Samoa Point Estates Limited holds sixteen leases in the region and will be discussed next. The remaining leases over larger areas of customary land are held by naturalized citizens—Dominique Dinh, Russet, Robert Monvoisin, and Bohn—through a web of companies. Other leases are held by local real estate agents, such as Francesca Grillo of Waterfront Real Estate. On a smaller scale, a number of mainly Australian and New Zealand expatriate residents have purchased lots within subdivisions and a number of other company and trust entities hold either a single or a small number of titles. Two leases have recently been transferred to Chinese investors to operate commercial and business developments. A local business, Lelepa Island Tours, holds two lease interests, and seven leases are held by local Lelepa or Mangaliliu men who have leased land to themselves either to protect it or to prepare the title for future sale.

Land Leasing: The Shifting Terrain of Dirty Deals

Speculative investments and the "rush" on frontiers often operate within these shifting terrains of opaque legal and illegal operations. Writing on logging in Kalimantan, Indonesia, Anna Tsing identified that the frontier exists in "the shifting terrain between legality and illegality, public and private ownership . . . violence and law" (2003, 5102). In Vanuatu, land deals take place in clandestine economies consisting of an opaque architecture of arrangements between investors, middlemen, landowners, and various ministers of lands. Within the North Efate landscape, the Samoa Point lease provides a revelatory case study of this architecture.

Initially used during the filming of *Survivor*, Samoa Point was described on the television program's website in 2004 as "a rocky headland in the north-west with a small sandy beach . . . there is good swimming and snorkeling." Here, the landscape is understood primarily as a playground for foreigners; no mention is made of the local meanings of the place. Samoa Point is named after the Samoan teachers who were stationed there in 1846, before dying of malaria. The leasing of Samoa Point has seen the imposition of foreign desires and the attempted erasure of local histories central to the place. The leasing and subsequent development of Samoa Point caused distress to Lelepa people as it involved the bulldozing of a large number of graves associated with the former missionaries who were stationed at Samoa Point. Today the landscape has been transformed into Vanuatu's only five-star resort, "The Havannah," which offers guests helicopter joyrides and rendezvous on Artok Island and the *Survivor* beaches. While guests may mistakenly believe these are empty landscapes, in reality they *are* peopled. The amorous daytime encounters of foreigners on beaches are the source of much discussion on Lelepa and Mangaliliu, with children and young men, in particular, sometimes racing to watch the show.

Acting on complaints from local custom owners, the leasing of Samoa Point by Russet was investigated by then Director General of Lands Joe Ligo. In their complaints Lelepa custom owners claimed not to have consented to the lease. After investigation, and in his subsequent report, Ligo found that the land transaction amounted to: "a dirty deal and stealing of land from Ni-Vanuatu land owners by a local businessman. The stealing was processed and approved by the Ministry and Department of Lands without the ni-Vanuatu customary land owners consent" (J Ligo 2011, 17).

In his investigation, Ligo described the customary land transaction as follows: Chief Andrew Popovi leased 17 hectares of customary land (approximately 17 football fields or 42 acres) of Samoa Point to Russet for the paltry amount of VT 2 million (approximately A$23,000) (2011, 17). One month after the original lease was registered and without any further development, the land was resold for VT 30 million (approximately A$342,000), although, to avoid stamp duty, the resale price was listed as just VT 8 million (A$91,000) (2011, 17–19). Documenting the amount that land sold for as less than the actual payment avoids stamp duty tax and is widely acknowledged as common practice in Vanuatu.

When the findings of the director general's report were made public, Russet responded by claiming that the original lease was made with Chief Popovi for an amount of VT 1 million (A$11,500), that the director general's claims were "false," and that the on-sale to the second investor was for an amount in the VT 10 million range (Neil-Jones 2011). Taking the VT 1 million amount as accurate, a resale amount of VT 30 million would represent a windfall profit to Russet of 3,000 percent for what was essentially the same unserviced area of customary land simply converted into leased property.

The Samoa Point land transaction illustrates that the amounts that supposed "custom owners" receive from leasing land, while large relative to local access to cash, are insubstantial relative to the actual market value of the land and the amount of profit that can be made from speculative land dealings. The opaque architecture of lease making, the clandestine economy of land dealings, and the associated windfall profits to the investor from the leasing of Samoa Point also offer a localized study of capitalist processes. In this instance, Russet won an extraordinary windfall profit, and Chief Popovi gained a small cash prize, but the material impact of this leasing is the dispossession of Indigenous people of a large area of customary land and the bulldozing of culturally significant graves.

This frontier of capitalism offers insights into both the commodification of landscapes and the operation of the global tourism sector, itself fueled by the manufacture of desire. Currently guests can book a room in a deluxe waterfront villa at the Havannah Harbour for one week for A$11,000, approximately the same amount as was paid to Chief Popovi for the original transaction over the entire seventeen hectares of customary land. These dealings make visible the spectacular scale of riches available to investors who are involved in land leasing, as well as the deep, driven inequalities that are present in these capitalist processes, both local and global. Here we can see the effective march of late capitalism, the process of value creation at the frontier of desire, and the consuming force of globalization. The commodity that is being consumed is the land adjoining Havannah Harbour—replete with foreign imaginings. In capitalist terms, the value is cultivated as the landscape becomes saturated with foreign desire. The material effect of these processes is to dispossess local Indigenous people and recolonize the landscape as a playground for foreigners.

Contested Authority and the Race for the Prize

But we must dive more deeply into capitalist relations to understand the nature of these lease transactions. Given the relatively small amounts that custom owners earn from customary land sales, why have so many powerful men been involved in leasing land? Careful ethnographic research suggests that customary land is leased both for access to cash and material goods and to assert personal authority over the landscape and rival claimants. The leasing of Samoa Point, for instance, cannot be understood without reference to the long-running chiefly title dispute over the landscape related to rival claims of chiefly authority over Udaone customary land. As the chiefly title case progressed, Russet leased the land from Chief Popovi, thereby bypassing the Island Court determination of who held the legitimate claim to the title and the land.

Where chiefly authority remains contested, the act of a powerful man leasing the customary land under claim represents an assertion of authority over a landscape through property. Across Vanuatu, male rivals engage in a competitive "race for the prize" approach to leasing customary land. While customary claims to landscapes remain in doubt, property transactions have the effect of fixing legal claims. In this approach, "the prize pursued in this race is not so much the land itself as its value; the winner is not necessarily the one who, at the end, holds legal possession but, instead, the individual who has managed to extract the maximum portion of the land's rent" (Benjaminsen and Sjaastad 2002, 129). It is apparent that these contests over land are as much about "the scope and constitution" of chiefly authority as they are about access to the actual land itself (Sikor and Lund 2009, 2). Possession of the landscape has been lost to the former Indigenous inhabitants. However, Chief Popovi asserted his chiefly authority over a rival chief and "won" what is locally considered to be a large cash payment for leasing the land.

Racing to lease customary land becomes a rational strategy when faced with a land rush and legal arrangements that ensure that another man can claim "custom ownership" over an area of land that is not rightfully his. The expert maneuvering by Russet allowed Chief Popovi to claim ownership to legal title regardless of the findings of the Island Court about who has the legitimate claim to the chiefly title. But it is Russet, not Chief Popovi, who won the ultimate pecuniary prize by extracting the windfall profit from the purchase and resale of Samoa Point.

In local discussions, the leasing of Samoa Point by Chief Popovi to Russet is widely condemned by Lelepa men as the stealing of customary land by one chief, so as to thwart the claims of a rival chief, rather than having the claims mediated through a dispute process. Lelepa men explained that much of the leasing along Samoa Point, including the leasing of the actual point itself, is a style of stealing land: "*fasin blong stil.*" Lelepa men consider that the stealing of customary land, rightfully under the authority of another man, has no place in *kastom*.

> Leasing along Samoa [Point] shows the *"fasin blong stil."* The proper chief goes to the tribunal to ask that it decides who the proper chief of Samoa Point is, but all "property" is sold already. Another man has already sold it.
>
> The proper chief of the island was waiting on Lelepa for the decision, but the others sold the land. We are challenging this in court, but they had already sold all the land.
>
> Now the graves have been bulldozed. The *paoa* of the *ples*, the spirit of the ancestors, has gone down because they have bulldozed the graves.
>
> We are challenging this in court, but they have already sold all the land. If we win the case does that mean we can win the big resort? No. Does that mean we can win the money? No. They have won all the money. The land is finished. (interview, June 2012)

This final statement, the *"graon hemi finis"* (the land is finished), represents an understanding not only of the way customary rights over landscape have been expropriated through lease making but also how this process of legal expropriation can lead to dispossession of the landscape of the broader landowning groups, with the result that the land is now a tourist resort. Property operates to assert a claim of authority against a rival chief. Property, backed by Torrens Title registration, ensures that leases, once made, are difficult to challenge. The creation of leased property effectively overrides all other legal and customary processes, resulting in a winner who captures the prize.

It is always important to remember who the ultimate winner is from these deals. As an expert investor, Russet has since employed the same strategy of creating a lease with one supposed "custom owner" while a chiefly title dispute is being judged in court in another part of Havannah Harbour.

Foreign Imaginings of World Heritage

Frontiers of desire create landscapes of compressed globalization. The years since 2000 have created, in North Efate, a period of compressed engagement between the global and the local (Hviding 2003, 542). Local people have formed engagements not only with global actors in the three *Survivor* television series but also with naturalized citizen investors (with their links to global tax havens) and real estate agents; archaeologists and cultural heritage scholars engaged to establish a World Heritage site; American and Japanese conservationists interested in reef preservation; Australian and American "Peace Corps" volunteers; "developers" intent on building in the landscape; hoteliers and restaurateurs; tourists; anthropologists; lawyers; and other foreigners intent on "development" projects. This is not to suggest that local people have not always formed attachments with the global world, but rather that in the period since 2000 this has developed more rapidly with a wider range of global actors, resulting in a confusing uncertainty as to what exactly is happening among locals and foreign expatriates alike and also the values that configure these relationships.

As an extension of this engagement with global actors, on 10 July 2008 the international World Heritage Committee recognized the Outstanding Universal Value of sites located in Chief Roi Mata's Domain as an example of a continuing cultural landscape. The site was inscribed on the World Heritage List with the issuing of the following statement: "The landscape reflects continuing Pacific chiefly systems and respect for this authority through tabu prohibitions on use of Roi Mata's residence and burial that have been observed for over 400 years and structured the local landscape and social practices" (World Heritage Committee Decision 32 COM 8B.27). The imagining of space as "World Heritage" brings with it a new series of actors with their own set of values around what the landscape of Chief Roi Mata's Domain represents.

Chief Roi Mata's Domain World Heritage site was established with conservation objectives that are often in tension with proposed large-scale developments in the region—developments such as wharves, subdivisions, resorts, and hotels. This tension means that, locally and globally, discussions of land leasing in the North Efate region often become interlaced with the story of World Heritage. Lelepa people continue to navigate their relationships with various outside actors in ways that may appear contradictory, seamlessly alternating between the supposed mantras of "conservation" and "development." In reality these changeable positions are deeply contextual responses to a particular confluence of people, agendas, and resources available at any given moment in time.

Lelepa people live and animate the cultural landscape of Roi Mata. At times, this has created tensions around the management of the site, in part because of the narratives of conservation and protection that mark the space of World Heritage. World Heritage functions as a designated sacred global space often oriented toward the enclosure of a particular monument within the landscape or what Chris Ballard and Meredith Wilson referred to as "the valorization of the monumental" (2012, 130). World Heritage is an elicitation of stories and values on a landscape that together represent an attempt to protect and conserve the landscape in the interests of the global community. Together these stories of World Heritage create a kind of "modern fairy tale" in which the heritage and the conservation project become a "magical, transformative commodity" (Peluso 2012, 80; West 2006). Key to World Heritage is the idea of the conservation of a site through the establishment of a "buffer zone" designed as a protective zone around the core area where development is restricted so that there is no impact on the heritage values of the site.

Legally, the attempted reenvisioning of the North Efate landscape as "World Heritage" creates tensions between the Vanuatu state's obligations under the United Nations Educational, Scientific and Cultural Organization's 1972 World Heritage Convention and constitutional claims that the ownership of customary land resides with custom owners. Inscription places obligations on states around protecting and conserving the cultural and natural heritage situated in its territory (World Heritage Convention, Article 5; UNESCO 1972). This article places an emphasis on state regulatory mechanisms but fails to recognize the existing customary law that manages the landscape and has done so for hundreds of years. The landscape of Chief Roi Mata's Domain has never had any operational regulatory framework and only minimal state resources have been allocated to the protection of the site. Actual protection of World Heritage has been dependent on the management of the site under existing customary arrangements under the guidance of the hardworking Lelema World Heritage Committee, the Vanuatu Cultural Centre, and a series of Australian volunteers and consultants.

The assertion of state territorial authority over World Heritage is practically and legally unworkable, as well as locally contentious. Many Lelepa people champion World Heritage due to a feeling of pride associated with the global recognition of their cultural landscape or because they benefit from small-scale livelihood incomes associated with the site. However, there are also powerful men who express resentment that the inscription of the site may limit their capacity to lease and develop their customary land, thereby impacting their constitutional rights as custom owners. Among some Lelepa people there is a concern that reconfiguring the landscape as World Heritage may privilege the state, global, and external stakeholders over the local custodians of the landscape. Creating tension is an imagined global space of World Heritage and conservation, and how these global imaginings translate as local meanings in a lived cultural landscape.

The Road to "Joint-Venture" Development

The lived landscape of the people of North Efate is named and narrated with reference to Chief Roi Mata. Recognition of the role that chiefs and *kastom* play in the management of the "continuing cultural landscape" of Roi Mata requires careful consideration of the values placed on the conservation and development of both the core area sites and the broader buffer zone (see map 2.2). In the long-running land-use planning project that I ran for years out of the Vanuatu Cultural Centre, chiefs and senior men repeatedly spoke of the need for protection of the core areas of the site—namely, Artok Island, Mangas Precinct, and Feles Cave—as all connected to the ancestral figure of Roi Mata. However, for many chiefs and senior men there is no necessary connection between the conservation and protection of these core sites, and the area currently listed as the World Heritage inscribed buffer zone. Accordingly, many of these men have leased, or plan to lease, substantial areas of the coast located in the buffer zone. Rather than leasing within the buffer zone, what is considered far more serious, in terms of *kastom* and the ongoing integrity of the World Heritage site, is the fact that Artok Island is held under a lease and that future leasing may impact the old *kastom* village of Mangaas. Leasing in North Efate presents a major threat to the core site areas as well as a challenge to the ongoing maintenance of a buffer zone around the World Heritage site.

The challenges posed by land leasing to the conservation ideals of World Heritage have created a series of conflicts around both the leasing of land and the establishment of roads to the leased areas of land to enable development to occur. Around the World Heritage site, the major leaseholder and potential developer is TransPacific. TransPacific currently holds dozens of leases across two areas: (1) at the *Survivor* beaches toward Tuk Tuk Point; and (2) around coastal areas located north past the Mangaas site at Punapangau and Mahwa beaches. In addition to these registered leases, TransPacific has negotiated a number of additional lease instruments throughout the buffer zone over areas of land that are awaiting registration. The leases currently held by TransPacific have no road access and so administratively should not have been registered.

For many years road access has been the crucial issue preventing TransPacific from developing the leases that it owns. Road access to many of these leases initially occurred with the filming of *Survivor* when a dirt track was constructed to allow the film crew access to the beaches. This road is an extension of the road that leaves the Efate ring road and travels down the steep escarpment into Mangaliliu Village. Leases registered by TransPacific and other investors over "*Survivor* men's" and "*Survivor* women's" beaches are located along this dirt track. In terms of requiring road access to existing leases, in addition to wanting the *Survivor* track to be redesignated as a "public road," TransPacific has requested a second access road to travel to leases on Punapangau and Mahwa beaches (TransPacific 2011). If an access road to these beaches was authorized, it would cause extensive damage to the Mangaas site, the former residence of Roi Mata and a core part of the World Heritage area. In an earlier attempt to secure road access to leases in 2007, TransPacific tried to enter into a memorandum of understanding with Lelepa and Mangaliliu Village councils and the Lelepa and Mangaliliu Council of Chiefs. The memorandum was based on meetings held between Munroe, his middleman, and various custom owners and chiefs at the Melanesian Hotel, an established venue for conducting land deals with easy access to alcohol and the hotel casino.

The location of the existing TransPacific leases and the proposed scale of development envisaged by TransPacific mean that leasing represents a threat to the ongoing integrity of the World Heritage site. The scale and type of development outlined in the memorandum are as follows, "The areas south of Tuku Tuku [*Survivor* beach leases] will be low rise residential, holiday village, boutique resort and small (commercial) tourism development.... Punapangau and Mahwa beach will be a low-rise residential holiday cottage with special resort precinct." Actualizing this vision would involve large-scale development on either side of Mangaliliu Village and the potential delisting of the World Heritage site. A subsequent Environmental Impact Assessment (EIA) located at Tope Estate in August 2008 was commissioned and paid for by TransPacific, in what appears to be a conflict of interest. The EIA is listed as a "report for a commercial subdivision" in which the proposed development is described as "a subdivision for a mini strata holiday unit with restaurant and shop." Far from being objective, the report reads almost as a promotional document endorsing the company and promoting a joint venture with fifty local landowners (Bani 2008, 6, 10).

Like many of the developments in the region, this particular project is described repeatedly as a "joint venture." The memorandum suggests that TransPacific leases will be developed as a joint venture along the following terms:

(a) The Developer *shall act* [emphasis added] for the Landowner in negotiating the best possible outcome for the Landowner...
(b) The developers and Landowners will share *equally* [emphasis added] in any financial benefit obtained from a first subsequent transfer of the lease. The financial benefit in this respect shall be defined as any net benefit made by the Developer in the sale of the lease including any equity obtained or negotiated by the Developer in the Company purchasing the Lease and developing the tourist/residential precinct.

This definition of "net benefit" is central to assessing the custom-owner benefits from the proposed joint venture. On closer inspection, the architecture of the leasing arrangements is "joint venture" in name only.

At the frontier of desire, speculative land dealings involve significant windfall profits to investors, as discussed. Comparisons can be made between the paltry annual rental payments made to custom owners and the publicly listed sale price for subdivided blocks of the same customary land. A closer look at "Tope Estate," the proposed TransPacific "joint-venture" subdivision development located just past the village of Mangaliliu, suggests how much equity exists in the shares afforded between investors and landowners. For Tope Estate, the listed price for the eight subdivided blocks is between VT 4 million and VT 8 million (approximately A$46,000 and A$90,000), yielding a total amount when sold of around A$550,000 for TransPacific. By contrast, the annual rent paid for seventy-five-year leases averages A$100 per year for each lease, earning each landowner around A$7,500 over the term of the lease. Together the group of custom landowners will receive A$60,000 for leasing their customary land, an amount that will depreciate over time in terms of real value. By comparison, TransPacific's profit from the Tope Estate is more than half a million dollars for a relatively small-scale subdivision on customary land.

There is a substantial disparity between amounts paid to custom owners for leasing customary land and the amounts yielded to investors from subdividing the same area of customary land. In the example of Tope Estate, the entire landowning group would earn just 1.5 percent of the final resale value of the subdivided customary land. This already paltry amount is, however, not the final amount afforded to landowners. In operating a legal clinic in the region, I have reviewed numerous payments made by TransPacific to custom owners. In these accounts, TransPacific's initial lease payments (premiums) have been paid over several years in smaller amounts rather than as a lump sum payment. In many instances, custom owners' relatively small premium payments have been paid based on a "net benefit" amount. This means that these payments have been whittled away to insubstantial amounts by TransPacific's deductions for inflated costs associated with "surveying," "advertising," and "administration." TransPacific's actual payments are far removed from the idea of custom owners equally sharing in the benefits from development—the idea associated with the supposed notion of a joint venture and the promise that investors and landowners will share equally from the development.

After failing to secure road access to their leases through the memorandum of understanding, TransPacific began to clear the coconut plantation located around its proposed Tope Estate subdivision, adjacent to Mangaliliu Village. In 2009, local opposition to TransPacific's subdivision coalesced on three main actors: Douglas Kalotiti, as the then chair of the Lelema World Heritage Committee; Reuben Kaloris, a custom owner with customary land along the track to the *Survivor* beaches; and Chief Mormor. Exercising his rights as a custom owner, Kaloris created a roadblock across the track. The opposition of these three actors was supported by Australian volunteer Adam Trau and was mobilized around protecting the buffer zone of the World Heritage site. Trau, Ballard, and Wilson described the contestations among Lelepa people at the time: "On the one hand, there are those within the community who see the buffer zone as a force which might inspire or elicit communal approaches to land similar to those of the past, while on the other, there are those who want to continue to move towards individual land ownership in order to capitalise on land leasing" (2014, 94).

Ongoing contestation relating to land leasing around the World Heritage site is best interpreted as a moveable dialogue that fixes at various points in time on different desires and imaginings—local and global—of the landscape: *kastom* narratives of ancestral beings and the idiom of land as a *saloa,* a shared communal resource; the imaginary of World Heritage and conservation; and the desire for development and cash payments. Each of these imaginings offers a distinctly different pathway for the future of Lelepa people. Local actors position themselves politically on the stage of North Efate choosing particular scripts at particular times and performing claims of authority over landscapes. Powerful men, who in 2008–2009 were vocal opponents of the development of the leases and the access roads subsequently, in 2011, signed a letter of support for the project. This performance of signing suggests that at that moment in time TransPacific managed to elicit support for road access. It shows the contextual, temporal act of signing as an act of chiefly authority over landscapes that, in customary tenure, properly belongs to others. The letter illustrates how places are perpetually made and remade, their contours fashioned temporarily against the prevailing winds of remembered pasts and imagined futures by the agency of a handful of men.

Conclusion: The Frontier of Property Relations

Saturated with desire, customary land belonging to Lelepa people along Havannah Harbour has been transformed into leased property. The rapacious leasing of the coastline continues. North Efate, just as in early colonial times, has been a frontier in the transformation of Indigenous customary landscapes. This transformation occurs through two processes. First, the regulation of social relations through property law backed by the authority of the state and the use of force or implied use of force, particularly the eviction of people from customary landscapes that they have lived in often for generations. Second, the development of leases to create the long-term dispossession of Indigenous people from land. The frontier of desire becomes the frontier of property relations, reconfiguring Indigenous relationships to customary land in socially transformative ways.

Management of landscapes under property law exists in contrast to preexisting customary arrangements. The inscription of a frontier is essential to this arrangement: "Inside the *frontier* [emphasis added] lie secure tenure, fee-simple ownership and state-guaranteed rights to property. Outside lie uncertain and undeveloped entitlements, communal claims, and the absence of state guarantees of property" (Blomley 2003, 124). Property law fixes particular geographical imaginings of landscapes that privilege the possession of landscapes by legal owners, to the exclusion of others. Transacting customary land involves privileging the rights of individual "custom owners" while the customary claims of other Indigenous people go unrecognized. At the frontier of property relations, Lelepa people with previous use and access rights under customary tenure become trespassers. Across Vanuatu, leases are walled, signs erected, gates built, and Indigenous access to landscapes denied; the spatial markers of property become fixed and must be obeyed on threat of violence. Along the coastline of Efate Island, real estate signs, trespass signs, walls, and gates carefully signal possession by lessees and the exclusion of Indigenous people from the landscape. Trespass signs operate as spatial markers of possession through claims of "private property." It is these spatial markers that serve to materially denote the frontier of property (figure 5.5).

Trespass and real estate signs are visual claims of ownership reminding viewers that property law regulates spaces and the performances permissible

FIGURE 5.5. A declaration of private property banning customary activities, 20 November 2014. Photo by author.

within those spaces. Property law can regulate access to spaces, or make spaces gendered as public and private. In this way, property can often become entangled with local social determinants of class, gender, and race. In Vanuatu, one of the main tensions around leasing land in rural areas is that property owners enact their exclusive rights of possession by building large gated and fenced boundaries that deny access to locals to beachfront, gardens, and coastal estates. Often these fences contain land and adjacent beachfront that is not legally owned. While the boundaries of all leased land finish at the medium-high-water mark, the physical fencing of these spaces marks out their enclosure and material possession. Lelepa people recognize that access to their land, gardens, beaches, and coastal areas is constrained once land is leased. Increasingly the space inside the frontier is racially segregated. Australians, New Zealanders, French, and Chinese owners of subdivisions and businesses live in gated communities. Resorts and restaurants for expatriates and tourists now dot the coastline of North Efate. Some Lelepa people are employees in newly formed businesses or are employed as house girls or gardeners in expatriate homes. However, most Lelepa people are removed and excluded from landscapes that they and their ancestors have gardened, fished, lived in, and passed through for thousands of years.

Although Vanuatu's constitution states that all land belongs to custom owners in perpetuity, leases for expatriate housing and large-scale development in rural areas, such as tourist resorts, often stipulate that there must be compensation for all infrastructure development and other "improvements" to the land at the end of the term of the lease. The inclusion of "improvements clauses" in lease instruments is now established practice in Vanuatu, and many leases located on the coastline of Havannah Harbour include them. While it is likely that these improvement clauses are unconstitutional, there is no instance where the validity of the clauses has been legally challenged. If these clauses were deemed to be legal, the result would likely be the alienation of Indigenous people from the land as it appears highly unlikely that custom owners could generate the cash required to compensate for improvements to the land. Accordingly, land built on by outsiders would effectively become alienated from the Indigenous landowners by the requirement of compensation.

The fiction of an empty landscape that marks tourism, real estate, and reality television reproductions is deeply political. It allows for possession by foreigners and dispossession of locals. Filmed, mapped, and surveyed—these "empty landscapes" are claimed. Integral to this process is the surveying and mapping of land that becomes a form of "organised forgetting" (Blomley 2003, 128), the extension of an ahistorical idea of landscapes unpeopled and unknown. Property itself is imagined as a relationship between an owner and an inert, empty space instead of the embodied and active landscape of Indigenous understandings. This relationship of owner and empty landscape obfuscates the violent relationships that dictate property ownership of land and rights of exclusive possession. The excluded "others" become "outlaws" or "trespassers" who have experienced the violence of dispossession (Blomley 2003, 132). Accounts suggest that some Vanuatu real estate agents extol expatriates interested in purchasing land to maintain violent colonial-style relationships in defense of property rights. In a report produced by Oxfam, the researcher, purporting to be interested in purchasing land, was told that she could "ensure the exclusive use of 'her' beach by keeping a couple of big dogs and a shotgun and making the locals believe that she would shoot them if they tried to land fishing boats there" (Slatter 2006, 8). The allusions to reenactments of colonial violence suggest the enduring logic of the frontier, in which colonial-style relations continue to haunt the landscape. This is the frontier where resorts are built on bulldozed graves. It is here that the tensions surrounding the deep inequities associated with capitalist relations at the frontier of desire endure.

Chapter 6
The Masters of Modernity

Vanuatu's national anthem describes the communal, shared nature of customary land as given by God to all Indigenous people. Ni-Vanuatu sing *"God i givim ples ia long yumi,"* which translates as "God gave the land to us," where *yumi* means the dual, inclusive form of "we." Early in my time in Vanuatu I held my first legal clinic in Mangaliliu under the shade of a meeting area set up for tourists traveling to the World Heritage site. An older Lelepa man came into the clinic with a number of leases and echoed while challenging the words from the anthem: "All my life I have heard people sing this 'Yumi, yumi, yumi.' Land does not belong to us. Land belongs to *mi-nomo*." The description of land as belonging to *mi-nomo* (only me) is a description of individual landownership rights exercised to the exclusion of others. It stands in contrast with conceptions of *ples* as a shared resource—a *saloa*—held through collective custodianship. It is also a description of gendered agency.

* * *

Exploring capitalist relations at the frontier of desire requires that we consider both the inequalities of lease making as well as the impact of these processes on social relations and, in particular, gendered relations. The opaque architecture of lease making provides insights not only into the riven inequalities that shape the global capitalist order but also the informal aspects of these relations that shape the "performances of personhood" (Bear and others 2015). Concepts of personhood in Melanesia have long discussed the tension between relationally constituted persons and Western, enlightenment constructs of the individual. This chapter adopts a feminist anthropological approach to consider how performances of property are gendered and enable particular aspects of personhood. The agency of powerful men engaged in leasing land is actively contoured by the specific legal identity of a "custom owner," increased opportunities to access cash and status available through leasing land, rival claims to chieftainship, and the desire to assert personal authority over landscapes and people. This agency is expressed in the context of social transformations in relationships to customary land as an expression of individual, masculine desire.

What happens when we consider capitalism not as a linear process, but as a process that is significantly "patchier" (Tsing 2015, 6), more human in scale, and variable in outcome? Can we adopt generative approaches that include considering the "fragile and intimate" contradictions that are present in localized studies of capitalist processes (Bear and others 2015)? Land dealings in Vanuatu remain speculative because it is not always possible for investors to recoup windfall profits. Across Vanuatu there are scenes of abandoned developments. Towering concrete ruins of investor dreams suggest that the value associated with land coalesces in particular places and at particular times. Value is dependent on the vagaries of cultivated desire and remains a gamble. The implications of climate change and global pandemics make investment outcomes increasingly precarious.

From the perspective of Indigenous actors, performances of leasing are better understood not as market transactions but as claims to personal authority in the landscape, against the authority of other rival men. The three key questions raised in this chapter are: (1) Why, if land dealings are so unfair in terms of the financial value received for customary land, do men not negotiate better deals, or why do they participate at all? (2) How is lease making related to an assertion of personal authority over land? (3) How are capitalist relations associated with land leasing enabled by the legal identity of a "custom owner"? In answering these questions, we can begin to understand that leasing functions as a response to a range of noneconomic factors that are not directly related to the cash payment received. The effect of investor demand for customary land has been to create new domains of agency that allow new sites for the production of masculine authority. In this process a new social identity associated with land leasing has become entrenched—that of a master of modernity.

Personhood and Possession: The Masters of Modernity

Ideas of personhood in Melanesia are often constructed as a dichotomy between relationally constituted "dividual" persons and Western constructs of the individual. Marilyn Strathern wrote that Melanesian persons are "dividual" in that they are "constructed as the plural and composite site of the relationships that produce them" (1988, 13). This "dividual" exists in contrast to a "possessive individual" who is "essentially the proprietor of *his* own person and capacities, for which *he* owes nothing to society [emphasis added]" (Macpherson 1962, 3). C B Macpherson's "possessive individual" operates as an exploration of how the individual functions with respect to institutional arrangements, namely democracy and the market.

Possession is central to Macpherson's idea of the individual such that a possessive individual is a description of a "proprietor" in possession of rights to property. Macpherson's "possessive individual" makes claims over property as an expression of personhood. Karen Sykes explored the "dynamic tension in the definition of possession" by considering different models of agency with respect to possession and enterprise in New Ireland, Papua New Guinea (PNG) (2007b, 258; 2007a). The expressions of agency associated with individual landownership are intimately entwined with ideas of possession. Individual landownership is a performance of masculine possession to the exclusion of others, particularly other male rivals. Colin Filer wrote that custom landowner ideology is best conceived of as "a form of public performance which reveals, displays, and dramatizes the social relations of everyday life, and thus provides a stage for the construction of male authority" (2006, 73).

Acts of land leasing offer insights into modernity wrought by desire, the desire of foreigners to possess a landscape and the desire of local men to lease land. Acts of leasing demonstrate the agency of masters of modernity, a term I use in homage to the important work of Margaret Rodman on the "masters of tradition," Ambae men who manipulate *kastom* as a basis for authority. Powerful men acting as masters of modernity manipulate various spheres of power and authority, including the introduced—modern—and *kastom* spheres so they can lease land. This description of agency is based on Lelepa people's discussions of the self-centered, individualized acts of a *masta-mi* in contrast with the relationally embedded *man-Lelepa*. The Lelepa man's statement that opened this chapter is that customary land belongs to *"mi-nomo";* it is the statement of a possessive individual, an individual who is the "proprietor of *his* own person and capacities [emphasis added]" (Macpherson 1962, 3). This is a claim of exclusive possession.

Across Melanesia, the property model has enabled powerful men to regularly lease land properly belonging in customary tenure arrangements to others. Before 2014 and the changes to the land reform package, if an individual man signed a custom owner form to *say* that he was the custom owner of an area of land, this was enough to create a lease instrument and protect the purchaser of land as "a *bona fide* purchaser for value, without notice" (*Land Leases Act*, Section 100). The *Land Reform Act* (Cap 123) protects the interests of people who have purchased land and includes the requirement for compensation from government for the loss of a registered interest in land. If a registered lessee is proved in court not to be the lessee and was not registered through fault or fraud on his part, then he will be entitled to compensation from the government (*Land Reform Act*, Section 14(2)). This situation has a parallel in Solomon Islands, where even without clearly defined "chiefs" akin to North Efate, "the concentration of control over logging in the hands of a small number of male leaders and entrepreneurs, and the exclusion of most women, must be understood partly as the result of the structural characteristics of rules and processes set out in legislation" (Monson 2012, 166; Maetala 2008).

The link between property and concepts of exclusive possession have meant that across Vanuatu leasing land is often the act of an individual man acting as the "custom owner." Embedded in the legal identity "custom owner" is the idea of a possessive individual, an owner of property. Leasing data for North Efate in 2015 shows that of the 129 existing leases in North Efate, 56 leases or 44 percent were signed off on by an individual. When an individual man leases land, this man is overwhelmingly a chief. The conflation of landownership with chieftainship means that over 80 percent of the leases signed by an individual were signed by a chief as the "custom owner" of the land.

The increasing conflation of chiefs with custom and the historical role of chiefs as "brokers" between outsiders and the village means that across Vanuatu the men engaging in land leasing are either chiefs or are heavily influenced by chiefs. Local authority is viewed as an important asset for investors who wish to conduct land sales with an individual in an expeditious manner, rather than a group. Chiefs offer investors both the "time-efficiency of dealing with an individual" and the authority embodied in leadership (Naupa and Simo 2008, 106). For these reasons, masters of modernity are overwhelmingly chiefs.

Chiefs overwhelmingly dominate land transactions in North Efate. As well as chiefs individually leasing land, they also play a major role in brokering lease transactions in a continuance of previous colonial models of the role of chiefs. In North Efate, of the leases that name more than a single individual "custom owner" as the lessor, over half (55 percent) list a chief as the first name on the lease instrument followed by the names of other men. Chiefs are thus the principal actors in transactions over customary land.

Acting as brokers, chiefs are adept at negotiating the spheres of modernity, including the financial, expatriate, and, to a more limited degree, legal arrangements. Chiefs usually have greater access to cash and other status commodities than other people. They are often extremely well connected to expatriate investors, which follows since they are recognized as *kastom* leaders of the villages or region. Chiefs are mostly highly mobile, moving seamlessly between village and urban areas; they are also more likely than other villagers to travel to other islands and overseas.

Masters of modernity are powerful men who possess both the skills to access the expatriate spheres of modernity and the status associated with their positions as men of stature in *kastom*. This combination of skills and status enables them to manipulate land leasing across the region. In this sense, they are the masters of modernity harnessing asymmetries of information—such as the sheer amount of knowledge to which they have access relative to other community members. They are a small group of men who are established local leaders and consequently have large networks of associates including expatriates, investors, and local politicians. They are men who, as leaders, often act as spokesmen on behalf of village populations. Accordingly, they are often excellent orators who are confident in public forums. Many men within this cohort have exceptional English-language skills and are therefore better able to manage complicated cross-cultural negotiations between the village-based custom owners and expatriates.

Compared to other ni-Vanuatu people from their villages, masters of modernity are seen as possessing more access to the expatriate sphere of Port Vila and are viewed as *savi,* possessing knowledge about how to conduct land sales and other business transactions that is not generally accessible. Many of the most entrepreneurial men were already powerful figures in existing domains of masculine authority. For example, Donald Kalpokas, a Lelepa man who is a former prime minister of Vanuatu and ambassador to the United Nations, was one of the earliest lessors to capitalize on the land rush. Lease making represents a new pathway for cementing existing claims of masculine authority, rather than a radical overhaul of existing hierarchies.

Embedded in the legal identity of "custom owner" is the "Western-like image of the individual (ideologically defined as an autonomous, self-animated, and self-enclosed agent)" (LiPuma 1998, 53–54). Individual land-ownership claims enable the assertion of possession over vast areas of customary land. For example, a recent lease on Epi Island involved an individual chief acting as a "custom owner" and transacting prime agricultural land amounting to almost 12 percent of Epi Island (5,343 hectares or 13,203 acres), including several villages and gardening land (Porter and Nixon 2010, ii). Recent fraudulent ministerial leases of large areas of tribal *naflak* land in North Efate were also signed off on by a single "custom owner." These individual acts in leasing land represent not only the signing away of the connections of a group of people to place but also relational connections—tribal identities mapped onto the landscape that connect people to others. The act of leasing land is a rejection of relational identity and of the claims of land and people as mutually constituted, in favor of the new individualistic identity offered by the law.

Copresent Aspects of Personhood

Land leasing offers a consideration of the individual agency of masters of modernity acting as custom owners. Discussion among Lelepa people contrasts the acts of self-centered men, who engage in leasing thinking only of themselves *(mi-nomo),* with the emplaced agency of a *man-Lelepa,* who acknowledges his obligations to the broader kinship group. Informed by Lelepa people's discussions of leasing, my starting point for thinking conceptually about personhood is that engaged relationality and individual agency should not be considered as oppositional aspects of personhood. Rather, they exist as copresent facets of personhood offering different aspects of agency, with individual agency held in tension with relational obligations.

A significant critique of the school of New Melanesian Ethnography, associated most closely with the work of both Marilyn Strathern and Roy Wagner, is that it creates a model that divides and differentiates between the Western individual and the Melanesian "dividual" in ways that are oppositional and essentialist (Wagner 1967, 1977; LiPuma 1999, 195; Mosko 2010, 216). The danger associated with this rendering of the person is that it contrives difference and fails to recognize that "*persons emerge precisely from that tension between dividual and individual aspects/relations* [emphasis in original]" (LiPuma 1998, 56–57). Categories of "individual" and "dividual" are porous, existing across all cultures. Rather than consider "individual" or "dividual" personhood as static states, agency is better understood as the locus of a multitude of acts, each of which represents a single temporal moment. Each act is formulated with respect to a specific set of circumstances and embedded in a particular matrix of social relationships. Personhood is structured by the coexistence of dividual and individual states interpreted with reference to modernity, capitalism, and other aspects of contemporary lives. A master of modernity, acting as a custom owner and signing a lease, functions in a temporal moment whereby individual agency is held in tension with relational "dividual" obligations. Leasing land functions as a particular aspect of individual agency in the commodity economy, viewed as part of the broader processes of modernity. Holly Wardlow raised important questions around how certain dimensions of modernity catalyze more individualistic expressions of agency, writing that "if one accepts these dual modes of personhood [relational and individual] can coexist, if in highly contested ways, then a variety of questions emerge. For one, might a transformation be occurring with more individualistic expressions of agency coming to the fore? . . . And if 'modernity' has something to do with an increase in individualism, what is it about modernity that has this effect? Further, how might the expression of a more individualized sensibility be gendered?" (2006, 8–9). Fantasies of modernity are made concrete in expressions of individualized and gendered agency, described by Lelepa people as the agency of a *masta-mi*. This is what was discussed earlier by the Lelepa chief as the processes of human change.

Acting as a *Masta-mi*

Lelepa men described the gendered agency of chiefs as masters of modernity engaged in leasing land in their own self-interest, in contrast with the proper role of chiefs in *kastom*. Then chair of the Council of Chiefs, Pierre Makmar stated:

> A chief must look after his people. He is not a chief of the land. He must tell all the people "you must work the land" but he is not the chief of the land. The chief must look after the people and direct them to do all of the work.
>
> Now people think becoming a chief is a chance. You win a chiefly title and after you sell the land to get the money. Now you become *"masta-mi"* now. It is no longer *"masta-yu"* he becomes *"masta-mi."*

The trend of stealing land is increasing. The land is there for everyone to work on. You should never sell the land. If you sell the land you become *"masta-mi."* (March 2012)

Placing these two words, *masta* and *mi,* together allows for an interplay of colonial and Indigenous constructions in the agency adopted in leasing land. It is a descriptor of contemporary agency that reaches back into past colonial relations. The idea of a *masta* is historically embedded in colonial social relations between foreigners and Indigenous people, with white male employers in the colonial period acting as *mastas* over male household servants or plantation workers termed *boes. Masta* also has a particular meaning in relation to land in Vanuatu. The *masta* was the name given to colonial plantation owners across the archipelago, including in North Efate (Rawlings 2002, 10; Rio 2002). While plantation owners had varying reputations, all relationships were characterized by inequality and the embedded power imbalance of a master and servant.

The linking of the two words *masta* and *mi* serves to critique land leasing as the act of a self-centered possessive individual engaged in improperly manipulating their chiefly authority to sell customary land. In describing the agency of masters of modernity, Lelepa people distinguish between the proper role of a chief holding land as a "caretaker" of a shared resource, a *saloa,* and land leasing, which transforms a chief into a *masta-mi.* In conversation, the identity of *masta-mi* is inevitably gendered male, in recognition that it is almost always men who lease land. It is not, however, applied to all males but rather is a category of masculine agency reserved for chiefs and other powerful men, who already possess knowledge, status, and power within a community. In contemporary leasing transactions in which one man becomes a *masta,* others are rendered *ol boe.* Leasing land is an exercise of strength, the performance of an autonomous individual that separates powerful men from other men and an agency expressed to the exclusion of women. As people are excluded from landscapes, men who have individually leased land must work to reestablish their relational status to others through the sharing of cash or status commodities gained from land leasing. Personhood with respect to land dealings embraces *both* the individualized agency of a *masta-mi* at the point of transaction and engaged relational sociality in the management of land dealings in the moral economy.

The action of a master of modernity as a *masta-mi* is contrasted by Lelepa people with the personhood associated with the relational, emplaced behavior of a *man-ples.* Selfish, individualized forms of possessive agency can be contrasted with those actions that are seen to "produce relations of symmetry and solidarity," including among extended kinship networks and the language-based identities of *man-ples* (Taylor 2015, 47). On Ahamb Island a person is judged to be morally "good" if they are humble, engage in sharing, and will *luk save* (see and consider) the needs of others (Bratrud 2021, 284).

Similarly on Lelepa Island, key aspects of the social self, such as the importance of sharing and kinship, are associated with being a *man-Lelepa.* People of Lelepa share language and kinship relations configured by both *naflak* and *blad laen* claims and, most importantly, a shared sense of *ples.* A *man-Lelepa* is embedded in *ples* and acts in accordance with *kastom.*

These idealized actions of a *man-Lelepa* are held in tension with the acts of a *masta-mi* who exercises his authority as an individual for the benefit of himself and his immediate family. In answer to the questions posed by Wardlow, land leasing is associated by Lelepa people with broader patterns of increasing expressions of individual agency:

> *Bifo* all family would go one place to make a wedding. *Bifo* there was not one man who would pay the school fees for his children on his own. Now it is easy to walk along the *road blong moni.*
>
> *Bifo* when one child went to school another man would offer and say come and use my plantation area to make copra and pay his school fees. . . . Now this doesn't happen anymore. Now every man must pay the school fees for his own children. Nobody plants coconuts now, they just lease the land. This is not climate change; this is human change. (interview, Nov 2014)

Changes in the customary practices of using land and sharing resources are described as the dramatic "human change" associated with the increasing expression of individualized agency. This is a fierce critique of the aspects of personhood—that of self-centered individual agency—associated with modernity. However, a *masta-mi* does not just function as an embodied masculinity responding to modernity; it is a masculine identity that restages past historical performances of lease making.

Performances of property endure. A master of modernity exists as a hybrid hegemonic masculinity reaching temporally into the past to echo the power relations over land associated with a *masta* of colonial inculcations. The performance of a contemporary master of modernity repeats the script of colonial *mastas* who reconfigured *ples* as plantations, creating new power relations of dominance over local men. While local men are now *mastas,* the hegemony has not been inverted. The agency of masters of modernity responds to foreign desires. The hierarchy of neocolonial masters over local men remains.

Modernity and Masculine Desire

The fantasy of modernity persists because it fulfills desires. Land leasing provides men with a pathway for the entangled desires for mobility, access to cash money, the consumption of status goods, and access to outside women. Nicholas Bainton described the entanglements of modernity, mobility, and masculinities among Lihiran men, writing that: "Lihiran men are characterised by their purchasing power and ease of mobility. Increased transport options—by sea, road and air—combined with larger incomes enable Lihiran men to travel greater distances, more often, to purchase more pigs for *kastom,* to attend other *kastom* events, to seek women, or simply act as 'local tourists' " (Bainton 2010, 136; Wardlow 2002).

Like many other Melanesian men, Lelepa men lease land as a means of accessing cash, consuming status-related commodities, and seeking out other women. Negotiations culminate in the act of signing a lease instrument in exchange for what is locally considered to be a relatively large amount of cash (termed a premium payment, as distinct from annual lease payments). Premium payments provide the motivation for leasing land. As one Lelepa man explained: "I don't have a truck. I can sell land past Mangaliliu to get a truck. Everyone is thinking this way" (interview, Feb 2011). Access to cash enables the purchasing of status-related commodities such as brick houses with corrugated iron roofs, cars, trucks, minibuses, boats, expensive "flash" mobile phones, televisions, and DVD players—the trappings of modernity. Access to cash also allows men to engage in the status-related purchasing of kava and alcohol for other men so as to create relationships of obligation.

Gift giving serves as an enticement designed to *switin* (sweeten) custom owners into leasing customary land. Investors regularly broker land deals by giving gifts of cash money or consumer goods. Investors also facilitate access to alcohol, kava, and the coveted spaces of modernity. For instance, investors interested in leasing "*Survivor* beach" land strategically promised development and offered gifts of both kava and beer, as a Lelepa man stated: "Andrew Munroe with his middleman Roy held a meeting at Mangaliliu. Every *man-Lelepa* went to that meeting. The two investors used *swit tok* [sweet talk]. They gave us beer, kava, bread sandwiches. Munroe told us, 'If you all give your land to me then I will give you development.' After the meeting almost every Lelepa man who had land at the *Survivor* beaches wanted to give their land to him" (interview, March 2012). Negotiating and signing lease instruments are often accompanied by excessive drinking of kava and alcohol. Promises of development suggest pathways to modernity and material possessions through acts of conspicuous consumption.

Relationships with investors offer local men access to otherwise inaccessible spaces of modernity, which form "new sites of power and praxis" (Rawlings 2002, 78). Land deals facilitate mobility through desirable destinations as investors host "custom owners" in restaurants, clubs, cafes, bars, and nightclubs. Certain venues in Port Vila, such as the Harbour View, the Melanesian Hotel, Chantilly's, Jill's Café, La Tentation, and the casino in the Grand Hotel, are all renowned places for brokering land deals, so much so that in these places the appearance of a chief sitting with an expatriate surrounded by papers is enough to create the expectation that a land deal is being conducted. As well as locals being hosted by investors, cash payments for land leasing make powerful men mobile and provide the means of accessing venues that other local men and women are less able to visit. Spaces of modernity are powerfully gendered. Most village women are unable to access "modern" spaces at night without being subject to vilification, such as being called prostitutes.

Conspicuous consumption of high-status commodities makes a claim to authority and stature, in competition with chiefly rivals or male kin. Men in Mangaliliu and Lelepa reported "competing" for authority by leasing land to purchase status commodities. As one Lelepa chief stated:

> All men make a competition to sell land. One man will sell his land and get a good house, a boat and a TV screen inside his house, when another man sees everything that he has he thinks, "I must sell land as well." So the second man goes and sells his land so that he can have all the same things. Then they start a competition to have all the best things, to *go antap*. If one man builds a good house and the house is really nice then every other man really wants that house. I will think I need to sell my land so that I can have a nice house to beat him again. All men do this. (interview, June 2014)

Ironically, much of this competitive behavior is designed to stop the inequalities that arise when one man has authority over others, locally described as to *go antap*. To *go antap* is a claim to masculine authority through the ownership of status-related commodities. These ideas are similar to metaphors of height used in northern Vanuatu, where height and climbing rank are often associated with masculinity (Taylor 2015). In North Efate, a man who wants to *go antap* is an ambitious man putting himself above others through the purchase of status commodities, thereby creating the potential for social rupture. The advancement of one man, or one family, leaves other men "behind" feeling jealous. These feelings of jealousy manifest as the desire to lease land to access similar status commodities such that social equanimity can be restored.

Chiefs as Brokers: Creating a "Wharf Development"

The role of chiefs as the brokers of customary land deals is highlighted in the process related to a supposed "wharf development" in North Efate. In April 2010, a letter was delivered to a village chief by Alick Kalmelu Motoutoura asking that the chief broker a lease over a large piece of customary land located adjacent to Lelepa Landing—the main landing site for boats from Lelepa Island to the mainland. The letter promises a "joint-venture wharf development" between custom owners and an unknown investor. According to the letter, the new joint venture company would run the wharf, develop a marina, process fish for export, and "create plenty of other commercial industrial business activities" (Kalmelu, letter to village chief, 14 April 2010; translated from Bislama by the author).

The customary land that was the proposed site for the development is beachfront estate with access to the Efate ring road, and due to these features the land was commercially valued at around A$800,000. The letter proposes a lease arrangement whereby the chief would sign a lease as *the* "custom owner" of the land, thereby allowing the investor the efficiency of negotiating with a chief rather than the twenty actual custom owners of the land. The letter describes the leasing arrangement with custom owners as follows: "The chief will be the lessee for a short period of time. When we transfer the strata title lease, a new company will be created that is a joint-venture investment between the investor and *all* [emphasis added] custom owners.... In this new company the custom owners will be the majority shareholders" (Kalmelu, letter to village chief, 14 April 2010).

The letter acknowledges from the outset that the chief does not have any rightful claim to the land. However, under the proposed arrangements the chief would sign the lease, rather than the group of custom owners who *actually* held the customary rights over the land. Confusingly even though a "wharf development" is described in the original Kalmelu letter, the letter also outlines arrangements related to transferring the lease title to strata title, a process only required if a residential subdivision was anticipated.

After receiving Kalmelu's letter, the village chief met with custom owners and highlighted the unproductive nature of the customary land (which is sandy and steep) where the proposed development would be located (interviews with custom owners, April–June 2010). The chief also promised that the wharf would help make North Efate the next "mini-township just like Port Vila." In discussions with custom owners the chief represented the wharf as an important development project, a *"namarwan,"* which literally translates as a dream or vision (interview with village chief, March 2011). The chief's expansive vision of the wharf development was: job opportunities for Lelepa people, access to transport and mobility, industry, housing, shops, and commercial development. The chief offered a seductive vision of modernity that both captured and fashioned local masculine desire. In response, people began to speak of the stores that would open and the jobs that would become available.

The chief's vision for the wharf development was informed by the colonial history of Havannah Harbour, as a former site of colonial settlement and shipping, and by previous proposals for a wharf development from other leaders. Following Vanuatu's independence, two prominent Lelepa leaders, Donald Kalpokas and Peter Taurakoto, repeatedly promised a wharf development for the region. Kalpokas was prime minister of Vanuatu (first in 1991 and later in 1998) and Taurakoto was one of the founders of the Independence Movement and the Vanu'aku Pati who later became Vanuatu's ombudsman. From the perspective of the chief, to create a "wharf development" where other leaders had failed would demonstrate significant personal authority (interview with village chief, March 2011).

Despite the powerful *namarwan* vision of development offered by the chief, some Lelepa people remained opposed to the wharf development. Douglas Kalotiti, then chairman of Chief Roi Mata's Domain World Heritage site, remained concerned about the environmental impacts of the wharf on the World Heritage site and maintained his staunch opposition to the development (pers comm, 2010–2011). These concerns were repeatedly raised by the director of the Vanuatu Cultural Centre in letters written to the village chief and copied to the minister of lands and the Department of Environment (Vanuatu Cultural Centre director to the village chief, 21 May 2011). As a result, many custom owners remained unsure about whether to lease their land for the development or not.

In this climate of uncertainty among custom owners, the chief secretly signed the large forty-hectare (ninety-nine-acre) lease. The lease was witnessed by only four members of the custom owner group, all of whom were younger men with strict *kastom* obligations to the chief as his immediate family. Once the lease was registered, the chief held a meeting with the remaining custom owners. He confirmed that the land was leased and told the group that he would transfer his rights as "lessor" to the custom owners. The chief claimed the best option for custom owners would be to sign the transfer document and receive a small cash payment from the investor (interviews with various custom owners, Feb–May 2011). The custom owners faced a dilemma—either sign on to the transfer instrument and have their "custom ownership" rights recognized or refuse to sign and begin legal proceedings in court.

Many custom owners were furious that the chief had leased their land. As an expression of their anger, they held discussions around the need to remove the chief's title from him. The custom owners could have taken the chief to court, but this was difficult given *kastom* obligations of *rispek* for chiefs. In court, custom owners would have needed to establish that the investor had engaged in fraud for the lease to be canceled—a claim made more difficult by the investor's strategy of keeping himself removed from lease negotiations. The custom owners remained concerned about legal fees and were convinced that the land was lost. They remained preoccupied with the question of who had received the "prize" for leasing—the premium payment made on signing the lease. Three weeks after the chief signed the original lease, the remaining custom owners signed the transfer instrument and were individually paid VT 50,000 (A$520). This represents a total payment to custom owners of A$10,400.

Masterful Investment: Joint Venture in Name Only

With the transfer completed, a media statement was issued that heralded the creation of a joint-venture company "MANLEP Investment Limited" (from the village names Mangaliliu and Lelepa). The media article made claims about the A$20 million wharf "joint venture" with 65 percent of the company held by custom owners. The development was described as "a privately owned project, the Vanuatu Government and the World Bank are in support of the development, particularly the populations of north and east Efate and the offshore islands plus developers who will benefit from commercial and industrial activities, particularly in the boosting of tourism industry not only on Efate, but for Vanuatu as a whole" (Toa 2011). Subsequent follow-up with the World Bank office in Vanuatu indicated they had never heard of the project (Milena Stefanova, head of World Bank Office, Vanuatu, pers comm, May 2011).

While both the media article and the original Kalmelu letter describe joint-venture arrangements with significant benefits accruing to custom owners, subsequent investigation suggests this might not be the case. Investigation of the company documents revealed that the investor, Robert Bohn, controlled the MANLEP company. Company documents showed that MANLEP holds the lease over the customary land. The documents contain no reference to joint-venture ownership. Ownership of all companies is determined by who holds the company shares. Of the 35,000 shares issued, half are held by Bohn's Pacific International Trust Company and the other half by another Bohn subsidiary company named Pine Limited.

Bohn's companies hold the lease and can make decisions to transfer the leased customary land without any reference to custom owners. Company documents also clarify who claimed the "prize" for leasing: each of the men involved in brokering the lease deal, namely Kalmelu and the village chief, were paid VT 3 million (A$37,000) (MANLEP Investment Ltd 2011). Bohn's companies now hold commercially valuable customary land worth A$800,000 for which he paid A$84,000—just over 10 percent of the value of the customary land with the largest payments being made to the village chief and the middleman, rather than the custom owners.

While the exact nature of the development remains unclear, lease negotiations have followed precisely the process set out in the original letter. The time frame, from the original letter being sent to landowners to the lease being signed by the chief, was around ten months, illustrating the momentum often associated with customary land leasing and the efficacy with which the investor was able to lease commercially valuable land at minimal cost. Which leads us to the question, who is really the master of customary land dealings in Vanuatu?

Masters of Modernity as Powerful Orators

Across Oceania, masculine authority in relation to land is often performed through oratory. Specific men in Vanuatu are famed for skillful speech that persuades—having a *swit maot* (sweet mouth). Having a *swit maot* refers to an almost magical skill of speaking "sweet" words that are easily digestible but also insubstantial. The term *swit maot* is often evoked in discussions about politicians or investors who *switin* people, that is, persuade, bribe, or coerce people. Local men in North Efate described how listening to speech by a *swit maot* can *turn turnem hed blong yu* (change your mind) or *kilim ting ting blong yu* (kill your thinking) so that any previous criticisms about the man's acts in leasing land are forgotten. During and after the "wharf development" land transaction, custom owners discussed being "won over" by the *swit maot* of the chief.

In Melanesia male leadership has often been associated with performative qualities and the cultivation of a public persona through oratory. The power of skillful speech is its capacity to persuade. Men who are good orators receive fame with a well-performed speech or shame if their speech is performed badly and fails to persuade (Bainton 2008, 200, 202). Performance of key aspects of ancestral *kastom* knowledge in public forums is essential to making land claims. Discussing the masters of tradition in Ambae, Margaret Rodman detailed how amid land disputes "men of knowledge who are also skilled at talking strongly and persuasively can exploit those who are unwilling or unable to defend their land claims or who are less capable of speaking in their own defence" (1987, 32, 48). *Kastom* narratives of place are political, and claims of the "rules of land tenure are one kind of strategic resource in interactions between people about access to land." Recounting land claims provides space for performances of male authority staged in a *nakamal,* land tribunal, or formal state court. These performances may include different, or even contradictory, customary tenure principles as "orators in land disputes are simply drawing on a wide range of cultural norms and precedents as these contribute to their position in a particular debate" (Ballard 2013, 52).

Weaving a "cloak of enchantment" (LiPuma 1994, 152), a speech performed well by a master of modernity can persuade people either to lease customary land or that their actions in leasing customary land that did not rightfully belong to them is somehow justified. As a powerful orator, the village chief, who promoted the wharf development, offered various narratives to reinterpret his acts of leasing property belonging to others, including that, as a chief, it was his role to promote development and that he, like the others, was fooled by the investor. Until his death the village chief retained his title, suggesting that these narratives were persuasive, at least to some extent.

Across Oceania it is widely understood that language carries concealed meanings. Writing of the Maring in PNG, Edward LiPuma explained the complexity in differentiating between the "skin" of the language in the words spoken, and the "interior truth" found in the intention of an actor in speaking specific words (1998, 65). Meaning exists in the space between the slippery performance of labile words interpreted against the supposed actual meaning and intention of acts. In Vanuatu, the hidden inner truth is described as the *stampa* (literally trunk of a tree); the idiom suggests the heart or core of meaning and self, the deep causal element that motivates a person to act in a particular way.

In the slippery space between language, meaning, and agency, people in Vanuatu are often described as multifaceted. People are referred to as having many faces, as many as there are sides to a slit gong, which is circular. A duplicitous person is named two-faced. A person who is understood to be overly concerned with cash or material possessions is known as money faced. Positions that appear to be absolutely held in one context will be regularly and completely reversed in another, as in the case of support for the World Heritage site already described. Speech is not heard as a claim to absolute truth but rather as contextual truth. In this context, speech is carefully calibrated against an individual's specific acts to find out the *stret fasion* (real meaning) of a person. This suggests the fluidity of representations of self through language as opposed to the *stampa* self that suggests a core, causal motivation of a person linked to some immutable origin. A person's name or their chiefly title is understood to alter their agency. Discussions of a person's true motivation, their *stampa* self, is often relationally linked to either their ancestral lineage, such as the character of a man's father or patrilineal ancestors, or the idea that people are connected to other people or ancestors of the same name. In this way, specific chiefly titles and *naflak* groups have become associated over the passage of time with land leasing. For certain specific titles, the action of a contemporary titleholder in leasing land will be understood as a relational extension of ancestral practices of land leasing and be deemed to reflect the *stret fasion* of holders of that chiefly title. Such local understandings reveal not only the continuities between colonial past practices and contemporary leasing but also how notions of spiraling historical temporalities can inform ideas of personhood and agency.

Chiefly Patrilineal Authority: Transformations in *Kastom*

Across Efate Island chiefly authority is increasingly equated with landownership. While *naflak* identities retain importance, they are being displaced by ideas of connections to landscape, following *blad laen*. Overwhelmingly Lelepa people describe "custom ownership" rights as following patrilineal descent. This has profound implications for personal claims of chiefly authority and the inheritance of chiefly titles. These issues are explored in a series of cases over the Arier chiefly title and dominion over customary land located along the coast of North Efate at Fatenlengi. Fatenlengi land is prime beachfront real estate and extremely commercially valuable. Accordingly, the right to benefit from leasing the land was a primary motivation for claimants in a long-running chiefly title case.

The original Arier chiefly title dispute case was heard in the Lelepa Island

Village Land Tribunal, appealed to the North West Efate Customary Land Tribunal, and subsequently appealed to the Efate Island Land Tribunal before finally being appealed to the Supreme Court.[1] The dispute involved alternate claims to "Fatenlengi" based on: (1) patrilineal *blad laen* (termed *nanatu*) rights to the Arier chiefly title and chiefly dominion; and (2) matrilineal *(naflak)* ancestral claims argued by a group of Lelepa men who claimed *laopeania* rights to the land. Claims to *naflak* and *laopeania* rights were based on arguments that rights were given to Lelepa Island men to garden on the land at Fatenlengi. It was understood that there were communal rights to work the land termed *kindamuna* meaning *yumi evriwan* (all of us) could work on the customary land—a *saloa*. The two claims represent competing visions of *kastom* practice and the ways of place.

In judging the Arier title, the Efate Island Land Tribunal was heavily influenced by Vaturisu customary land laws that privilege patrilineal claims to landscapes. Quoting extensively from the Vaturisu laws, the tribunal determined that "the authority for Fatenlengi custom land boundary has been held under the Chiefly 'Arier' title for over 300 years" and that this title was passed following "the *blad laen* and passes through the father to his son." The tribunal decided that *laopeania* land-use rights could only be asserted where there was no "custom owner" of the land. The tribunal went on to find that all customary land on Efate Island is held under the authority of a chief as "custom owners" and therefore there are no *laopeania* rights (*Peter Taurakoto, Chief Arier Kaltang v Chief Nearutalo Napalaunaot, North West Efate Area Customary Land Tribunal,* Land Appeal Case 1 of 2003). This judgment demonstrates the wholesale adoption of the Vaturisu vision of patrilineal landowning arrangements across Efate Island.

Evidence of seven generations of patrilineal ancestry was traced by the Arier family group as a lineage of chiefly titleholders that predated missionary influence. Accepting this evidence, the tribunal found the Arier chiefly title was held by Chief Arier Kaltang Matuele Sakarie and that on his death Lapsar Felix passed underneath the coffin to claim the title as the current Chief Arier. Writing in 1956, Jean Guiart (2013) described the act of "kicking" the coffin as a way of subverting the matrilineal *naflak* system and of transferring chiefly titles. In the instances recounted to Guiart, successor sons acted on their titleholding fathers' death by placing their foot on the coffin thereby laying claim to a chiefly title. Guiart's account of this practice is strongly disputed by Lelepa people who point out that a man cannot kick the coffin without the agreement of all the important members of the deceased's family.

Lapsar Felix Kaloruk described his patrilineal claim to the title as follows: "My right comes from blood alone. It is like a light switch where my patrilineal ancestors turned on the light, after the light came through my father to me. It is the true line because it is blood" (interview, Aug 2011). The effect of patrilineal descent structures is to create a narrowing base for chiefly authority, passed from fathers to sons. As chiefly authority is increasingly linked with landownership, chiefs and their sons are franchised to the exclusion of others who previously claimed connections to landscapes.

In North Efate, chiefly titles are increasingly passed on following *blad laen* rather than *naflak* descent patterns. Transformations in chiefly title inheritance from *naflak* to patrilineal descent models are associated with the selfish, increasingly individualized, chiefly behavior of a *masta-mi:* "Now we have knowledge, but we are ignoring the *kastom* way. . . . All chiefs today don't think about their people, they don't look after the people in need. All chiefs today just think about themselves and their lives as individuals. One chief just thinks about himself and his immediate family he doesn't think about his people, the only times he thinks about his people is when he decides they must pay a fine" (interview with Lelepa men, March 2012). Linked with ideas of patrilineal descent, chiefs are criticized for being concerned with the needs of their immediate family only rather than the broader customary group.

Changes to chiefly title inheritance are viewed as an expression of the individualization associated with modernity and contrasted with the proper *kastom* practices from *bifo:*

LELEPA CHIEF: Now all families dispute chiefly titles. One man says he will have the title and another man says he will have the title. . . . *Bifo* chiefly titles passed through *naflak* but after it changed. Now today chiefly titles are held by *blad laen.*

SIOBHAN MCDONNELL: What is the reason for this change from *naflak* to *blad laen?*

LELEPA CHIEF: Men go to school now, they have knowledge. Now if their father is the chief they want to be the chief. It is in their own interest. If you are a chief and you have a son and you like him, then you want him to have your title. When he is still a boy his father will have said to him, "When you grow up you will be chief." So from the time that boy is small he is already thinking about his chiefly title.

Men no longer want to pass their titles to their sister's children following *naflak.* They are greedy for the titles and want to pass them to their own son. (interview, Nov 2014)

This discussion was a critique of the way chiefly titles are fought over as a means of accessing rights over land and authority over rival claimants. Increasingly men holding chiefly titles are claiming individual possessory rights over those titles, as well as the right to pass their title on to their son. Recent examples from Lelepa Island clearly illustrate the preference for passing chiefly titles through *blad laen.* For example, in recent years the chief "Niarangsu" title was passed from Meto Kalotiti to his firstborn son Sefo Kalotiti and then, on his death in 2013, to his firstborn son Gideon Kalotiti. The chiefly title of "Mawsepong" associated with the domain of Tuktuk Point was also passed from father to son.

Turning Titles into Titles

Chiefly title disputes reflect conflicting claims of authority to govern people and land and are a major source of conflict within villages and between families. Across Efate Island numerous cases exist of contested chiefly title claims between two or more rivals. Determining through the formal state legal system which man holds a chiefly title in accordance with customary law has demonstrated the schisms in attempts at legal pluralism in Vanuatu. Contention over chiefly titles has been linked to claims over the right to manage conflict and govern at the local level, as well as instability and violence (Forsyth 2009, 114). Chiefly title disputes are sometimes associated with physical violence or with accusations and fear of sorcery *(nakaemas)*. One report on a chiefly title dispute discusses how "violence became the norm and many people left the village fearing for their safety" (Kalontano, Vatu, and Whyte 2003, 117). Chiefly titles are now viewed as a pathway to claim legal authority to lease customary land. This is not simply a perception among claimants, it is also established practice in the Department of Lands as government officers regularly accept chiefly titles as the basis for custom-owner status and the right to lease customary land. The idea that chiefly titles convey the right to lease land was discussed by a group of Lelepa men, "When the court made their finding about who was the right Chief Arier, the court said, 'He owns the chiefly title and the land' " (interview, Nov 2014). Receiving recognition as the holder of a chiefly title is increasingly being understood by tribunals, land administration officials, and local people as being the "custom owner" over an area of land.

Ironically, leasing land has also been used by chiefly rivals as a way of subverting the findings of a tribunal or court, as described in the leasing of Samoa Point. Property rights once registered become cemented in form and in time. Registration of titles removes the flexibility associated with customary land-tenure arrangements. The leasing of land by a "custom owner" is an act of exclusive possession to the exclusion of all others. In this sense, ownership "curtails relationships between persons; owners exclude those who do not belong" (Strathern 1996, 524). The effect of leasing land can be to "cut the network" of customary relationships between people and *ples*. Land leases fix in time the statement of masculine authority exercised over property. Leases, once made, are protected by Torrens Title arrangements and are difficult to cancel. Land titles are increasingly seen as a way of future-proofing claims to authority over landscape—a view often supported by judicial processes. This places land sales in yet another context—as a means of asserting authority over a customary landscape, beyond the claims of chiefly authority supported in customary tenure systems. Powerful men are strategically using the legal identity of "custom owner" as a way of leasing land to assert their ongoing dominance over rival claimants, people, and landscapes.

Problems of forum shopping mean that decisions of a tribunal or court are regularly appealed. In a case similar to the leasing of Samoa Point, investor David Russet began to negotiate a subdivision over the valuable Fatenlengi customary land at the same time the Arier chiefly title was being contested through legal institutions. Even while the chiefly title was before the courts, the resolution of title became of secondary interest to the rival parties compared to the "prize" cash that could be earned through subdividing. From 2013 to 2014, as the Arier title case was appealed to the Supreme Court, Russet approached Jimmy Kalsau—the claimant who had lost his tribunal case—to sign the "custom owner" consent to subdivide the Fatenlengi land. Despite being the claimant to a chiefly title case that he had ostensibly lost, Kalsau still managed to sign the consent and receive a small cash payment from Russet. Felix Lapsar, the established "Chief Arier," then began legal action to prevent the registration of the forty-one subdivision instruments. Legal efforts made by Lapsar eventually resulted in Russet making a second agreement with him for his transfer consent for around A$100,000 for the Fatenlengi land.

The Arier case clearly indicates the effect of property transactions in which legitimate chiefly titleholders can be left with authority over a landscape that has already been leased and subdivided by a rival claimant. This is locally described as providing a legal pathway to stealing customary land, a *fasin blong stil.* Legal title trumps any determination of chiefly title.

But who is the real master? In contrast with the relatively small amounts paid to the rival claimants for the Arier title, Russet stands to earn another windfall profit from subdividing the Fatenlengi land. Real estate advertisements currently advertise the Fatenlengi land as a subdivision of thirty-two oceanfront lots and eight larger lots with oceanfront access. Subdivided lots range from VT 13 million (A$150,000) for waterfront lots to VT 6.5 million (A$74,000) for lots with oceanfront access, suggesting a total resale amount of around A$3,500,000 (LJ Hooker Vanuatu 2014; see also L J Hooker Vanuatu 2021). These amounts indicate that while chiefs are pivotal actors in this transformation of customary landscapes, it is investors who ultimately have the most to gain from speculative land dealings.

My Land, My Life

As well as a performance of authority, land leasing is a performance of gender (Butler 1990a, 1990b). Just as Wardlow has used the identity of *pasinja meri* (literally passenger women) as a way of exploring modernity and gendered relations among the Huli in PNG (2006), the performance of custom ownership operates as a particular script of masculinity, articulated in relation to modernity. Leasing land is a way of asserting masculine authority over landscapes—particularly when coupled with ideas of development—as well as authority over people. Discussions of masculinity must acknowledge the many "moving" diverse and fluid masculinities that exist in North Efate and in Vanuatu more broadly (Jolly 2008; Taylor 2008a). Oceanic masculinities are best considered "relationally and historically, between pasts, presents and futures" (Jolly 2008, 3). Masculinities are performed in particular ways as "embodied discourses" produced by history, power, hierarchy, and agency and are reflective of cultural context (Dvorak 2008, 61). Produced by capitalist property relations, a master of modernity operates as a type of "hegemonic masculinity." It is an assertion of male authority that renders other masculinities, particularly those of younger men, marginal and subordinate (Connell and Messerschmidt 2005). It functions as a style of masculine agency in response to the entrepreneurial possibilities associated with the "race to the prize" of land leasing, suggestive of the effects that economic transformations can engender on social identities (Taylor 2015). Acts of powerful men leasing customary land effectively strip other men of their relationships to the land. Leasing customary land removes livelihood opportunities for younger men and particularly those who have low levels of formal education who need to have access to land and coastal estates to garden and fish.

Increasingly the authority of chiefs is being challenged by young men in angry public displays. Many young Lelepa men described a lack of *rispek* for contemporary chiefs that engage in leasing land. On Lelepa Island, the building most visibly associated with chiefly authority is the chiefs' house, termed *farea* (the Efate word for *nakamal*), which hosts *kastom* courts and proceedings as well as regular meetings of the Lelema Chiefly Council. In recent years, meetings of the council have been impossible due to tensions between chiefs over land leasing or rival claims to chiefly titles. Young Lelepa men, who feel that their future has been challenged by leasing, spoke derisively of the problems of the chiefs in convening meetings. Recently, a young man's anger flared into protest and he nailed shut the doors of the chiefs' *farea* with planks of wood. This presented a public and aggressive challenge to both the space of the chiefs to meet and the authority of the chiefs to judge others. It also represented a public display of disrespect that was alternately celebrated and criticized by other Lelepa people.

Across Efate Island, young men have increasingly begun to rally around their anger at the sale of their "birthright" by older men. In areas such as Pango on Efate Island, which has been subject to large-scale leasing, young men who no longer have adequate access to gardening land or coastal estates are facing increasingly constrained choices. Young Pango men often have a reputation of being ineligible marriage partners as they are regarded as land poor. In North Efate, I had numerous conversations with young men about their anger at chiefs, fathers, and uncles who have leased their "birthright." Young Lelepa men were concerned that they, like Pango men, may find it difficult to marry as they had no way of supporting a future wife and family through subsistence gardening or fishing. Vigilante gangs of young men from Pango and Port Vila—who are increasingly disenfranchised given the lack of choices available to them in contemporary Vanuatu society—are forming. As their anger and feelings of dispossession grow, these young men may come to embody the tensions and dislocation associated with land leasing.

Chiefs Speak Like an Empty Drum

Lelepa people routinely critiqued the actions of chiefs in leasing land as failing to observe the proper *kastom* ways of *ples*. The acts of masters of modernity in leasing land are critiqued against the ideal acts of a proper *kastom* chief. Distinctions are drawn between a *masta-mi,* concerned only with his personal authority over land, and the remembered practices of former chiefs acting in the ways of *ples,* thinking and caring for others. In discussing the proper role of a chief, many Lelepa men drew on accounts of the former paramount Chief Natmatsaru who, at the end of each day, would stand on the edge of Lelepa Island to make sure that all his people returned safely. He would not rest until all canoes were accounted for, and all his people safely returned (interviews, 2011–2012). The exercise of masculine authority by leasing has often led to circumscribed authority in *kastom,* with diminishing *rispek* for chiefs who lease customary land:

> For chiefs who have leased land, when they come to a meeting and talk no one will respect them. *Bifo* if a chief said we had to work, every man would work. If you did not work you would be in trouble, you would be sick or have an accident and you would have to apologize to the chief. Now chiefs say we should work together but men do not follow him because the chiefs no longer have power. This is because when they ordain the chiefs the chiefs no longer know all the *tabu* places. These are the places that bring power to the chief. (interview with Lelepa men, June 2012)

Among the local population, chiefs who lease the land of their people or lease land belonging to others lack *rispek*. Diminishing authority is also associated with an inability to access the sacred power of *ples* (McDonnell 2015). The power associated with place continues to be closely bound to the authority of chiefs in North Efate, just as it was in the past. Ellen Facey wrote of the historical practice of one form of investiture of chiefly titles, in which the central element of the rite was the "pulling up" of the sacred spirit from the predecessor and the instillation of it within his successor. This involved transferal of a potentially fatal power and so it had to be performed by other chiefs within a sacred enclosure of coconut husk stems constructed especially for the occasion. If non-chiefs approached this area they could be killed by the force of the sacred spirit (Facey 1981, 300). Ancestral beings have agency and continue to affect the course of peoples' lives and their claims to chiefly authority over land.

A Lelepa man described his chiefly anointment, termed *patnanu,* which involves a current chiefly titleholder passing the sacred *kastom* power, held by a chief, to another man. The *kastom* ceremony necessitates a complicated and particular placement of coconut *(nanu)* husk stems underneath the current titleholder so he is able to assume his chiefly position and appropriate his power. The man detailed what occurred as this ceremony took place: "At the time when I passed the coconut stems underneath, I turned the leaves. I had not meant to turn them, but the spirits of the ancestors are alive today. When I pushed the leaves, another man was there, the power of the chief moved all about. The spirits of the ancestors made their work" (interview, April 2012). Ancestral spirits subverted the chiefly anointment ceremony and stole the sacred power from the supposed successor, passing it to another man who today retains the chiefly title. In this narrative, the agency of the ancestors intervened to promote the interests of one man over another. Ancestors are very much alive. Place is embodied by ancestral beings such that chiefly authority means, among other things, being able to harness and channel the sacred power of place.

A regular criticism of contemporary chiefs is that because they no longer access sacred power, they speak "like an empty drum." Their speech no longer has weight or meaning. Pierre Makmar contrasted the chiefly judgments of the former Paramount Chief Natamatewia with current chiefs: "When I was young, I worked with Chief Natamatewia. When he judged you in the village court *(farea)* you could feel his power. When chiefs judge you now you don't feel any power, there is nothing. Their judgment is not heavy because they are just playing at being chiefs and with their chiefly titles. There is no real power" (interview, June 2012).

Discussions of "empty drums," as opposed to decisions that are heavy and saturated with sacred power, illustrate the etiolation in masculine authority of contemporary chiefs. Decisions by chiefs are no longer heavy with sacred power and, accordingly, are no longer considered binding. This is often described by local chiefs and Lelepa people as a situation in which the *paoa blong ol jifs i ko daon* (the power of all chiefs is diminishing). The lack of "heaviness" of chiefly decisions creates further tension as local village courts or council of chiefs' decisions in land matters are increasingly considered nonbinding on the parties. In some instances, when village courts or chiefs have made a decision about who the correct custom owners are for an area of land or how a leasing process should proceed, a single individual chief, in a display of personal autonomy, has acted against the decision. Pragmatically the *kastom* authority of chiefs over the landscape in North Efate has waned considerably in recent years. Bans and *tabus* placed on certain areas, or on the collection of certain species of fish, are often no longer properly observed.

The Sacred Power of Place

Men who lease customary land disobey *kastom* and can face retribution from the ancestral power of place or from rivals who resort to sorcery (locally termed *nakaemas*). Anger at those chiefs who have acted as masters of modernity and leased land belonging to others is often expressed subversively as narratives of *nakaemas*. These narratives of *nakaemas* increasingly distinguish between: (1) the power of *ples* that attacks those who have not adhered to the correct practices in *kastom* by leasing land that rightfully belongs to others; and (2) the marauding dangers of commodified *nakaemas* that can be purchased by those with access to cash to use against rivals in land claims.

Accounts of *nakaemas* in North Efate have included incidents of poisoning, bodily possession, transformation of people into dogs and devils, control of bodies and minds, and, ultimately, *nakaemas*-related deaths. *Nakaemas* accusations cannot be interpreted in and of themselves but are more properly viewed as an ongoing process of circumspection that takes place around specific sources of tensions within social groups, one of which relates to dealings over land. The tapestry of narratives of *nakaemas* is woven over time; with each death comes a new set of explanations and accusations that must be carefully considered and analyzed before a conclusion is reached. With each subsequent, otherwise unexplained, death the process is repeated. Temporally a narrative becomes woven from a series of events that may have taken place before and after the most immediate circumstances of a death. Together these competing and contested narratives in North Efate weave a complex critique of land leasing in the region and of the failure of powerful men to observe the appropriate protocols in *kastom* to care for *ples*.

Many of the accusations of *nakaemas* around recent deaths on Lelepa Island are linked to the involvement of men in land disputes. The actions of five dead men in facilitating land leasing or, as in the case of one of them, in opposing land developments in the area against the wishes of his immediate family members, have resulted in claims and counterclaims of *nakaemas*. In North Efate, the conflict and jealousy surrounding land leasing and chiefly title disputes are increasingly associated with the fear that a disgruntled party may resort to *nakaemas*. As one Lelepa man stated: "If I make a problem with another Lelepa man about land that man will go and find a *nakaemas* practitioner from another place to come and kill me. All men on the island are really frightened of *nakaemas* when there is a land problem" (interview, June 2013).

In North Efate, powerful men who lease land are viewed as being more able to access *nakaemas* practitioners than others because of their greater access to cash and their larger networks in Port Vila. They are also perceived as using the threat of *nakaemas* as a strategy to defend their involvement in leasing land belonging to others. Threats of *nakaemas* create compliance among broader groups of disenfranchised custom owners or community members with the land dealings undertaken by chiefs. Many men that I have interviewed who have had their land "stolen" and leased by a chief reported that they are frightened to challenge the authority of the man involved because of the ongoing social tensions that this would create and of their deep and unassailable terror of *nakaemas*. This palpable fear means that leasing by these chiefs may go unchallenged.

The final narrative about the recent deaths in North Efate relates to the sacred power that resides in key places within the landscape, so if these places are disturbed, ancestors and spirits of the place may seek retribution. People in North Efate talk about the *kastom* curse invoked when a powerful man steals the land of other people. This occurs when powerful men: (1) claim rights that are not theirs in *kastom* over land such as asserting claim to a chiefly title that does not rightly belong to them; or (2) engage in leasing land over which they have no right. In each of these cases, *kastom* dictates that men who engage in these practices run the risk of being cursed: *graon hemi kaekae yu* (the land will eat you). The embodied landscape has agency and can curse the living who do not correctly follow the *kastom* ways of place. The agency of the *ples* resides in key *kastom* sites, and its capacity to injure informs claims and accusations of *nakaemas*. The land is suffused with stories of deaths related to men who have engaged in land dealings. Deaths and sicknesses are explained as caused by men claiming authority over landscapes or leasing land to which they have no "rightful" ancestral claim.

Conclusion: The Tensions Surrounding Performances of Property

At the frontier of desire, specific legal identities actively script the performance of personhood by defining possessory relationships to property. The idea of a possessive individual is foundational to claims of custom ownership. At the scale of the village, leasing is dominated by masters of modernity acting as custom landowners. While, under the constitution, citizenship is commensurate with custom landownership, in practice it is only a handful of powerful men who are so enfranchised. Custom landownership is repeatedly assumed by a few masters of modernity who assert power over landscapes and people.

Leasing land provides powerful men with a pathway for mobility, access to cash, the consumption of status goods, and, therefore, enhanced personal authority relative to rival chiefs and kin. Individual chiefs compete to lease land to legally register their claim in property against rival claims. Leasing land becomes a "race to the prize" in which the winner receives cash income as well as having their claim over land registered. Registration of a lease fixes in time the name of the man purporting to be the "custom owner." The discussion in this chapter illustrates that men lease land for a range of reasons that are not related simply to the cash amounts made from leasing.

Increasingly acts of leasing by masters of modernity are being critiqued. Land leasing is described as the act of a self-centered individual *masta-mi* who fails to consider his relational obligations to others. Young men, concerned about the sale of their "birthright," are publicly challenging chiefs by displaying a lack of *rispek*. Narratives of *nakaemas* weave a complex critique of land leasing in the region and of the dangers of failing to observe the *kastom* ways of place. Narratives around a series of deaths in North Efate represent a critique of land leasing and in particular the leasing of key *kastom* sites, the most centrally important of which is the burial site of Chief Roi Mata on Artok Island. Together *nakaemas* narratives represent a direct challenge to the authority of masters of modernity who have acted in a way that has abrogated their responsibilities in *kastom*.

These various critiques suggest some of the tensions associated with the contemporary performance of property adopted by various masters of modernity and describe the dual, contemporaneous aspects of personhood by which individual agency is held taut—in tension—with relational obligations to family and kinship groups. Ultimately men who fail to meet their relational obligations risk being cursed—either by another person who will literally speak the curse or through the agency of the landscape itself. The land has ears and eyes.

The land will eat you.

Chapter 7
Mama Graon

Performances of leasing land and the stages where lease negotiations take place are starkly gendered. The exclusion of women from decision-making around land leasing and natural resource management is common across Oceania (Bolton 1999, 2009; Maetala 2008; Monson 2010, 2011; Naupa 2017; Naupa and Simo 2008). Lelepa women are often prevented from participating in decision-making over the leasing of customary land or in accessing a substantial share of the benefits from leasing. This is not, however, the whole story. Sometimes, some women do speak about land. Consideration of Lelepa women's role in decision-making around land should begin with the perspectives and voices of women themselves.

Women in North Efate offer complex and nuanced understandings about the operation of women's *raets* over land, demonstrating "vernacular" translated, local meanings of "rights" that build from "sociocultural understandings of gender, family and justice" (Merry 2006b, 38; 2006a; 2009). To be meaningful to women themselves, discussion of women's land *raets* in Vanuatu must be grounded in an understanding of local relational identities; for this reason, I have termed them "grounded *raets*." Women's land *raets* and agency must be interpreted with reference to power relationships, decision-making, and the gendered exercise of property rights and chiefly authority over landscapes. These vernacular ideas of *raets* do not equate with Western, liberal claims to equality that inform discourses around individualized human rights. Rather than posit a set of rights, this discussion explores local women's agency in land dealings in North Efate to clarify how vernacular land *raets*, or grounded *raets*, operate for women.

Grounded *raets* for women are informed by ideas of appropriate *kastom* practice, as well as embodied and genealogical claims to place. Relationships between *kastom* and *ples* are "extremely important to the claim that women have *kastom* too" (Bolton 2003, 67). Lelepa women's *raets* to land are explored in this chapter through a detailed account of the *kastom* practice of *paumaso*, the gifting of land from a father to a daughter on her marriage.

Practices of land leasing show that the agency of local women is actively contoured by interpretations of *kastom*, as well as the idea of land as property owned and leased by a masculine possessive individual. This chapter explores land leasing as a form of individualized masculinized agency exercised by masters of modernity and largely unavailable to women. Defining and interpreting *kastom* with respect to land is overwhelmingly the provenance of these men. *Kastom* narratives can work to emplace men and displace women in the landscape, as occurs with the alternate claims of *blad laen* and *naflak* rights. Discussions of appropriate *kastom* behavior can also restrict the agency of women by functioning as claims that "women should not speak about land." In practice men often assume the role of speaking about land in public forums, suggesting that these "public" forums are gendered spaces.

Some women can, and do, speak about land in the *nakamal*. *Kastom* narratives that link women to *ples* allow women a voice on land matters. The idiom of land as the mother—termed *mama graon*—allows women *kastom* narratives for critiquing land leasing. In documenting the voices of local North Efate women speaking about land and how *kastom* can provide pathways for women's agency, I seek to avoid the essentializing dichotomy that informs debates around culture versus human rights (Levitt and Merry 2011; Merry 2001). These debates often present a simplistic analysis of women in Oceania as victims of the intersection of patriarchy and culture (or its metonym in Melanesia, *kastom*). Instead, I hope to offer a discussion of women's emplaced agency and their grounded *raets* to speak as women of the *ples*.

Exploring Women's *Raets* to Land

Historically women in North Efate have held both primary access and use rights over landscapes as either: (1) *paumaso raets* held by an individual woman over a specific area of coastal land; and (2) other "use rights" accorded to women such as rights to garden, collect resources from the land, or build houses on a particular area of land. A widow can also claim access to a deceased husband's plot of land. This can, however, be a fraught process based on whether family members consider the widow behaved as a moral and proper woman such that her claim should be supported against other male relatives or male children (Naupa and Simo 2008, 84–85). Being a proper woman involves going to the locally approved church (the Presbyterian Church in North Efate), meeting relational obligations such as preparing for family events, caring for children and other family members, showing deference to senior men in the family, knowing and properly following *kastom* practices, being demure and humble, dressing appropriately, and not engaging in activities that are gendered masculine such as drinking kava or alcohol.

Women's *raets* to land in North Efate closely align with marriage relationships. When a woman marries a man from another place, according to *kastom*, she must move to her husband's land and be allocated gardening *raets*. Locally this is explained as follows: "When women marry out they have rights to their husband's land. When the woman marries out and leaves, then her brothers own all the land. She does not have rights to her father's land because she has left. When this happens, the father may want to pass some small piece of land to his daughter" (interview with Lelepa chief, Nov 2014).

Historically, women's role of bearing children to place is central to the idea of women belonging to *ples* (Bolton 2009, 11). It is women who garden and produce food, women who work the landscape, women who birth and nurture children, and through these acts cumulatively assert the ways they belong to *ples*.

In *kastom* in North Efate, women are referred to as *pounakar*, a type of stinging nettle that wherever it is tossed it will put down roots and grow. Describing women as *pounakar* offers an emplaced role for women, but it can also be a negative term meaning that when women are married out they then belong to that *ples*, rather than their original home. During a dispute, a woman and her children can be reminded of their status as *pounakar*, which means that they cannot claim land rights in their original birth *ples*. In this context, the term *"pounakar"* becomes an insult, used as a way of disputing a woman's claims to land.

The *kastom* practice of *paumaso* also offers important insights into local vernacular ideas of women's *raets* to land. *Paumaso* refers to the practice of ritualized gift giving that can include giving specific parcels of land. Historically older male relations often passed *paumaso* land to women. More recently *paumaso* land has been gifted to both men and women on marriage, at funerals, or for other significant occasions as part of a ritual exchange. Local Lelepa chiefs described the practice of *paumaso* and gifting land to women as follows: "If a father wants to make *paumaso* he passes a piece of land to his daughter when she is married. That woman has the *raet* to pass that land to her sons or daughters" (interview, May 2012).

Once gifted, plots of *paumaso* land are described as land belonging to a specific woman. *Paumaso* plots of land are usually allocated from coastal gardening land to ensure that a woman and her family would always have gardening land within their family plot. For this reason, plots of *paumaso* gardening land are located predominantly along the coastline of mainland Efate. In relational terms, the act of gifting land also creates an expectation that the woman will reflect on and think about the man who has gifted the land to her. This is a relational obligation that entwines both parties even beyond the death of the often-older man.

Lelepa women repeatedly described individual men's *raets* to land as following patrilineal descent rights *(blad laen)*, contrasting gifts of *paumaso* land to women as follows: "Men's land rights come from their father. Women's land rights come from when a woman gets married, her father must give her land" (collective statement, Women and Land Workshop discussion, Oct 2010). This statement encapsulates the different ways that individual men and women can be recognized as the "custom owners" of specific coastal areas of land. These individualized "custom owner" rights are different from the use and access rights that women are entitled to as part of marriage, family, or kinship arrangements. Specific individual male rights over family plots of coastal land can be contrasted with *naflak* land that is held by a group and managed under a chiefly title, as already discussed.

Locally, Lelepa women articulated their absolute *raet* to *paumaso* land and described how the practice of *paumaso* is changing. Leisara Kalotiti provided an example: "Women too have got *raets* to land. For me and my sisters my father gave us all individual plots of land when we married. When we married, we held the small pieces of land that our father gave to us. But this is changing. If there are too many children or not enough land then fathers don't have enough land to give some to their girls on their marriage" (interview, May 2011). The coastal land rush on Efate Island has caused a rapid transformation in the practice of *paumaso.* For women aged around forty years and over living in Lelepa and Mangaliliu, *paumaso* was common practice, with daughters of high-status men, in particular, receiving large plots of land from their fathers as part of their marriage exchanges. Recognition of these *kastom* practices of gifting land is long established in the literature (Guiart 2013; Naupa and Simo 2008). Writing based on ethnographic work conducted in 1956, Jean Guiart described the *kastom* practice present across Efate Island of allocating women rights over land as follows: "On her marriage, the wife brings in her dowry some plots of land called *paumaso,* which she and her husband benefit, and which will be passed on by her to her daughter when the latter marries" (2013, 22).While Guiart described a *kastom* practice of land being gifted exclusively to daughters, contemporary accounts suggest substantial changes to this practice.

Growing land shortages suggest significant alteration to the practice of gifting *paumaso* land with land increasingly being divided among sons rather than gifted to daughters, although there are still a small number of recent instances in which land has been divided between sons and daughters. As land becomes scarce, it is daughters rather than sons who are losing access to gardening land, indicating the gendered nature of land transformations, processes of commodification, and the associated vulnerability of women who are "falling through the basket"—the social safety net provided by access to customary land.[1] Land as a *saloa* is a shared basket of overlapping use and access rights that binds people to place. Customary land functions as an important safety net providing ongoing access to land for Indigenous people, including vulnerable women and men. Land is central to the operation of the *kastom* economy with women working as the primary producers of food for families, as well as the weavers of ceremonially important textiles. The commodification of land through land leasing and the associated land rush has led to profound social and cultural transformations in the allocation of *paumaso raets.* As a result, the position of women in Efate is increasingly precarious as they are no longer supported by the social safety net that customary land provides not only in Vanuatu but also across Oceania.

Can Women Be Custom Owners?

Increasingly, the ideology of landownership informs how Lelepa women articulate their own land *raets*. Women themselves claimed *raets* to *paumaso* land as rights of individual ownership equal to those of men: "A woman has the same right as a man who *owns* land. The two of them have the same rights [emphasis added]" (collective statement, Women and Land Workshop discussion, Oct 2010). While Lelepa women's *raets* over *paumaso* land are widely recognized, these *raets* rarely correspond to the ability to lease land. Local chiefs identified *paumaso* land as being controlled by individual women, and they stated, "Woman should be the boss of that land. Men have got other land that their fathers have given them" (interview, March 2011). Lelepa chiefs stated that while a woman *should* be the boss of her land, this does not necessarily translate into women acting as custom owners and leasing land. The experience of North Efate appears to be replicated in Solomon Islands. Writing about matrilineal land arrangements that operate in Guadalcanal, Makira, and Isabel, Ruth Maetala asserted that even where women are considered the "bosses" of land this rarely results in their being involved in decision-making about the land or in any receipt of benefits from logging contracts (2008, 51). While Lelepa women stated that women's *paumaso raets* are equal to the landownership rights of men they also acknowledged that most women have difficulty asserting their rights in any decision-making about land. This is the tension between supposed rights and actual decision-making capacities with respect to land. Anna Naupa and Joel Simo posited that where the rights held by a woman are primary rights, defined by them as rights that a woman can claim direct ownership over, "she is much more likely to be included in major decision making" as compared to when she has only secondary access and use rights (2008, 85). But the questions remain: Even if a woman has primary *paumaso raets* over land can she embody the legal identity of a custom owner? Can she exercise the authority of a custom owner over property and lease land?

Responses to the question "Can women be custom owners?" often involve lengthy discussions among Lelepa women. Lelepa women asserted that while it is theoretically possible in law given that land *raets* are held by women, in practice the performance of leasing is gendered. Women articulated *raets* as relational claims mediated through *kastom* and kinship, rather than absolute statements of individual possession that translate into "custom ownership." For Lelepa women, the question of whether a woman can be a "custom owner" becomes a complicated consideration of who in *kastom* has the *raet* to speak about land, as well as access the spaces in which land claims are made and where land transactions take place. Both *nakamals* and the spaces where lease transactions are conducted operate as gendered spaces, largely inaccessible to Lelepa women. The agency and modality of personhood associated with the legal identity of a custom owner is overwhelmingly gendered male.

Unbeknown to Lelepa women, the Vaturisu Council of Chiefs is clear in its customary land laws that only men can be custom owners. Chapter Ten of these land laws is titled “Men who can own land,” in a clear gendering of the identity of custom owners. The laws go further. In the chapter titled “Men who cannot own land,” the laws state: “Following the proper custom law of Efate, women *do not have a raet to own land* [emphasis added]” (Vaturisu Council of Chiefs 2007, 6). The Vaturisu Council of Chiefs has written laws that specifically deny the possibility of women being custom owners or owning land. The legal identity, “custom ownership,” is not just a conflation of the twin ideologies of landownership and chieftainship, it is specifically understood, and now dictated in customary law, as gendered male.

Gendered Spaces of Land Claims

Supposedly “public” forums, designed to allow for public discussions of land disputes or consultations on land reform are, in practice, overwhelmingly gendered male. This gendering of spaces applies to meetings held in the Malvatumauri Nakamal (the national chiefs’ house located in Port Vila opposite Parliament House), as well as in courts, land tribunals, village courts, or local village *nakamals*. Naupa poignantly described her experience of presenting on the need to protect women’s land rights at the gathering of overwhelmingly male participants during the National Land Summit of 2006 held in the Malvatumauri Nakamal. In making this presentation, she bravely endeavored to “speak about the unspoken,” namely women and land, and to speak herself as a woman, in a culture where women rarely speak before chiefs and do not often speak publicly in *nakamals*. Naupa concluded that because of the gendered nature of these spaces, women are largely absent from land decisions as well as from broader national policy discussions around land reform (2017, 313).

At issue in public spaces is the right of women to speak about land. Speeches about land are largely given by men, regardless of whether the stage is a *nakamal* or a court. Oratory is a famed performative model of masculinity, one that women may be denied. The Vaturisu Customary Land Law for Efate Island, written by the Vaturisu Council of Chiefs and regularly used as the basis for determining land disputes in *nakamals* and land tribunals, states under the chapter titled “Practices of *kastom rispek*,” “following the *kastom* of Efate a woman does not have any right to stand up in a court to talk about land” (2007). This powerful edict about *kastom* from the Vaturisu Council of Chiefs is strongly disputed by women and men in North Efate. The effect of this edict may be to silence ever more women from speaking about land. Even aside from its potential effects, the edict functions as a further reminder of how chiefs have the power as the authors of customary law to confer or remove *raets* from women. Rather than creating a “breathing space,” the elision of *kastom* into pronouncements by masters of modernity on "custom" has the potential to become a choke hold on the voices of women.

Women in the Kitchen Not the *Nakamal*

Aware of the difficulties faced by women speaking in public spaces and having already run a series of "public" workshops on land, I decided to run a series of workshops specifically for women on land issues. On the first day, the workshop was delayed as I faced a wall of opposition from men led by a number of chiefs pointedly questioning why I wanted to speak to women about land. A careful negotiation ensued, and eventually some women were allowed to participate. Many women were, however, not allowed to attend the workshops by their husbands on threat of reprisal. During the workshop, women repeatedly raised concerns about husbands and chiefs stopping women from attending meetings about land and leasing, telling them instead to "stay in the kitchen" where women belong. A local woman recounted her experience of these workshops:

> We had workshops with women so that the women could share their thoughts about leasing land. All the women said during the workshop that men always make the decisions without us, these men say that we women "belong in the kitchen and *only* in the kitchen." So women have to stay in the kitchen while men go and travel into Vila and sell the land.
>
> The men lease the land and then they come back but almost all of the money has been spent by the men by the time they come back. They give the women small money and say this money is for food for the family. Men just think about *"mi-nomo,"* they just think about themselves and their own interests. (interview, March 2011)

This account of leasing is a narrative of masculine mobility and consumerist desires. It is an account of the agency of powerful men fulfilling their own desires rather than meeting the needs of their families. It is also a description of gendered spaces where men are highly mobile, in contrast with women who are confined in the kitchen. These narratives of mobility and stasis speak to relations of power by which public and private spheres are actively delineated and maintained by men as gendered spaces. This assertion that women's place is in the private, domestic sphere of the kitchen acts as a narrative that removes women from supposedly "public" spaces of discussions about land.

Women's right to speak about land has often been associated with their general status in society. Writing about women and land, Dorosday Kenneth and Henlyn Silas argued that "however low now the status of women in Vanuatu, or however secondary their rights to land; as society changes, other things inevitably change. As women improve their qualifications and take on more [leadership] responsibilities in Vanuatu it is hoped that their status in custom with regard to land will also improve" (1986, 85). Experience from across Melanesia suggests that education and employment are not necessarily enough to enable women to exercise their *raets* to speak about land. Martha Macintyre offered a poignant illustration of the silencing of three educated Papua New Guinean women attempting to speak about land issues. The result was that the women were "put in their place" by men and told they were acting "against custom" (2012, 245; Monson 2012, i). Across Melanesia, claims that women speaking are "against custom" operate to remove women from public spaces of speaking about land.

Locally, women in North Efate described ideas of *kastom* and *rispek* as central to understanding the discriminatory treatment of women by men. Women who participated in land workshops described *kastom* practices as the basis for the oppression of women: "When they are at school boys and girls are equal. Our *kastom* means that all men look down on us women" (collective statement, Women and Land Workshop discussion, Oct 2010). Roslyn Tor and Anthea Toka described the transformation to *kastom* practices and the increased inequality of women as a response to the intensive experience of colonization and Christianity in Vanuatu: "Christianity, colonialism and independence in a relatively short period... has inevitable consequences. What is being realized today is that women bore the cost of these changes much more than men. In the cultural soup of today's society, the contemporary 'kastoms' and beliefs that have evolved are discriminatory to women and some quite contrary to past practice" (2004, 62).

The changing attitudes associated with colonization and the introduction of Christianity have led to what Naupa and Simo argued is a growing lack of respect for women (2008, 102). The lack of respect for the role of women in *kastom* informs customary land law, such as that prescribed by the Vaturisu Council of Chiefs, which removes the capacity of women to speak on land in public spaces. Ancestral authority associated with *kastom* has been concentrated and intensified through Christian and colonial pressures, as well as more recent processes of modernity. Margaret Jolly wrote, "Perpetuating *kastom* in South Pentecost has meant just this. The male domination inherent in the ancestral culture has been challenged but also in some ways intensified through its relation to colonial pressures. This has generated a strange paradox whereby men both mediate and monopolize modernity, and struggle to keep women apart from it. The self-conscious need to 'hold women tight' becomes not just an internal imperative but part of the resistant relation to external pressures" (1994, 257). Jolly offered a cogent analysis of gender and agency that hinges on the control and manipulation of *kastom* and modernity by men. Masters of modernity have the capacity to manipulate both lease making and *kastom* in their own individual self-interests in the style of a *masta-mi.* Women are held tight by these edicts about *kastom,* told to *"stap kwaet"* (shut up and be quiet) in the kitchen and not interfere in land issues, which are widely discussed as the business of men.

Across Vanuatu, women are repeatedly told that they cannot speak about land in public forums as this is disrespectful to men and not proper in terms of *kastom*. A chief from Raga in North Pentecost described these restrictions: "When a woman stands to speak [in a *nakamal*], she can disrupt the community's harmony because of the huge role she plays as a mother of the tribe and the home, as a mother and a sister. If she takes these into consideration she will not assert herself or speak out because of her important role to maintain peace among the two tribes" (Naupa and Simo 2008, 103).

In this quote, female identity represents the embodied values of *kastom*, with women acting in deference to men (termed *rispek*). At issue for many ni-Vanuatu women in participating in *nakamal* meetings is *rispek* for *kastom* practices. Women who fail to follow *kastom*, or act with *rispek*, risk widespread disapproval and shaming for failing to act as a "proper woman." Many ni-Vanuatu women themselves described the importance of deference toward male leadership, customary institutions, and processes. In making these statements, women articulated the value they place on aspects of *kastom* in their lives and in maintaining the social fabric of kinship and daily existence. The significance of these relational, shared values associated with *kastom* and *rispek* actively contours the agency expressed by women.

Moving beyond "Saving Our Sisters"

Discussion of women's land rights must recognize that for many ni-Vanuatu women customary institutions and processes are highly valued. To be meaningful for women, vernacular *raets* must emerge that enable women access to these customary institutions without destabilizing the institutions themselves or attempting to rewrite *kastom* to better accord with simplistic Western individualist notions of formal equality. Naupa and Simo critiqued women's land-rights discourse that "typically incorporates Western concepts and terminology into discussion around women and land... which risks undermining women's traditional land rights and altering custom norms for women's participation in land management" (2008, 86). Claims of rights to gender equality are viewed as a largely "foreign import" that fails to recognize the agency of local women in negotiating their *raets* through customary institutions (Naupa 2017, 308; Jolly 1996). Naupa and Simo suggested that rights-based approaches also potentially undermine customary processes and institutions that may offer better access to land for women than the formal state mechanisms of either legislation or court processes. Moreover, state-centered, rights-based approaches fail to take account of the limited ambit of the state in Melanesia.

A further critique is that human rights discourse is implicitly constructionist, assuming Western models of personhood that too often envelop women in the secular garb of modern persons exercising individual agency (Merry

2009, 385). Jolly wrote that one of the problems with human rights approaches is that they often assume Western models of personhood such that "one of the hazards of this kind of debate is that the human slides imperceptibly into the western" (Jolly 2000, 126; Merry 2001). Human rights discourse is often the "language of individual empowerment" such that individuals can protect themselves against injustices (Ignatieff 2003, 57). By contrast, as already discussed, in Melanesia relational and kinship obligations also create "dividual" obligations allowing women to make choices that may appear different to those deduced only by individualistic human rights models of personhood (Merry 2009, 400–401; Gewertz and Errington 1999; Strathern 2004). This is not to suggest that "the West" or the "developed world" has a monopoly on values of gender equality or notions of individual rights (Lawrence 2013, 2014). However, Sally Engle Merry argued that human rights discourse appears to create a binary between the "rational" choices made by modern [read Western] women and the oppressive nature of women choosing to live by "tradition" or "custom." She suggested that it is important to challenge this binary by "mapping the middle" between the positions (Merry 2009, 401; 2001). Unfortunately, the presumption of much of women's rights discourse in the Pacific adopts this binary and remains focused on acts of "imperial maternalism" in which women from "developed" countries seem intent on "saving our sisters" (Abu-Loghod 2013; Jolly 2016).

Resistance to Foreign Ideas of Women's Rights

Efforts to "save women" in the Pacific through countries becoming signatories to international agreements on women's rights, such as states signing on to the United Nations Convention for Elimination of Discrimination Against Women (CEDAW), have met with limited success (Jolly 2012a, 3; Zorn 2012). CEDAW includes a number of provisions related to women's rights of access to natural resources and land (Article 14 (2) (g)). CEDAW remains controversial in the Pacific because the convention documents maintain that women are oppressed by culture. This is discussed in Article 5 as the requirement that all states modify cultural and customary practices to eliminate prejudice against women. Judgments of local courts across the Pacific often operate against the principles of CEDAW and in favor of state legislation or supposed community values (Zorn 2012, 190; Lawrence 2014, 4). Even where efforts have been made to recognize the principles of equal rights, these efforts are of themselves unlikely to provide solutions to entrenched discrimination and gender violence. Jolly commented that "emphasis on the power of the law and especially of international law to combat gender violence has not only been unduly optimistic but has somehow failed to acknowledge how changes in the broader economic and political situation in which Pacific women are situated powerfully molds and often constrains their capabilities to address gender violence" (Jolly 2016, 364–365). Law is a blunt instrument in addressing the complex intersections of patriarchal control over women's bodies.

The experience of CEDAW in the Pacific suggests the limited efficacy of legal arrangements informed by a formal rights-based approach to gender equality. Formal equal rights approaches also run the risk of male resistance and suggestions that such reforms will elevate women's rights by diminishing those of men (Naupa and Simo 2008, 86). John Taylor documented a group of men claiming that rights-based approaches undermined Vanuatu's "natural" *kastom* and the Christian patriarchal gender order (2008c, 165). Rights-based approaches can often challenge[2] some of the underlying cultural norms and power dynamics operating in Vanuatu. The result is that much of Vanuatu's male leadership has not been receptive to a formal rights-based gender and land approach (Naupa 2017). The eleven-year struggle over the passing of the *Family Protection Act* in Vanuatu amid opposition from the Malvatumauri and the Vanuatu Christian Council illustrates the difficulties associated with gaining the support of influential male leaders for what are perceived to be imposed Western ideas of equal rights. It is even more concerning that some women, in advocating for formal rights-based equality, may perhaps be interpreted by men as threatening their status, thereby placing women in vulnerable positions at risk of physical violence (Macintyre 2012, 246–247).

Moving toward Grounded *Raets* for Women

In contrast with formal equal-rights-based approaches, Naupa and Simo argued for consideration of the vernacular *raets* that exist in a "customary tenure approach," which acknowledges "the range of women's land rights, from visible participation in decision-making processes at the family and village level, to less visible representation through family members in the nakamal" (2008, 86). This suggests that even if women are not visibly participating they may still be influencing decision-making. Throughout Vanuatu following customary tenure arrangements, it is often a brother, father, uncle, son, or group of men who advocate on behalf of a woman's access to land suggesting the nexus of relational rather than individual concepts that inform discussions of women's *raets* to land.

From an advocacy perspective, framing women's *raets* in the context of family cohesion and *kastom* has proved a more effective strategy than a formal equal rights approach in Vanuatu (Naupa 2017, 317). This provides an advocacy and land-reform strategy that situates women's land *raets* in broader understandings of the social fabric of women's lives and as steeped in *kastom*. However, Naupa and Simo cautioned that "relying on the flexibility of customary tenure alone will not achieve fuller group involvement in land decisions," and that for this reason a middle pathway that operates in the space between "rights" and customary tenure is needed to adequately recognize women's land needs (2008, 86). This approach can be described as "mapping the middle"—the space of women's agency in articulating land claims in customary institutions and forums—in much the same way that Merry discussed the role of local human rights "translators" who operate in "the middle of a field of power and opportunity." People who work as "translators" must present their rights claims in vernacular, cultural terms that are acceptable to local communities, including communities dominated by male leadership (Merry 2006b, 42; Levitt and Merry 2011).

Women across Vanuatu make active choices around whether and how to pursue land claims based on assessments of customary tenure rights and appropriate *kastom* practices. These are nuanced and careful decisions that belie the agency of women in negotiating *raets* far beyond those understandings of equal rights as mediated through shades of "imperial maternalism." Women present claims to *raets* in ways that demonstrate a pragmatic understanding of *kastom,* the role of "proper women," as well as the relative status and agency of individual women. The agency of individual women is informed by their status within the customary group and their age. The ability of individual women to express their claims over customary land becomes a complex matrix informed by: (1) *kastom* ideas of the behavior of a "proper woman" and how a particular individual has performed her customary and relational obligations; (2) a woman's status within the customary group as the wife or daughter of a chief or as a woman who is deemed expert in *kastom* knowledge; (3) a woman's age, with seniority allowing some women the *raet* to speak, whereas it is often significantly harder for younger women to discuss land issues in public forums; (4) whether a woman is a *woman-ples* or has married in from another island; and (5) whether a woman speaks with the backing of male relations or in opposition to their claim, including the status of any men she speaks against. The interplay of this matrix means that older women who are expert in *kastom,* or whose claim is supported by a chief and who are *women-ples,* are more likely to be able to articulate their claims to land. This offers a matrix of land *raets* grounded in the everyday realities of women's lives.

Pragmatically, local women in North Efate are adept at expressions of agency that follow the contours of *kastom* practice in this "middle space" of grounded *raets.* This idea of grounded *raets* acknowledges that women often negotiate their interests collectively through kinship and extended family relations. Adequately accounting for women's agency in their expression of land *raets* also requires movement beyond modes of personhood as framed by the dichotomy of individual/dividual. The agency of women over land suggests the copresence of individual and dividual aspects of self, and many women in North Efate articulate claims to landscapes as individuals through male relations. Women's grounded *raets* function as claims of personal autonomy expressed as extensions of their relational claims as mothers, sisters, daughters, or nieces. These *raets* are informed by understandings of the reciprocal work and roles of men and women in maintaining and producing the ways of *ples.*

Across Vanuatu women often advocate for land access through male relations. This means that single, divorced, or widowed women can be particularly vulnerable to acts of "intimate exclusion," whereby male kin deny their access to land (Hall, Hirsch, and Li 2011, 145; Jolly and others 2015). The difficulties faced by widows in maintaining access to land were described by Trudi Kalotiti, a widow on Lelepa Island. Trudi contrasted her claims to *raets* over customary *paumaso* land gifted by men to her late husband Douglas Kalotiti with entitlements to Douglas's father's land:

> For the land that was gifted to Douglas... I need to stand up and talk to my sons to make sure they can access the land. I have told the boys that they must work the land, must make gardens and build a house so that we can hold the land for the future.... But for the other land, land that belonged to Douglas's father I would never talk about that....
>
> ...When Douglas was sick he told me I was not allowed to talk about any of Douglas's father's land. He told me before he died, "Don't fight for the land, wait for my brothers to look after you so that you can work on the land." So that is what I am doing, I am waiting for the family to pass some land to me and my sons to work on....
>
> ...I am hoping the family will look after me.... It is not easy for widows to go into a family and make a land claim. The men look down on me because I am a woman that has married into the family, so I must push my sons to talk about our *raets*. (interview, Nov 2014)

Trudi Kalotiti's agency in maintaining access to land illustrates the meaning of grounded *raets* expressed in recognition of the contours of *kastom*. In her discussion of land *raets*, Trudi acknowledged her role within her smaller and larger familial structures, as well as her identity as a woman from another *ples*. Recognizing these contours of relationality and island identity and the way they confine her individual capacity to express her claims to land, she pragmatically adopted an approach in which her land *raets* are expressed through the customary tenure claims of her sons.

In workshops in North Efate where women were given a series of problems around securing their access to land, such as being widowed or divorced, they overwhelmingly advocated for strategies of articulating grounded *raets* through relational modes of agency. Maternal uncles are often key figures in *kastom*. They can advocate for nieces in their claims to land. This role of uncles reflects the reciprocal exchange associated with *braed praes* payments made to uncles for a niece, and the role that these uncles continue to play in mediating relationships between a married woman and her new kin, including ongoing land access. Land access is closely tied to marriage relationships and these relational, respectful, and emplaced modes of women's agency represent a middle pathway in the recognition of vernacular *raets*.

In Vanuatu, women's agency is actively contoured by interpretations of *kastom*. This includes women's own understanding of *kastom* and roles of "proper women" in discussions about land, as well as the interpretations of *kastom* offered by masters of modernity. The idea of grounded *raets* acknowledges salient expressions of women's agency with respect to land as articulated with reference to *kastom, ples,* and *raets* expressed with, rather than in opposition to, men. In this way, grounded *raets* are claims that operate in a middle path—the search for a meaningful vernacular regarding women's *raets* as they exist in customary spaces, rather than formal rights that flow from introduced notions of equality and are mediated by introduced laws controlled by a state that is part of an international system. Importantly, the articulation of pragmatic, grounded *raets* removes the potential vulnerabilities of women that can be associated with using destabilizing narratives associated with formal rights-based equality.

Grounded *Raets*: Women Speaking about Land

While women in North Efate acknowledged the difficulty faced by many ni-Vanuatu women in speaking in *nakamals* and attending public meetings, they maintained that in North Efate women *can* and *do* speak in public spaces about land issues. Lelepa woman Leisara Kalotiti described her understanding of *kastom* and women's *raet* to speak in *nakamals* across Vanuatu, informed by her many years as a woman *filwoka* in the Vanuatu Cultural Centre:

LEISARA KALOTITI: I have been going to women *filwoka* workshops for many years. I have heard women field-workers from Tanna who have said, "Women are not allowed to talk in the nakamal." In North Efate we do not have any rule that says women cannot talk. . . .

. . . For example, if there is a meeting that happens in the community when there is a woman in the meeting she can just raise her hand and then she can talk.

SIOBHAN MCDONNELL: But what if it is a meeting about a specific piece of land like a land tribunal meeting? Can a woman talk in that meeting?

LK: Sometimes women are busy and they can't come to the meeting because they are too busy. But if the meeting was very important then women would come and sit in the meeting of the *nakamal* and, if they wanted to, they could talk. Women too can talk.

SM: Have you heard stories about women talking in land tribunals?

LK: Yes. For *paumaso* land particularly women can speak. Women do speak in land courts or land tribunals. (interview, Nov 2014)

Leisara Kalotiti's account of North Efate women speaking in public forums was supported by her late husband Chief Kalkot Mormor, who stated, "Just last week we had a woman who had been given land by her father, but her uncles [father's brothers] were disputing it. She came to the Council of Chiefs meeting and told her story and we all listened to her. It was a big meeting and she talked about what her father had said to her about the land. Her two uncles wanted to ignore her land claims so she had to tell all of us chiefs what her father had said so that we could judge" (interview, Nov 2014). The resulting decision of the Council of Chiefs found in favor of the woman who spoke about her claim to land. Lelepa woman Naomi Williams, who served as the secretary of the Council of Chiefs for almost ten years, confirmed the presence of numerous women speaking before Lelema Council of Chiefs meetings and of the chiefs finding in favor of women (interview, Nov 2014).

Accounts of *raets* must be *grounded* in the experience of women. Lelepa and Mangaliliu women's ideas of grounded *raets* emerge as an entanglement between "exogenous and indigenous epistemologies and values" (Taylor 2008c, 166). The articulation by local women of *raets* over land represents a statement of claim to land, made in relation to others, and offered in relation to the localized Indigenous values of being a woman of the *ples*. In customary tenure arrangements, discussion of formal rights to equality, as opposed to the grounded *raets* of women, risks creating assumptions and policy formulations that further alienate women from being active participants in defining and interpreting *kastom* as it applies to land.

Accounts from North Efate suggest that women in North Efate can articulate *raets* to land in public meetings of chiefs without usurping *kastom*. It is true, however, that women who speak in public meetings are usually able to express particular relations of power and claims to authority; they are more likely to be senior women well versed in *kastom* who are *women-ples*. Moreover, a woman's claims are more likely to succeed if they are supported by male relations. Regardless, these accounts of women speaking about land serve as important reminders of the need to move beyond simplistic women's rights discourses that describe *all* women as oppressed or the commonly held refrain across Melanesia that women cannot speak about land. Some women do speak.

Grounded *Raets* Not Property Rights

Women's grounded *raets* over land do not easily translate into the property right claims of possessive individuals. Women in North Efate make personal claims to relational *raets* exercised through a prism of "dynamic strategies and relations of power" (Taylor 2008c, 177). These grounded *raets* can be contrasted with the property right claims of individual possession that inform the legal identity of custom ownership. Experience from North Efate suggests that even where primary rights are recognized as being held by women over parcels of *paumaso* land, it is extremely unlikely that these women will be recognized in any of the legal instruments as the "custom owners" of the land. Of the 349 names listed on the lease instruments located along coastal North Efate in 2015, fewer than 1 percent of all recorded names belong to women. Land-lease documents and ethnographic data for North Efate demonstrate that only four women have been involved in leasing land in the region. Of these four women, two are women whose fathers are unhappy with their sons' repeated leasing of customary land and so have put leases under the names of their daughters to avoid the land being on-sold, and two are women whose husbands have placed the lease in both of their names. Having considered the nuanced way by which women negotiate customary tenure *raets* to land in North Efate, these *raets* can be contrasted with the stark masculinization of possessive individual custom owners engaged in leasing land.

The land rush that has taken place on Efate Island has substantially undermined the customary land *raets* of women. In articulating their own understanding of women's roles in customary tenure arrangements, Naupa and Simo identified land sales as major threats that weaken women's traditional role in the governance of customary land (2008, 86). It is clear in North Efate and across the archipelago that the act of transacting land by custom owners is overwhelmingly male dominated. The effect of lease making is to draw into stark relief the gendering of possessive custom-ownership claims informed by Western-derived models of the masculine individual. The property rights of custom ownership remain largely unavailable to local women whose grounded *raets* over land are relational, embedded in family and *kastom* practice, and exercised with or alongside men.

Women Displaced by Acts of Intimate Exclusion

Land legislation that was created post-independence in Vanuatu has assumed a particular model of a custom owner that has further exacerbated existing gender inequalities in relation to land (Naupa and Simo 2008). Maintaining gender-neutral language in the drafting of land legislation, rather than enabling equality, permits the sliding of a possessive individual as an owner of property into a masculine identity. Custom ownership is routinely identified as a legal category pertaining only to men. While there is no legal reason why women cannot be custom owners, the practical reality is that women are less able to access the public expatriate spheres in which lease transactions are conducted, just as they have difficulty speaking about land claims in customary institutions because "this is not *kastom*."

When plots of *paumaso* coastal land are leased, it is the names of men as brothers, husbands, and chiefs that are recorded in the registered instruments as the owners of the land. Using the instrumentality of the law and adopting the identity of custom owners of property, men become *emplaced* and women *displaced* from the landscape. Transactions of property operate as a second wave of displacement of women from the landscape of North Efate, in addition to the earlier transformations of systems of customary tenure from *matrilineal* to *patrilineal*. Once *matrilineal* arrangements that embedded people of the place held in the wombs of their maternal ancestors *(naflak)*, the landscape of North Efate is increasingly parceled as property retaining only the names of local men as custom owners. This process has meant that property rights have increasingly been claimed and asserted by a small powerful group of masters of modernity in acts of "intimate exclusion" of women and other members of the community (Hall, Hirsch, and Li 2011, 145; Smith 2017).

Locally, women in North Efate are critically aware of the role that signing a lease instrument plays in an assertion of future legal ownership rights to a landscape. The first recommendation that a large group of Lelepa women put to the Lelema Council of Chiefs meeting was that for *paumaso* land and "family land," "the husband and the wife must both sign the lease." Echoing the resolutions from the National Land Summit, women from Lelepa and Mangaliliu articulated an idealized decision-making process through which husbands and wives decide together to lease customary land: "When men lease land it should be discussed with their wives. They should sit down together and decide they should talk about how they want to lease the land and what they will use the money from leasing land for" (collective statement, Women and Land Workshop discussion, Oct 2010).

Many women stated that for *paumaso* plots of land it is the woman alone who should decide whether the land is leased or whether to hold it for her children or grandchildren. In contrast to this idealized decision-making process, a chief and his wife recounted their experiences of decision-making with respect to leasing in the region:

CHIEF: It is men who decide to lease land, they don't give women a chance.

WIFE: Yes, husbands make all the decisions they never call out to their wives so that the two of them can sit down and decide. The husband should say to his wife "I have been thinking we should lease this land, but I want us to sit down together and talk together and decide whether to sell the land or not."

But what happens now is that the man runs to town to sell the land and the woman is in the kitchen, in the house. Women cannot go to the buildings where land is sold. (interview, Nov 2014)

The spaces of land transactions are gendered, as are the transactions themselves. Land transactions take place in gendered spaces, such as nightclubs or bars, where it is inappropriate for village women to be seen. Similarly, in formal courts and chiefly title determinations, it is largely men who make land claims. Formal state court and *kastom* forums function as spaces where land claims are overwhelmingly performed and adjudicated by men. Acts of leasing are overwhelmingly executed by a man acting as a possessive individual over property. As one Lelepa woman related:

> Most of the time men say, *"Mi bae mi mekem"* [I will do this alone] and then they will lease the land. When everything is finished sometimes men and women will share the money but sometimes a man will think about buying a truck or house. Sometimes a woman doesn't even know what her husband has done....
>
> ...Many women complain that when their husbands sell the land, they don't give their wives anything. They promise to share the money but, when they sell the land and have the cash, they buy alcohol and then the money is gone. (interview, Nov 2014)

Cash made from leasing land often supports men in their performance of masculine excess, as described by Lelepa women: "Men think too much of their own self-interests like drinking kava, drinking alcohol, smoking cigarettes. When men lease land, money comes sometimes; women get some small money but mostly men look after themselves" (interview, Nov 2010).

Locally, women in North Efate critiqued leasing practices where the benefits of land leasing accrue only to a small handful of men. Ruth Maetala wrote in Solomon Islands of a similar experience of logging royalties accruing mainly to men with women receiving only token payments for areas of land for which they were landowners. Maetala suggested that this situation occurs because women are absent from negotiations and timber hearings as they are not recognized as trustees for logging agreements; therefore the men do not need to consult them to seek their consent. Legal identities in Solomon Islands and Vanuatu are manipulated by powerful men to exclude others from sharing in the benefits of land leasing, logging, or resource extraction (Maetala 2008, 51–52; McDougall 2011, 140–141).

Overwhelmingly women across Melanesia, like those in Vanuatu, want to be more involved in decision-making about land. In practice, women in North Efate are rarely involved in decision-making about customary land, including *paumaso* land. A broader survey of Efate villages by Naupa and Simo demonstrated that women's participation in decision-making over land "was minimal, if it occurred at all." Women in North Efate overwhelmingly expressed the desire to be informed about meetings that related to leasing or any other decision-making about customary land, as opposed to current practices where men monopolize information and husbands actively bar wives from attending meetings. Naupa and Simo described similar situations across Efate Island where land deals have occurred without women's prior consent or even their knowledge (2008, 106–107). It is men who are approached to create leases by investors, men who negotiate the sale of land, men who sign the legal documentation (certificate of negotiation, lease documents, receipts of payments), men who receive the money from the principal lease payment, and men who receive the annual rent payment. When leasing land, just as in colonial times, men deal with men.

Masters of Modernity Manipulating *Kastom*

The act of transacting land by "custom owners" is starkly gendered. The authority of men to lease land comes from: (1) the model of a possessive individual exercising property rights as a form of capitalist relations; (2) the gendered spaces of land transactions; and (3) the power of masters of modernity as the authors and arbiters of *kastom* in the *nakamal,* land tribunal, and court processes. Increasingly ni-Vanuatu women argue that contemporary *kastom* practices are being manipulated by masters of modernity who utilize their authority to define and interpret *kastom* in the *nakamal* and in land tribunal processes (Naupa and Simo 2008, 103; Naupa 2017; Tor and Toka 2004). Following Margaret Rodman's earlier work, I have argued that men are manipulating *kastom* in their roles as masters of modernity.

Kastom narratives entail a conscious and selective representation of key aspects of self. Nowhere do the fraught and political nature of opposing narratives of *kastom* and *ples* become more apparent than in the customary and legal entanglements related to opposing claims over land. Here, the narratives of self are fought over by a handful of powerful men vying for authority over land and each other. Masters of modernity are powerful orators who offer authoritative *kastom* narratives when they speak about land in court and in *nakamals.* By not allowing for the voices of women in these spaces, the construction of *kastom* becomes the domain of such men. The effect of these narratives is deeply political in that they operate to reproduce particular models of place making and structures of relatedness. Increasingly in North Efate, these modes of place making privilege *blad laen* over *naflak* claims to chiefly titles and result in *blad laen* gaining authority over landscapes.

Lelepa women repeatedly claimed that powerful men manipulate *kastom* in a variety of ways. Following the land workshops, women in North Efate called on male leaders in the Lelema and Vaturisu Council of Chiefs to ensure that all land tribunals were fair and that *kastom* narratives did not become a "false history" of people (collective statement, Women and Land Workshop discussion, Oct 2010). Women critiqued, in particular, the practices of bribing land tribunal judges, and they condemned the practice of "land stealing" in which powerful men lease land that in *kastom* properly belongs to others. While the women wanted to make these and other recommendations about land leasing and women's *raets* public by speaking to the media, they were told by the council of chiefs to *"stap kwaet"* (be quiet) and that they were "not to wash dirty laundry in public" (meeting with Lelema Council of Chiefs, April 2011). Once again women were pushed back to the domestic sphere, their voices removed from the wider public domain.

Transforming Narratives of Place and Displacing Women

Transformations in connections to place may also have the effect of displacing women. In earlier chapters, I discussed the changing nature of customary tenure arrangements in North Efate from *naflak* (matrilineal descent) to *blad laen* (patrilineal descent), including the endorsement of patrilineal descent by the Vaturisu Customary Land Law. These customary land laws, ironically signed off on by Chief Mormor (a major advocate for *naflak* rights), privilege *blad laen* systems of landownership. At issue is whether women who hold *raets* over land can exercise practical decision-making authority over customary landscapes, and whether this is influenced by changes to customary tenure from matrilineal to patrilineal descent structures.

Ethnographic work has long posited the idea that in the numerous matrilineal areas of Vanuatu (the Torres and Banks islands, Maewo, North Pentecost, East Ambae, Espiritu Santo, and Efate) there are "strong prima facie grounds for expecting a higher status accorded to women and a marked reduction in male hegemony" (Allen 1981, 2; Demian 2007; Lepani 2012, 2015; Lepowsky 1994). Recent work by Milne Bay scholar Salmah Eva-Lina Lawrence (2013, 2014) offers further support for claims that matrilineal arrangements lead to the higher social status of women, lower levels of violence toward women, and higher levels of political participation among women. By contrast, research from Pentecost and Efate Islands in Vanuatu, as well as matrilineal areas in Solomon Islands suggests that, even where matrilineal systems exist, men retain control over land use and decision-making (Maetala 2008, 51; McDougall 2011; Naupa and Simo 2008, 85). Maetala gave an account of one matrilineal woman landowner from the Weather Coast in Guadalcanal: "Even if I am a landowner, I am seen as a nobody, only good for home making and baby rearing" (2008, 51). This suggests that while matrilineal systems provide the potential for female authority this potential is not always realized in the performance of property.

The increasing dominance of patrilineal descent narratives of ownership over *naflak* conceptions of *place* has implications for the ongoing connections of women in the landscape of North Efate. This is because matrilineal descent functions not just as a basis for the inheritance of land and chiefly titles but also as "a constitutive configuration of persons, land and identity" (Demian 2007, 167; Scott 2007). Returning to the idea of *na"flak"*—"as from the womb," tribes birthed from the mother—the idea of birthing people of the *place* creates a particular narrative in which women are central to the construction of *place*. Women birth people so as to actively create *place* as constituted through people as *man-ples*. This narrative allows women a material and spiritual connection to *place*. Lissant Bolton recognized women's connection to *place* through the birthing of children and in the role that they play, alongside men, in productively utilizing the land: "Women practice their relationships to land by bearing children to it. Both men and women practice their relationship to land by using it for gardens and by living on it. By correctly asserting that men hold rights to land, it is possible to emphasize the connections that men have to land in a way that obscures women's connections to it" (2003, 95).

Here the role of women is emplaced, acknowledged for actively constituting personhood and identity. While these roles that women play are important, it is men's role in public forums that remains crucial to both the assertion of land claims and the practices of land leasing, and it is the absence of women from these forums that allows men to assert rights that obscure the claims of women.

If women are recognized through *naflak* systems as birthing the people of a *ples,* then what happens to the status of women with respect to land as alternative *blad laen* narratives of *ples* gain precedence and authority? Sitting in my first land workshop on Lelepa Island in 2009, I watched a brave, angry, young woman raise the importance of women and *naflak* to land claims in a *farea* full of chiefs, men, women, and elder people versed in *kastom.* In true Melanesian fashion, there was no response to her question around the transformations in connections to *place* that now inform *kastom* in North Efate. The elder man, a *kastom* expert who had been speaking on land, shrugged his shoulders. Silence filled the hall. It is this silence into which many of the questions around women, *kastom,* and relationships to *place* continue to drift. Irreconcilable, unanswerable questions emerge from a society that is increasingly transformed into recognizing only patrilineal *blad laen* claims to land. These questions are catalyzed by claims made through Christian missionization, capitalist commodity economics, chiefly authored "customary" land laws, and by contemporary land-leasing practices that privilege masculine individual possession. These entangled processes work to ensure the ascendancy of *blad laen* narratives over *naflak,* thereby circumscribing women's relationships to *place.*

During discussions I had with a group of Lelepa Island chiefs, they described the way women's relationships to land are increasingly eroded and cautioned against men forgetting the importance of women to the practice of *kastom*: "Now because of *blad laen* men are not thinking too much about women and land. But women have a big role to play. If I don't recognize my sisters' claims to land then, when I have some business, will my sisters still help me? We men must remember that women weave mats. Women work making all different things" (interview, Nov 2014).

Here a group of chiefs acknowledged the dependence of men on the work of women, recognizing the centrality of women to the maintenance of *kastom* as the ways of *ples.* Women are central in the production of food, in maintaining the *kastom* practices of ritualized exchange associated with marriage and funeral ceremonies, and as the preeminent weavers of textiles as ritual exchange items. These comments of the chiefs pointed to an understanding of the reciprocal nature of men and women's work in maintaining *kastom* in North Efate. Land claims informed by ancestral *blad laen* and lease making by men over land, particularly *paumaso* land, vitiates against this perceived reciprocity.

The Vaturisu Customary Land Laws inform local customary tribunal and island court determinations of what is correct in *kastom.* Masters of modernity have dictated the removal of the *raets* of women to speak and own land, while at the same time privileging their own land rights as chiefs. It is this same handful of masters that arbitrates land disputes in *nakamals,* Council of Chiefs' meetings, land tribunals, and island courts. In this way the Vaturisu Customary Land Laws function as a monstrous reanimated cadaver, a "Frankenstein's corpse," authored not only to intimidate women but also to silence them in the *nakamal,* with the effect of potentially stripping women of their *raets* to place. The act of codification of "custom" land law presents, as Grace Molisa predicted, a challenge to the grounded *raets* of women. Customary processes and institutions informed by these customary land laws have the potential to impact on women's *raets* to land in ways that are almost as detrimental as lease making itself.

Speaking as *Women-Ples*

This is not to suggest that *kastom* narratives always favor men and oppress women. *Kastom* is not monolithic and cannot be viewed *only* as a domain used by powerful men to intimidate women and "the weak." *Kastom* is actively created and contoured; it is fluid and changing. *Kastom* belongs to women just as it belongs to men. Determining customary tenure and identifying custom owners involves mapping processual claims to land, claims that women can be actively engaged in framing. In this way customary tenure offers potential for nuanced articulations of grounded *raets* for women, far beyond those historically created by land dispute judgments in the formal state legal system.

Kastom and customary tenure systems may also allow women agency that they are often unable to access in formal state-based proceedings. Customary institutions allow a greater level of access to rural women than formal state institutions that are located only in the urban centers of Port Vila and Luganville and remain largely inaccessible to local village women. Women may also play a far greater role in judging disputes, in customary institutions that actively name women in legislation, than they have done to date in formal state-based courts. Statistics suggest that for the period from 2001 to 2007, just over 20 percent of the adjudicators of land tribunal disputes were women, a recognition of women's *kastom* expertise in land matters. This experience suggests that for women to be able to exercise *raets* over land they need to participate in the processes that relate to interpreting *kastom.* Women must be able to voice their interpretations of *kastom* within customary institutions (Naupa and Simo 2008, 86, 93). This, in turn, requires access to customary institutions and the *raet* to be heard, as included in the 2014 land-reform package.

Kastom can offer a powerful pathway for women to exercise agency. Former Minister of Lands Ralph Regenvanu, in his discussion of the implications of the land-reform package for women, has repeatedly extolled women "to learn their *kastom* and to speak as custom owners within the *nakamal*" (pers comm, National Land Law Consultation Tour, 2013). Here Regenvanu, as the former director of the Vanuatu Cultural Centre, articulated the long-held mantra of the Vanuatu Cultural Centre women's field-worker program that there must be an acknowledgment that women *can* speak for *kastom* (Bolton 1999, 53). This project has included gathering *filwoka* women together every year to hear women speak about aspects of *kastom* in Vanuatu. The Vanuatu Cultural Centre has also been instrumental in demonstrating how women produce *kastom,* through, for example, the weaving of textiles as claims to attachment to *place* (Bolton 1999, 2003, 2009). Regenvanu's position assumes, however, that women can actively author *kastom* and be involved in defining and interpreting land *raets.* These assumptions are not unproblematic, as demonstrated by the Vaturisu Customary Land Law, which was drafted by men alone to the exclusion of women.

Despite all their limitations, customary processes may still provide better access for women than formal state-based mechanisms. Court arrangements function as gendered spaces controlled overwhelmingly by men. Prosecution of claims to land through the formal state system involves access to vast financial resources often unavailable to women, particularly women based in the village without ready access to the cash needed to hire lawyers and to travel to Port Vila and Luganville.

Conclusion: Land as the Mother, *Mama Graon*

Emplaced feminine identities associated with *kastom* actively link women to *ples* and can provide a basis for women to speak about land issues. Women from Lelepa and Mangaliliu often exercise their agency by embracing the identity of women who care for *ples* in the interest of their children and future generations. Articulating their agency as *women-ples* enables women to claim connections with land through relationally embedded modes of being. Central to this agency is the idiom of land as the mother—*mama graon.* Women in North Efate spoke, as mothers and grandmothers of the *place,* about their concerns for *mama graon.* As Leisara Kalotiti adeptly explained: "We eat from the land, when we die we return to the land. Land is our mother. Land takes care of the children. It provides food, gardens to feed children and grandchildren in the future. You make your house on the land. The land keeps the family safe. The land is *mama graon* (interview, Nov 2014). Here land is gendered and embodied as a mother echoing the famous words of Sethy

Regenvanu, widely held across Vanuatu, that land is *"mama graon."* The framing of land—so central to self in Vanuatu—as female, enables the agency of women to speak about *ples*.

The agency of Lelepa women is most visible in their articulation of these emplaced narratives as critiques of land leasing and the use that men make with money from leasing land. These are relational agencies articulated with an understanding of people embedded in *ples* and of women as carers and nurturers of children and *ples*. While women rarely assert claims based on matrilineal *naflak* descent, their agency is informed by the understanding of birthing people of the *ples*. In North Efate, women use their roles, as mothers and grandmothers, to argue that land should be held for future generations or that resources from leasing should be properly utilized for school fees or shared resources, such as housing. Speaking as *women-ples,* Lelepa women regularly raised concerns about land and resource management during our conversations. They repeatedly expressed concerns about outsiders' overuse of local resources through overfishing, the collection of firewood, and sand mining and their impacts on local freshwater resources and communal forest resources. Local women argued that, with respect to land, women's agency is defined by emplaced relationality in ways different from that of men: "All women must think about the future, we are worried that there will not be enough land for our children and grandchildren" (interviews, Oct 2011).

Women also articulated *raets* as *women-ples* as against other women who are not following proper *kastom* practices. Thus, one of the key recommendations of local women following the land workshops was that a woman who marries a man from another place on Efate Island, or other islands, must go and live with her husband's family rather than continue to live on Lelepa Island or in Mangaliliu. This was articulated as proper *kastom* and as a way to deal with increasing land scarcity and population pressures.

The ability to speak as *women-ples* has allowed local women to take up leadership positions in key community organizations in the region. These include the Nuwae Water Project, which delivers fresh water across Lelepa Island and is led by chairperson Naomi Williams, and the Lelema World Heritage Committee, which manages the World Heritage site and has more female than male members. The four-year Nuwae Water Project successfully located fresh water on Lelepa Island, where previously there was no water supply other than rainwater tanks, and also provided water tanks across the island. By electing Naomi Williams over other male applicants, members of the committee and the Lelepa Island community concluded that women were more able than men to allocate precious water resources based on need. This was due to the relational agency expressed by women as "carers" and "nurturers" and "mothers" as opposed to the locally perceived fear of self-interested male leaders acting as *masta-mi.*

Consideration of women's land access and use rights must be informed by an understanding of "grounded *raets*," the vernacular women's *raets* that exist in customary spaces, rather than rights that flow from introduced notions of formal equality. Discussions of grounded *raets* illustrate that the agency of women is actively contoured by interpretations of *kastom,* as well as the idea of land as property owned by a possessive masculine individual. Women articulate grounded *raets* as relational claims mediated through *kastom* and kinship, rather than absolute statements of individual possession that translate into "custom ownership." This means that plots of *paumaso* customary land, which are understood as belonging to individual women, are nevertheless leased by men.

Discussion of grounded *raets* allows for a more nuanced discussion of aspects of female agency with respect to land claims informed by status, authority, age, adherence to *kastom,* and whether claims are made by a *woman of the ples.* The ability of individual women to express their grounded *raets* is informed by *kastom,* ideas of the behavior of a "proper woman," a woman's status and age and whether she is a *woman-ples,* and, finally, whether a woman speaks with the backing of male relations or in opposition to their claims.

Speaking as a *woman-ples,* a Lelepa woman spoke at the end of the women's land workshop, describing the act of "owning" land as a source of potential rupture with *kastom,* both in the contentious politics of local disputes and as a direct challenge to the *kastom* practices of future generations:

> In the time of our ancestors every tribe and clan had land. People cannot live without land. In our *kastom* land belongs to the people and people belong to the land.
>
> Without land people don't exist. Without people the land is useless.
>
> In our *kastom* our ancestors thought about land and told us: the land is our mother; the land protects us and holds us; the land shelters us; the land provides for all our human needs; the land is our cemetery, and the land holds our identity.
>
> Now we are losing our traditional system. We have not maintained it. People have come up with a new idea about owning the land. This new way leads to disputes. If we are not careful, in time we will lose our *kastom* for our future generations. (Closing address, Mangaliliu Women and Land Workshop, Oct 2010)

Exercising their agency, women in North Efate *do* speak about their grounded *raets* to customary land in *nakamals* and before chiefs. Speaking as *women-ples* about *mama graon,* they expertly utilize the narratives of *kastom* to speak about land issues. Lelepa women offer salient critiques of leasing by masters of modernity. The question is: will the men listen?

Conclusion

Refusal: Attempts to Decolonize Law

Stories of Indigenous dispossession are never simple, linear narratives of global capitalist expansion. This book offers insights into the complex exchanges that take place between investors, middlemen, and Indigenous landowners at the frontiers of land transformations. It shows how capitalist relations not only penetrate all corners of the globe but also increasingly confine the ideas and practices that govern our lives and bodies. However, links between paradise and capitalist processes, land alienation, and the associated dispossession of people, are complicated by critique and acts of resistance. Ultimately, these stories are partial, uneven and their processes incomplete. And in their midst, we find fertile spaces of refusal.

Across the Indigenous world, the commodification of land as property is understood as socially transformative, precisely because land is such a powerful site of ontological meaning and identity. The centrality of terrestrial and marine landscapes to epistemological framings and relational identity is why "the dispossession of land and access to the ocean . . . [is] so materially and spiritually destructive for Indigenous people" (Arvin, Tuck, and Morrill 2013, 22). For Lelepa people, landscapes are named and narrated by the acts of Chief Roi Mata and his consort and are animated by the nightly and diurnal movements of little people, *sengalengale,* who are increasingly angered by the leasing and development of sacred places. Place is animate. The land will eat you.

Across Oceania, acts of dispossession often become sites of resistance coalescing as movements against evictions, political sites of occupation, and resettlement (Filer, McDonnell, and Allen 2017; Foukona 2015; Foukona and Allen 2017; Rooney 2017). These movements serve as acts of refusal, as expressions of Indigenous sovereignty against the nation-state. Writing in a settler-colonial context, Audra Simpson shared her account of a Mohawk Kaianere'kó:wa National Lacrosse Team refusing to travel internationally on passports other than those of their own nation, thereby challenging the relationship of people to territory, as well as the supposedly settled boundaries of nation-states. She theorized that these acts of refusal "necessarily upset the conceits and premises of settler states . . . that Indian people as a condition of their Indigeneity, lose their territory and somehow disappear" (Simpson 2014,

185). In Vanuatu, the movement for land reform to better protect custom landowner rights emerged from a ten-year process involving numerous acts of refusal that challenged the role of the state and, in particular, the minister of lands in leasing customary land without the consent of landowning groups. So, what then do these acts of refusal mean in postcolonial self-governing Indigenous territories? What does it mean, for a movement to form that challenges the operation of the state and its governance of land? And if land is the basis of sovereignty, do these acts of refusal and the political movement that they built create a new expression of Indigenous sovereignty?

In Vanuatu, as knowledge about the national scale of the land rush became more widely available, a political movement grew that critiqued the actions of powerful political figures and chiefs who engaged in land leasing, calling for changes to the land laws so as to better protect Indigenous rights. In 2013, Ralph Regenvanu became the minister of lands, and I became his legal adviser and the principal drafter of a land-reform package designed to slow the rush to lease customary land and to halt the illegal leasing of customary land without the free, prior informed consent of customary landowning groups. The laws also offer a model for decolonizing law, in that they create constitutional legal pluralism by allowing customary institutions, rather than formal state courts, to identify custom landowners and determine land disputes.

An entry from my journal marks the passing of the new land laws in the Vanuatu Parliament in December 2013:

> The land reforms have passed Vanuatu's Parliament!
>
> Ralph rings me: "It's passed! We are celebrating! You should celebrate too." He laughs down the phone. "I am listening to *My Land My Life* on repeat."

So the story that began with a song, completes its circle...
Or so we thought...
Some stories are never finished.

Pendulum Swings

Globally land-reform debates are often characterized by pendulum swings, or "double movements," between arguments for the idea of customary land as a barrier to development and counterclaims that customary land functions as the basis of the social safety net and therefore needs greater protection. Discussing capitalist relations and the commoditization of land, Karl Polanyi argued that land transformations are often subject to a "double movement" whereby different actors either facilitate the commodification of land through the establishment of property rights and markets, or challenge these processes by asserting the socially embedded nature of land (Polanyi 1944; see also discussion in Cotula 2013, 1606). As elsewhere in the globe, discussion of land reform in the Melanesian region has been characterized by these "double movements" between advocates for neoliberal reform of customary land and those who defend customary landholding arrangements (Weiner and Glaskin 2007, 1; Fingleton 2005; Gosarevski, Hughes, and Windybank 2004; Hughes 2003). As the commodification of land or resource extraction gains pace, the pendulum often swings in the other direction toward efforts to protect and safeguard Indigenous land and resources.

In Vanuatu, countermovements for the return of Indigenous land have long been associated with large-scale political movements. The period before Vanuatu gained independence was defined by renewed conflict over large-scale colonial land alienation that coalesced around two major political movements. The first was the Nagriamel movement based out of Santo Island and led by the charismatic Jimmy Stephens, and the second, was the party famed for bringing independence to Vanuatu, the Vanua'aku Party. Beginning in the early 1960s the Nagriamel movement initially formed to help people hold on to their customary land and then, subsequently, to regain access and control over alienated land. While the movement originally began on Santo Island, with a particular resettlement of Tanafo near Sarakata River, groups of supporters also flourished on all northern islands. In 1967 Stephens and the other head of the Nagriamel movement on Santo, Chief Buluk, were jailed for two months for convincing Ambrym people to resettle on land owned by a Frenchman, arguing that only Chief Buluk had the authority to allocate land and not the colonial government (Van Trease 1987, 138–140).

In the 1970s Stephens unfortunately became involved with a group of American speculators headed up by Michael Oliver who were determined to purchase customary land and set up a tax-free "Republic" (Van Trease 1987, 141–150). Faced with the potential of further large-scale alienation of customary land by Oliver's American-based Phoenix Foundation, a new group of leaders formed an Independence Movement and named it the Vanua'aku Party from the words *vanua,* meaning land or home, and *aku,* meaning to stand up, translated as "Our Land Party" (Patterson 2006, 324–326). Writing as early as 1973, Barak Sope, the secretary general of the Vanua'aku Party, argued that: "The unity of many New Hebrideans is possible if based on a common struggle for the regaining of alienated land" (1974, 33). The Vanua'aku Party led the country to independence on the basis of the return of customary land alienated during the colonial period.

Twenty years later, as the leasing of customary land became a rush, another political movement began to form in ways that echoed the pre-independence movements.

Acts of Refusal

In Vanuatu, growing public concern over the commoditization and leasing of customary land provided the momentum for a broad-based countermovement for land reform that developed from the mid-2000s onward. Development of the movement took around ten years and was led by civil society organizations. As Vanuatu's land rush became increasingly rapacious, civil society—led by the Vanuatu Cultural Centre, the Malvatumauri, and the Vanuatu Association of Non-Government Organizations—began to organize in opposition to the widespread leasing of customary land, openly challenging the role of successive ministers of land who leased customary and state land without either the consent of landowning groups or any reference to public interest. The then director of the Vanuatu Cultural Centre, Ralph Regenvanu, became involved:

> After Vanuatu went through its Structural Adjustment reform program in the late-1990s many of us were worried about the speed with which leases of customary land were being granted by the government without proper processes being followed. Customary land leases were being approved without custom land-owner consent or planning approval.
>
> Our thinking around land reform started with the Traditional Money Banks project which involved workshops across Vanuatu. These workshops came up with the idea of needing to have an urgent national meeting to talk about land issues because the leasing of customary land was out of control....
>
> ...The National Land Summit happened the following year, and made twenty resolutions around changes needed to land law and administrative arrangements. (pers comm, May 2015)

The need for changes to the land laws resonated particularly with people on islands that had experienced the greatest leasing of customary land such as Efate, Santo, and Epi. However, as the land rush became more rapacious, people on other islands also began to experience the impacts of customary land leasing, such as a growing awareness that certain outer islands or parcels of customary land had been sold to investors by the minister or individual chiefs. From the mid- to late-2000s a growing number of Vanuatu's smaller outer islands were listed as "for sale" on international websites, often without the knowledge of local custom landowning groups.

Organized by civil society, the National Land Summit in 2006 was a key turning point in the debate for better protection of customary land. Attended by around eight hundred people, including the prime minister, ministers, members of Parliament, chiefs, civil-society representatives, men, women, young people, and members of the business and legal community, the resolutions from the summit identified five main problems with land dealings on customary land: (1) leasing without the consent of custom landowners was possible because there were no established processes for identifying custom landowners; (2) ministers of land were leasing customary and state land in their own interests and without the consent of the custom-owner groups; (3) individual men leasing customary land that in *kastom* is generally understood as being held by a group; (4) leases being issued without adequate compensation being paid to custom owners; and (5) environmental, planning, and cultural sites' safeguards were not being met in the leasing of customary land. The twenty resolutions from the Summit were widely covered by print media, television, and radio and formed the basis for public debate on land issues across Vanuatu.

Resolutions from the National Land Summit were subsequently endorsed by the Council of Ministers in 2007. However, this seems to have had little actual impact in practice with ministerial leasing of customary land continuing unabated. This lack of political response led Regenvanu to move into politics. As he stated:

> The failure of Parliament to implement the resolutions from the National Land Summit led to me deciding to go into politics. I stood as an independent and won a seat in Port Vila.
>
> My frustration at being an independent led me to form a political party. The name of the party needed to reflect where we came from. It needed to reflect the impetus for my involvement in politics; I called it the *Graon mo Jastis* party [Land and Justice Party].
>
> We won four seats in the 2012 election which meant I could negotiate to become the Minister of Lands early in 2013. That's when the real land reform work began. (Regenvanu, pers comm, Nov 2014)

Catalyzed by Regenvanu's move into politics, the widespread social movement for land reform transformed into support for the Graon mo Jastis Pati that ran on the platform of both ending corruption and implementing the resolutions of the 2006 National Land Summit. In the following election, Regenvanu was able to negotiate to become minister of lands, a position he held from 23 March 2013 to 11 June 2015. At this time, I took on the role as his legal adviser as well as the principal drafter of a substantial land-reform package specifically designed to address the resolutions of the National Land Summit.

As drafting of the new legal arrangements began, our ministry of lands team decided that, given the significance of the reforms and the implications that they would have in peoples' land rights, nationwide consultations would be necessary to ensure that people understood and were supportive of the reforms. Nationwide consultations across Vanuatu were subsequently led by Minister Regenvanu and the president of the Malvatumauri, Chief Seniomao Tirsupe, with a total of twenty-five separate consultation meetings held in Bislama in various provinces over key aspects of the laws. Separate consultations were also held with the legal, business, banking, and investment communities. Finally, a working group of technical experts was formed to meet regularly to offer drafting input based on key constituencies including representatives from the legal sector, key government agencies, the nongovernment sector, women's groups, youth groups, and business and investor groups. These consultations led to detailed discussions around many of the aspects of the proposed land laws. Numerous areas of the drafting were substantially amended because of consultations both in village-level meetings and in technical working groups.

National consultations across all provinces culminated in a National Land Law Summit held in Port Vila on 16–17 October 2013 and attended by the acting prime minister, Edward Natapei, and other ministers, the president of the Malvatumauri, the director of the Vanuatu Cultural Centre and Vanuatu Cultural Centre field-workers from across the island, representatives from key government departments, and nongovernmental organizations. Delegations of chiefs, women, and youth from all provinces also attended the national meeting. The resolutions from the National Land Law Summit provided support for the package of reforms, as well as suggesting additional changes. The land reforms were also considered at length in detailed consultations with the Malvatumauri who provided their endorsement of the reform package.

Constitutional amendments and new land laws were debated at length in Parliament before being supported by an overwhelming majority of members in December 2013, with the laws coming into effect in February 2014. The land-reform package of 2014 is contained mainly in two pieces of legislation: the Custom Land Management Act to replace the operation of the existing Customary Land Tribunal Act and substantial amendments to the existing *Land Reform Act*. The operation of this new legislation was supported by significant constitutional amendments. The central elements of the land-reform package include: (1) the passing of jurisdiction to customary institutions to make final determinations of disputes and identifying custom landowners; (2) removing the power of the minister over customary land and state land; (3) improvements to the leasing process to require prior informed consent and so as to take account of environmental, planning, and cultural safeguards; and, perhaps most contentiously, (4) the land-reform package recognizes a specific set of *raets* for women including what has been defined as "a *raet* to be heard in the *nakamal*."

Attempts to Decolonize Law

Property is an idea that has remade worlds. Ideas matter, concepts matter. Reflecting on the work of Marilyn Strathern and her statement that "it matters what ideas we use to think other ideas [with]" (1992, 10), Donna Haraway wrote that "it matters what stories make worlds, what worlds make stories" (2016, 12). Property is a concept that has transformed both the landscapes of Oceania and the identities of people belonging to those places. This is true in post-independent Pacific nations, just as it was true in colonial times. Masculine performances of property endure within the contemporary garb of landownership. They are staged across Melanesia often at the behest of logging, mining, and gas companies. In Vanuatu, the alternately fickle and yet global tides of capital create landscapes saturated with desire, commodified, and resold to foreigners either as beachfront estate or as holiday packages replete with images of "sand, sex, and sea."

The research practice of "staying with the trouble," as mentioned in the introduction (Haraway 2016), means attention to the neocolonial, capitalist configurations that inform the trouble and the damage that they bring. Anna Tsing argued, in her own reflections on our damage to the planet, that we need to reconfigure the idea of the Anthropocene so as to draw attention, not to the "human" or the *"anthropo,"* but rather, with the advent of capitalism and its associated environmental destruction, to "imagining the human since the rise of capitalism entangles us with ideas of progress and with the spread of the techniques of alienation that turn both humans and other beings into resources" (2015, 19). This involves the removal of kin, the essence of becoming alone. Imposed ideas of property represent a point of rupture in Indigenous spiritual, emotional, intellectual, and embodied practices of belonging to land. Processes of Indigenous dispossession center on the remaking of land into property.

In this book, staying with the trouble has involved a deep dive into property and how it has the potential to reconfigure Indigenous relationships to land. It involves acknowledging that colonial relations endure and are instrumental in ways of seeing and knowing the world, even in supposedly postcolonial regions such as Oceania and Africa. Returning to the famous words of Sethy Regenvanu, "Land as the Mother," that began this book, the quote follows: "For ni-Vanuatu, land is more than a simple commodity to be used for gain and to be disposed of when it has been stripped of its value. [For ni-Vanuatu] Land is an intrinsic part of themselves and their whole being" (1980, 67). Property is a central tenet of Indigenous dispossession in that it allows for land to be remade into a commodity able to be purchased. In Vanuatu, landscapes previously held under custom governance structures become parceled individualized units of property held under Torrens Title registration. Law continues to define Indigenous relationships to land, thereby impacting being and belonging as well as political power and sovereignty. Attempts to decolonize law must challenge the authority of legal systems that remain centrally informed by colonial legacies.

Historically in Vanuatu there has only been very limited recognition of custom and customary institutions in the constitution and the legal system. Recognition of customary processes and institutions within Vanuatu's legal system has been tempered by the continuation of the previous Anglo-Australian common law system post-independence. This follows global trends in which many postcolonial legal institutional arrangements have remained informed by colonial legacies, which then provide the "matrix in which consciousness, identity, and life chances take shape" (Merry and Brenneis 2003, 26). Many postcolonial legal systems are characterized by a lack of recognition of customary law and existing customary institutions. Recognition of customary law in Vanuatu has also been further limited in part because the legislature and judiciary have failed to provide guidance as to how the recognition of customary practice and institutions could occur (Forsyth 2009). This has implications for the practical operation of legal arrangements with respect to land, namely how property law creates legal identities that enable powerful men to manipulate their individual "landownership" claims to land, as well as entrench their personal authority.

Efforts to decolonize legal arrangements must begin with land. The starting point for drafting new legal arrangements with respect to land should be an acknowledgment that all institutions—formal and customary—have strengths and weaknesses. As discussed earlier, Vanuatu has historically been characterized by a plurality of state institutions, rather than deep legal pluralism that would allow recognition of customary institutions and the role of chiefs in resolving land disputes. Vanuatu's land reforms of 2014 were an attempt to decolonize law, creating new spaces for the jurisdiction and authority of customary institutions within the existing legal institutional architecture of the Vanuatu state. To do this, I drafted constitutional amendments to allow *nakamals,* or customary institutions, the power in law to both identify landowners for customary land across Vanuatu and make final and binding determinations of land disputes.

Nationwide consultations on the land-reform package highlighted widespread support for the use of *nakamals* to determine land disputes. This was supported by earlier findings of three reviews of the operation of the customary land tribunal, which all indicated widespread, popular support for the use of *nakamals* to resolve land disputes. The resolutions from the National Land Law Summit read:

- We want *nakamals* to be the authority to make decisions about customary land ownership in Vanuatu.
- We want the Constitution to be clear that decisions about the ownership and use of customary land must be made under customary law and not in formal courts. (Resolutions, National Land Law Summit, Port Vila, 16–17 Oct 2013)

In practice, *nakamals* exist across Vanuatu as customary institutions operating as seats of governance for particular areas. Members of a *nakamal* include all men, women, and children who come under the governance jurisdiction of that *nakamal.* Women are specifically named as members of the *nakamal* within the drafting to avoid any claims that women are not allowed to attend meetings of the *nakamal.* A *nakamal* may be related to a single landowning group or an extended family group, or it may be related to a number of landowning groups or extended family groups living in a village or larger area. Given the immense cultural and linguistic diversity of Vanuatu with around one hundred different languages, there are many different vernacular language words for the term *nakamal* in different localities including *farea* in parts of Efate, *gamal* in parts of Malekula, *naumel* in Motalava, and *jaranmoli* in parts of Santo.

Support for *nakamals* was based partly on their perceived accessibility relative to state courts. Formal state-based courts remain largely inaccessible to rural people and women, and young people in particular. One of the major criticisms of previous arrangements was that a person with resources could appeal through the levels of tribunal and court arrangements, winning their case against others who did not have resources to pursue the dispute (Simo and Van Trease 2011). Access to higher courts in Vanuatu involves the payment of expensive legal fees. Large areas of land have been leased in Vanuatu without recompense to the rightful custom landowners who have not had the opportunity to access legal assistance. At present there is no free legal advice service to custom owners in Vanuatu, and land-related matters represent a substantial area of work for most lawyers. The Custom Land Management Act includes limited rights of appeal on grounds of improper process: for example, a meeting not being held correctly. But it requires that final binding determinations that identify custom-owner groups can only be made by *nakamals*. As Minister Regenvanu explained, "The new laws bring determination of custom owners back to customary institutions, it removes the power from courts and the government to determine who the custom owners are and puts it back under rules of custom" (pers comm, April 2014).

Widespread support for *nakamals* was also closely related to a desire for the use of customary law for resolving land disputes. The Custom Land Management Act uses meetings of *nakamals* to both identify custom-owner groups and manage disputes about custom ownership in accordance with the rules of customary law. In national consultations, people voiced opinions that the resolution of land disputes by *nakamals* would allow for recognition of broader sets of land-use and access rights, rather than the win-lose nature of court disputes that often allocate absolute property rights to individuals.

Decolonizing the law to recognize the jurisdiction of *nakamals* to determine land disputes, by removing substantive appeals to formal state courts, required an amendment to the constitution. This was necessary because a previous Court of Appeal decision related to a land dispute resolved by a chiefly tribunal had established that "the only bodies that have lawful jurisdiction and power to make a determination that binds everyone are the Courts" (*Valele Family v Touru* [2002] VUCA 3[1]). The amendment I drafted to Article 78(3) of the constitution states that "the final and substantive decisions reached by customary institutions or procedures... after being recorded in writing, are binding in law and are not subject to any appeal or any review by any Court of law." This constitutional amendment is designed to allow customary institutions to determine landownership and land disputes.

Land is the mother. It was anticipated that the effect of these changes would be that people would meet in *nakamals* and determine their own relationships to land, in accordance with customary law. The new laws represented an attempt to move beyond the model of alienated property held by a single owner, so as to allow for the diverse and complex ties of being and belonging that inform ni-Vanuatu relations to land. Rather than a court process that results in a winner and a loser, *nakamal* processes of deliberation may allow greater recognition for the complex and overlapping relational use rights that so often encompass customary systems of landholding.

Enhancing the Power of Chiefs

Drafted to decolonize the legal system and give effect to legal pluralism, the land-reform package provides further recognition of the authority of chiefs within the state. Chiefly structures are given a number of roles under the Custom Land Management Act, including supervising the processes for identifying custom landowner groups. Passing jurisdiction to *nakamals* is also likely to strengthen the authority of chiefs as the authors and arbiters of customary arrangements with respect to land. On Efate Island, this has the potential to further condense chiefly power over customary land. The Vaturisu Customary Land Laws may prove an ominous portent for the recognition of *kastom* arrangements with respect to land, particularly in relation to matrilineal landholdings and women's *raets*.

The role of chiefs as central pillars of the state is further strengthened by constitutional amendments that ensure a role for the Malvatumauri in reviewing land law. Following the amendments to Article 30, Parliament is obliged to consult with the Malvatumauri before making any changes to land law in Vanuatu. This mandatory requirement to consult means that the Malvatumauri must provide advice on any new laws, and this advice is then tabled in Parliament alongside the proposed bills. These provisions are designed to allow for public awareness of any proposed changes to land laws, as well as consideration by Parliament of the advice of the Malvatumauri before any changes are made.

The role of chiefs as the arbiters of *kastom*—and in particular customary rules with respect to land—is entrenched within the institutions of state by the amendments to Article 30 of the constitution. At the scale of the state, Vanuatu has become a nation of chiefs; chiefs represent their respective area of the archipelago and arbitrate on land law, supposedly in the interests of landowners. The result may be that chiefs influence the legal recognition of "custom" with respect to land in ways that Grace Mera Molisa reminded us could impact on "women / the timid / the ignorant / the weak" (1983, 24). I have described in this book how chiefs often broker relationships with overlapping interests, traversing the different scales of the politics of land transactions. Some chiefs act as masters of modernity, brokering land deals in their villages. Amendments to the constitution may further politicize the role of the Malvatumauri by including them directly in parliamentary processes and the ties that link them not only to the village but also to the broader networks of investor and political influence.

The Obdurate Significance of Custom Landowners

The idea of land as property is, in itself, implicitly constructivist. In this book, I have discussed how the property model informs the legal identity of "custom landownership" and is therefore largely incommensurate with the complex, overlapping access and use rights that inform customary land management. The ideology of landownership amplifies the transactional nature of property; the "customary" becomes entrenched in the territorialization of customary land by the state and the processes of capitalist expansion. The legal identity of "custom landownership" also creates a particular politics of land dealings in Vanuatu. In this process, the rights of larger landowning groups become truncated by land dealings initiated by a small handful of powerful men.

The concept of property profoundly alters the way we see the world. It has the capacity to remake Indigenous identities and cut the socially embedded relationships to place. Ideas matter, concepts matter, as Strathern reminded us (1992, 10), and as Sally Engle Merry stated: "Law is not simply a set of rules exercising coercive power, but a system of thought by which certain forms of relations come to seem natural and taken for granted" (1988, 889). The enduring legacy of the colonial model of property may be that it erodes Indigenous attachments to landscape by changing the way people themselves conceive of their relationships to land. Landownership as a term represents a claim in property to exclusive possession, allowing individuals to own land wholesale that is thereby more easily commodified. Claims of "custom" landownership are increasingly transforming customary relationships to land. On Efate Island, this approach is entrenching patrilineal claims to land and chiefly titles that have historically been understood as grounded in matrilineal descent. Claims to *ples* are also central to women's capacity to assert their authority in *kastom*. The effect of titling and registration has been to ignore women's claims to customary land, even land over which they are understood in *kastom* to hold absolute rights. Together, changes in understandings of "custom" and land leasing have the potential to "cut the network" to place—the binding of people to place and to each other through kinship structures—by eroding women's claims to belonging to the land (Strathern 1996).

Concerned by the distortions created by the ideology of custom landownership, in my initial drafting of the land-reform package I created a broader legal identity attached to landholding rights in an attempt to better accommodate customary land-use practices. The legal identity of a "custom owner" was replaced with the term "landowning group," meaning that a broad group of Indigenous people could be recognized as holding ownership or use rights to an area of land or any adjacent waters. However, this broader legal identity was rejected in consultations on the reform package. Powerful male leaders criticized this definition, arguing that it weakened their constitutional rights as custom owners. The resolution from the National Land Law Summit illustrates the degree to which custom landowner ideology is now entrenched as *the* legal identity attached to Indigenous property rights: "We request changes to the term 'land-owning group' to 'custom owners': and define 'Custom owners' to mean any lineage, family, clan, tribe or other group who are regarded by the rules of custom following the custom of the area in which the land is situated as the perpetual owners of that land and, in those custom areas where an individual person is regarded by custom as able to own customary land, such individual person" (Resolutions, National Land Law Summit, Port Vila, 16–17 Oct 2013). In the drafting of this resolution, many powerful men argued for the retention of individual custom ownership rights over certain parcels of land, particularly on Efate and surrounding islands.

Across Melanesia, the identity of "landowner" remains of obdurate significance in ways that are best described as ideological but that also increasingly shape local agency in the transaction of land and other resources. Masters of modernity dominate the negotiation of benefits from large-scale resource extraction projects, just as they monopolize payments from the leasing and rental of customary land. More and more, the ideology of custom landownership is influencing the ways in which *kastom* is defined, as seen in the Vaturisu Council of Chiefs' Customary Land Laws. The elision of *kastom* as custom means that manufactured legal identities are increasingly framing local articulations of Indigenous agency, and these in turn distort conceptions of *ples*.

Allowing for individual ownership of customary land may enable an individual man (a *masta-mi*) to once more lease land that in custom belongs to a group of people, although attempts have been made in the drafting of the new law to ensure that the processes of land leasing are broadened beyond the decisions of a powerful individual man. The amendments to the *Land Reform Act* include strict, free, prior, informed-consent processes consistent with the United Nations Declaration of the Rights of Indigenous Peoples requirements contained in Article 10 (UNDRIP 2007). To ensure proper consultations with custom landowners, applications for negotiation certificates must contain significantly more information (see Part 6A), and they must be written in Bislama. The amendments include a new role for a land ombudsman to provide administrative oversight of *nakamal* and leasing processes to ensure that all processes have complied with the requirements of the Acts. Rights of appeal to the land ombudsman are included to ensure the leasing process meets the strict requirements of the process laid out in the *Land Reform Act*. The new leasing processes also require that environmental, planning, and cultural safeguards be met. Together, these processes aim to ensure a more thorough leasing process with decision-making over leasing, subdivisions, or changes to the type of lease made by the landowning group.

Mapping the Middle: Women's *Raets* in New Land Reforms

Women in Vanuatu want to be involved in decisions about land. The land transactions detailed in this book illustrate the gendered nature of land leasing in Vanuatu, with masculine claims often obscuring both women's *raets* over land and matrilineal landholding arrangements. The land-reform package attempts to find a middle path—"to map the middle"—between recognition of customary institutions dominated by powerful men and the international obligations imposed on the Vanuatu State to recognize the "rights" of women (Merry 2006b). A series of safeguards have been included in the land-reform package in an attempt to allow the voices of women and young people, in particular, to be heard in meetings of *nakamals*.

The new land-reform package recognizes a specific set of *raets* for women linked to consent to the leasing of land and other processes. Consent processes included in the *Land Reform Act* require that "any other community or group of indigenous citizens that may be affected by the agreement must have had an adequate opportunity to express its views to the custom owner group." These affected groups "must include, but are not limited to all *women* [emphasis added] and young people living in the area concerned, any indigenous citizens who are not custom owners and any community in whose locality the land is situated" (see 6J[8]). Where this requirement is not met, the affected group can appeal to the land ombudsman. This drafting ensures that women are given a *raet* to be heard in the *nakamal*. This is a relational *raet* recognizing that women need to be part of the decision-making process rather than an assertion of individualist human "rights" in a formal legal sense. Elsewhere the legislation specifically includes women in key processes. This drafting ensures that the legislation does not reinscribe gender privilege and that "custom owners" cannot be simply understood as masculine possessive individuals.

Allowing women the *raet* to speak in the *nakamal* remained extremely contentious in discussions of the land-reform package among powerful men. In consultations with the Malvatumauri, many chiefs remained opposed to these sections of the reforms, claiming that it was not *kastom* for women to speak in the *nakamal*. Speeches about land are overwhelmingly given by men. However, some women can and do speak in *nakamals*. Offering women the opportunity to express themselves in the *nakamal* permits women a space to exercise their own agency. Allowing for these grounded *raets* of women to speak in a *nakamal* may support those who do speak, as well as challenge ideas so often proffered by chiefs that women cannot speak about land. Finally, the drafting is designed to support all women, not just *women-ples*, to speak about land. These rights also extend to young people, to other ni-Vanuatu who are not custom owners (people who married into families or *man kam*), and to other community groups, perhaps church groups, who may be affected by the decision.

Who Are the Real Masters?

Struggles over resources produce winners and losers. At the scale of the village, I have termed the handful of powerful men who dominate the transaction of customary land "masters of modernity." These men lease land not only for access to cash and as a pathway to modernity but also as a claim of power and authority over other men. Masters of modernity exist across Oceania and perhaps broader afield. Engaged in brokering deals with outsiders, it is these men who negotiate trustee arrangements with logging companies in Solomon Islands or who sit on the boards of incorporated land groups in PNG receiving the lion's share of royalty payments. These are the men who extract the majority of the benefits that accrue to "landowners" from resource extraction projects. Increasingly, they are also the men who either negotiate agreements with settlers in receipt of payments or initiate what are often violent processes to evict others from land. As a group of men, they are dynamic, skillful, and opportunistic, able to manipulate the custom and modern arenas in their own interests. They exhibit oratorical prowess and are often positioned as the "spokesmen" for Indigenous groups co-opting locals and outsiders alike in their attempts to garner power over rivals.

Property is enacted within the architecture of power. Real estate investment, with its often indeterminate value and potential for appreciation, provides opportunities for money laundering and criminal activities. In Vanuatu, the speculative land market operates in parallel with the country's status as a tax haven with financial capital held by a privileged few expatriate and settler elites. The clandestine economy of land dealings occurs in part because of the windfall profits that can be made by investors from property transactions. These investors are, in turn, willing to make illicit payments to state actors who help to facilitate property transactions over customary and state land. Ministers of lands have historically played a dual role: as the supposed regulators of land dealings and as rent seekers who personally benefit from dealings in land (McDonnell 2017). As a result of this dual role, development, planning, and environmental regulations are regularly subverted through alliances of investors with politicians (McDonnell 2017).

In Vanuatu, the processes of land transformation are often dominated by Indigenous actors who move seamlessly between their various roles as custom landowners, chiefly brokers, middlemen facilitating land transactions, Department of Lands staff, members of Parliament, and ministers. But we must also ask: who are the ultimate winners, who are the "masters" who made the most gains from the land rush in Vanuatu? While Indigenous actors are often inveigled into transacting land, they are generally performing property at the behest of investors. Former Minister of Lands Regenvanu described the operation of the clandestine economy in Vanuatu, "All Ministers of Lands have been involved in accepting payments from investors. It happens across other Ministries as well: you want something, you pay. But Lands and Public Works [Ministries] are the most obvious areas where payments by investors are made" (interview, Nov 2014).

Distinctions between illegal and legal acts or licit and illicit payments become blurred when the actors are legitimized by the authority of the state. Regenvanu described the exchange of illicit payments for consent to property transactions: "In the Ministry of Lands it is about leases being signed. Some Ministers have been very transparent, they tell investors, 'You pay and you get a signature.' The bigger the project, the bigger you are [as an investor], the more money you have, then the more you pay" (interview, Nov 2014).

Land transactions are staged at various locations across Port Vila and Luganville. Various high-end restaurants are renowned as meeting places between key ministers and investors. The stage for the performance of leasing generally involves a lunch with the minister, a bottle or two of wine, and a cash payment exchanged for signatures on various lease instruments. Almost 40 percent of all registered leases in Vanuatu are missing key lease terms, including the following: the lessor, term of the lease, year of registration, lease type, and area under lease. This suggests a widespread and long-term subversion of the proper legal and administrative processes associated with formal registration of legal instruments (Scott and others 2012). Consent to leases, transfers, and subdivisions by ministers of lands have been available—at a price—and there is widespread discussion of land deals facilitated through the Department of Lands and ministers' offices.

Removing the powers of the minister of lands to lease customary land breaks the legal identity so central to the governance of customary land by the state. These changes were extremely difficult to achieve politically and are a major contribution of the land-reform package, as described by Regenvanu:

> The first hurdle was to remove the power of the Minister, and this was always going to be the most difficult and politically sensitive hurdle to overcome, which is why it had not been overcome by successive governments despite this being a principal recommendation of the Land Summit years ago.
>
> There have been no new leases over customary land since the package came into effect, through the new process. The land-reform package has slowed things down and made creating a lease over customary land a much more thorough process. It has ensured that communities have control over their land again, and no one is just going to take it away. There is now consideration by custom-owner groups around how they want to deal with their own land.
>
> Now that we have removed the unilateral and unfettered powers of the Minister of Lands, which have resulted in so much customary land being leased against

> the wishes of custom owners and local communities, and now that the constitution requires the government to consult with the chiefs before making any further changes to the land laws, I feel we have now securely established a new paradigm for dealing with the leasing of customary land into the future. (pers comm, Nov 2014)

Political support for the passing of the land-reform package shows that it is possible for government to act against the interests of influential investors engaged in speculative land dealing. Ensnared in patronage networks, politicians are often viewed as responsible for villages of constituents and are themselves Indigenous landowners. National consultations generated broad-based popular support for the land-reform package and provided the political momentum for reform. As the momentum for land reform grew, politicians proved responsive to constituents, including many politicians who had previously been implicated in customary land dealings or partnerships with investors.

Pendulum Swings and the Politics of Land Reform

The 2013 land reforms passed with the support of over two-thirds of the members of Parliament. But, some months after the passing of the reform package, the political currents changed when a new Kilman-led government was instated. The new minister of lands, Paul Telukluk, discussed the importance of repealing the land-reform package so as to "boost economic development," pointing again to the ongoing influence of the shadow state in the space of land reform (G Ligo 2015). These attempts at repealing the land reforms stalled in October 2015 when Telukluk was found guilty of accepting a bribe—along with many of his other parliamentary colleagues.

In discussions around land reform, we need a continual reminder that law reforms can only ever be part of the solution to complex societal problems. I remain wary of the way that legislation is touted as the response to almost every development issue in the Pacific region (Forsyth 2014). Political processes, operating at the levels of the state and the village, will dictate the degree to which legislative reform will translate into practice. Laws are easily sidestepped or changed by political actors. Similarly, laws can easily be disregarded in village politics and chiefly determinations, which are made largely beyond the ambit of the state. Accordingly, changing land laws is only part of the solution, albeit an important part. Altering legal identities can change the means of transacting land, at least for a period of time. Ultimately, legal arrangements must be supported by broader social and political change.

Politically engaged anthropology retains the tension of working in practical spaces. Those of us involved in writing law must always be conscious that we can exacerbate the problems of institutional arrangements or provide even less access to justice for "the timid and the weak." The land-reform package is far from perfect, but hopefully it offers a better prospect than the rapacious land leasing that occurred before the reforms were instituted.

Decolonization as Practice: Returning Land to Indigenous Control

Decolonization is not a metaphor (Tuck and Yang 2012). At its core, the practice of decolonial research and activism involves a commitment to the principles of Indigenous self-determination and to the repatriation of Indigenous land. Eve Tuck and Wayne Tang argued that "decolonization specifically requires the repatriation of Indigenous land and life" (2012, 21). Beginning with our understanding of land as sovereignty, it is clear that all acts of decolonization, as well as attempts at creating alternative development pathways that center on Indigenous self-determination, must begin with returning land to Indigenous control. Globally various contemporary movements such as those organized around "Land Back" or "Idle No More" call for, among other things, the return of public land to Indigenous control (LANDBACK 2021). Increasingly, these global voices are joining in songs with those in Oceania, building on existing coalitions, such as the Melanesian Indigenous Land Defence Alliance (MILDA), that strongly oppose the alienation of land and sea from customary landowners and who met in 2014 on Lelepa Island. Here, the scales of the story collide; where better to hold a meeting of a regional group of Melanesian land rights activists than in a location that had seen so much rapacious leasing? Increasingly a flourishing collection of global, transnational, and national movements of activists convene in person, or on social media, creating spaces of political engagement both outside and occasionally, as occurred in Vanuatu, within the spaces of government.

As I finish writing this book (May 2021) three new bills have been introduced to Parliament by the Vanuatu government that provide significant amendments to the 2014 Land Reform Package. The explanatory memorandum written to describe the purpose of each of the bills discusses the need for amendments that "provide a platform for the Government policy of developing the productive sector and utilizing lease [*sic*] as a tool for development." The 2014 land laws are understood as impeding development and the interests of people who hold leases, such that the rights of custom landowners must be now wound back accordingly. To supposedly enable development, the proposed amendments remove the power of customary institutions—*nakamals*—to resolve landownership over custom land when there is an application for a negotiator's certificate to lease land. They also hand significant powers to the minister of lands, while at the same time significantly impacting on the rights of Indigenous custom landowners to engage in processes of free, prior, informed consent over the issuing of a negotiation certificate or a lease over their land.

In the 2014 package, all powers were removed from the minister of lands so that they could no longer be abused, and land could no longer be leased without the consent or knowledge of the custom landowner group. The new laws return the powers to the minister to consent to a lease, meaning that the minister will again have the power to sign consent to a lease agreement on behalf of a custom landowning group in place of members of the group signing themselves.

And, in response to this latest pendulum swing in the land-reform debate, there comes another act of refusal. A coalition of civil-society groups has formed to oppose the latest amendments. The chairs of the Vanuatu Association of Non-Government Organizations, the Vanuatu Council of Churches, the Vanuatu National Council of Women, the Vanuatu Cultural Centre, the Vanuatu Youth Council, the Melanesian Indigenous Land Defence Alliance, and the director of the Vanuatu Cultural Council jointly wrote to the Malvatumauri asking that the minister of lands and the president of the Republic not support the amendments on the grounds that they are unconstitutional and will have major impacts on Indigenous land rights. As I write this conclusion, it is uncertain what the outcome of all these moving parts will be. It is unclear if the amendments will pass and come into law or not.

So, to return to the questions that I began with: what then do acts of refusal mean in postcolonial self-governing Indigenous territories? Increasingly, acts of refusal function as claims of Indigenous sovereignty against the operation of a relational state, operations that so often dominate the politics of Melanesian nation-states in ways that undermine the formal institutions of government. Acts of refusal challenge the clandestine economy and the actions of state actors and investors who engage in land dealings over customary and state land. They are acts of protest, of resettlement, of criticism, of *nakaemas*. And they are acts of song. They are directed at the powerful leaders involved in transacting land in ways that benefit few and dispossess many.

It seems that the story that began with a song is not yet over. These latest bills are a reminder that the work of returning land to Indigenous control is never done. Decolonization is not a metaphor; it is an ongoing process, and, in the midst of it all, the constant reminder that land is life.

Notes

Introduction: My Land, My Life

Song lyrics translated from Bislama by the author in consultation with Stan Antas and Ralph Regenvanu.

1. In 2013, I worked with Professor Don Patterson and the State Law Office to redraft the Strata Titles Act so that the act no longer allowed for the subdivision of land and instead applied only to buildings (1B Strata Titles [Amendment] Act 2013 [No 8 of 2013]).

2. See *Ifira Trustees Ltd v Kalsakau* [2007] VUSC 119, Civil Case 183-06 (14 Nov 2007); Office of the Ombudsman, *Public Report on the Improper Sale of Government Houses by the Office of the Prime Minister under the Former Prime Minister Maxime Carlot Korman* [1998] VUOM 7 (3 March 1998); Office of the Ombudsman, *Public Report on the Granting of Leases by the Former Minister of Lands Mr Paul Barthelemy Telukluk to Himself, Family Members and Wantoks* [1999] VUOM 6 (22 April 1999); Office of the Ombudsman, *Public Report on the Improper Granting of Land Lease Title 11/OE22/016 by the Department and Ministry of Lands* [1998] VUOM 10 (9 April 1998); Office of the Ombudsman, *Public Report on the Mismanagement of the Tender Sale of the Ten (10) Deportees' Properties by the Former Minister of Lands, Mr Paul Telukluk* [1999] VUOM 9 (28 May 1999); Office of the Ombudsman, *Public Report on the Conduct of Messrs Vohor, Dope and Boulekone Regarding an Attempt to Contract with Volani International Ltd* [1998] VUOM 4 (20 Feb 1998); Office of the Ombudsman, *Public Report on the Improper Conduct by Government Officials in dealing with Mondragon's Proposed Free Trade Zone in Big Bay, Santo* [2001] VUOM 3 (6 Sept 2001).

3. A$1 is approximately US$.67.

4. One Vanuatu vatu (VT) is approximately US$.01.

Chapter 1: Reciprocity as a Fugitive Anthropologist

1. Journal entries and interview transcriptions have been lightly edited for style and consistency.

2. *Nakamals* is a colloquial term for places where kava is drunk, and it also has a more formal meaning as a chief's house. Sometimes this is the same place, but often these are physically separate places.

Chapter 2: Weaving Narratives of Place

1. After much local discussion, these titles have been adapted in discussion with Lelepa people from the titles described in works by Guiart (2013) and Rawlings (1999a, 77–78). My discussion is based largely on detailed interviews with Lelepa chiefs and senior *kastom* knowledge holders conducted between June 2012 and October 2018.

Chapter 3: Performing Property, Throwing Silver Dollars

1. In 1849, just a year after Geddie sailed into the harbor, the commander of HMS *Havannah* found a deep, calm anchorage between Lelepa and Moso Islands and thereby named the waters after his ship (Miller 1981, 90).
2. Land Appeal Case 01 of 2002 (26 April 2002).

Chapter 4: Custom Landownership a Frankenstein Corpse?

1. Civil Appeal Case 11 of 2007 (30 Nov 2007).
2. Land Appeal Case 021 of 1984 (21 May 1986).

Chapter 5: The Frontier of Desire

1. While I provided legal assistance, the case was led in Vanuatu by Garry Blake. See *Monvoisin v Mormor* [2019] VUCA 6; Civil Appeal Case 1935 of 2018 (22 Feb 2019).
2. For example, before 2015 when customary land was leased, a stamp duty fee of 7 percent was payable to the Government of Vanuatu. However, if customary land was held by a company, the stamp duty fee was only 4 percent, creating an incentive for investors to create a company to hold the lease title over customary land. One legal firm in Vanuatu advised its clients that "many properties in Vanuatu are held in company names" (Geoffrey Gee and Partners and Ashurst 2014). Land reforms that I drafted in 2015 were designed to address this inconsistency.

Chapter 6: The Masters of Modernity

1. *Peter Taurakoto, Chief Arier Kaltang v Chief Nearutalo Napalaunaot, North West Efate Area Customary Land Tribunal,* Land Appeal case No 1 of 2003. The Arier chiefly title dispute has been heard in four different customary and legal institutions, demonstrating the institutional pluralism that existed in dealing with land disputes prior to 2014.

Chapter 7: Mama Graon

1. This analogy is an extension of women in the Pacific "falling through the net" of informal networks of social protection, such as that provided by customary tenure (see discussion in Jolly and others 2015).
2. *Family Protection Act* (No 28 of 2008).

Conclusion: Refusal: Attempts to Decolonize Law

1. Civil Appeal Case 01 of 2002 (26 April 2002).

Glossary

The Glossary is mainly Bislama and Lelepa language words. Lelepa language entries have been marked with "(L)" and Papua New Guinea tok pisin "(PNG tok pisin)."

aelan dres	island dress
aina (*kanaka maoli*)	land
aku	stand up
alenan vanua (Sia Raga)	the correct ways and ideas belonging to the place
antap	to *go antap,* meaning to claim authority over another man
atafi (L)	assistant chief
atafi kutu (L)	assistant chief "mosquito"
blad laen	patrilineal descent
boes	plantation workers
evri man hemi tink tink wan-wan	we are in a new time of individuality
fakalé	someone who acts like a mother, someone who cares for the children or the people
fanua tabu	land is sacred
farea (L)	word for *nakamal* on Efate
fasin blong stil	a new behavior of stealing land from others
filwoka	field-worker
gamal	word for *nakamal* in parts of Malekula
girl-Lelepa	younger woman from Lelepa
"God i givim ples ia long yumi"	"God gave the land to us"
go finis	leaving ceremony
graon hemi finis	the land is finished
graon hemi kaekae yu	the land will eat you
Graon mo Jastis Pati	Land and Justice Party
jaranmoli	word for *nakamal* in parts of Santo
karam (L)	sugarcane
karaw (L)	clamshell
kastom	tradition
kastom gavnans	customary governance
kastom hemi laef yet	*kastom* continues to animate the day-to-day lives of the people
kay (L)	shellfish
kilim ting ting blong yu	kill your thinking

kindamuna (L)	all of us together
lakantamas (L)	a stone
laopeania (L)	claim that if you plant food or fruit trees on land that is not held under a chiefly title, you can hold rights to the land
lawya	lawyer
lawya blong yumi	our lawyer
levsepsep (L)	little people
likol kliniks	legal clinics
luk save	see and consider
makaru (L)	arrowroot
malu (L)	wild yam
man-kam	a person from another *ples*
man-Lelepa	being from Lelepa Island
man-ples	the correct and proper way of behaving as an emplaced person; literally a man belonging to the land
man-Vila	being from Port Vila
mase/masei	star
mastas	masters
mau (L)	workman of the chief
mi-nomo	men who engage in leasing thinking only of themselves; only
munawae (L)	sorcerer
mwalala (L)	dancing ground
naflak	matriclan; matrilineal kinship
naflak nawita (L)	octopus matriclan
nakaemas	sorcery
nakainanga (L)	totemic system
nakamal	place where kava is drunk; chief's house; seat of customary governance
namale	very culturally significant tree—leaves are sacred and are used to mark *tabu* or sacred places
namarakiana	description in Pango of village areas of land held under *naflak* matriclans
namarwan (L)	dream or vision
namataisu (L)	chief's carver
nambanga	banyan tree
nanu (L)	coconut
napeas (L)	slit gongs
napetaw (L)	breadfruit
nasautonga (L)	annual payment of homage
natale (L)	taro
natamate (L)	power of ancestors
natamwate (L)	feast
natkar (L)	chiefly power
naumel	word for *nakamal* in Motalava
nawi (L)	yam
nawota (L)	chief
nefao (L)	tree
ol tabu ples	important cultural sites

paoa blong ol jifs i ko daon the power of all chiefs is diminishing
pasinja meri (PNG tok pisin) passenger women
patnanu (L) chiefly anointment
paumaso (L) land gifted to women, usually practiced as the gifting of land from a father to a daughter on her marriage
ples place
pounakar (L) a type of stinging nettle that wherever it is planted will put down roots and grow
powa/paoa power
raets rights
rispek respect
road blong moni think only about money
rong (L) basket
saloa (L) a wooden plate representing shared access and use rights to land
savi possessing knowledge not generally accessible about how to conduct land sales and other business transactions
sengalengale *levsepsep;* little people
silowa Southern Efate spelling of *saloa*
stampa inner truth; literally trunk of a tree
stap kwaet shut up and be quiet
stret fasion real meaning
stret fasion blong onem wan kastomary graon the proper way of owning customary land
strong hed stubborn; not likely to give way
switin sweeten
swit maot sweet mouth
swit tok sweet talk
tabu prohibition or ban; sacred
taem bifo time before
taem blong tu dak the time of heathen “darkness”
Taloa devil spirit
tasinga (L) the ear of the chief
turn turnem hed blong yu change your mind
vanua land or place
Vanua‘aku Pati Vanua‘aku Party; Our Land Party
vatu (L) stone
wan-wan (one-one) rights belonging to an individual person, usually a man
wantoks “one-talk” from the same language group, family, or tribe
wita/weita (L) octopus
wita loa (L) black octopus
wita taw (L) red octopus
woman-ples the correct and proper way of behaving as an emplaced woman; literally a woman belonging to the land.
yumi evriwan all of us

References

Abu-Loghod, Lila

2013 *Do Muslim Women Need Saving?* London: Harvard University Press. https://doi.org/10.4159/9780674726338

Alexeyeff, Kalissa, and Siobhan McDonnell

2018 Whose Paradise? Encounter, Exchange, and Exploitation. *The Contemporary Pacific* 30:269–297.

Allen, Jafari S, and Ryan Cecil Jobson

2016 The Decolonization Generation (Race and) Theory in Anthropology since the Eighties. *Current Anthropology* 57:129–148. https://doi.org/10.1086/685502

Allen, Michael

1981 Introduction. In *Vanuatu: Politics, Economics and Ritual in Island Melanesia,* edited by Michael Allen, 1–8. Sydney: Academic Press.

Articles of the Australian Association of the New Hebrides Company

1889 National Library of Australia (NLA), Canberra.

Arutangai, Selwyn

1987 Vanuatu: Overcoming the Colonial Legacy. In *Land Tenure in the Pacific,* edited by Ronald G Crocombe, 261–302. Suva: University of the South Pacific.

Arvin, Maile, Eve Tuck, and Angie Morrill

2013 Decolonizing Feminisms: Challenging Connections between Settler Colonialism and Heteropatriarchy. *Feminist Formations* 25 (1):8–34. https://doi.org/10.1353/ff.2013.0006

Bainton, Nicholas A

2008 Men of *Kastom* and the Customs of Men: Status, Legitimacy and Persistent Values in Lihir, Papua New Guinea. *The Australian Journal of Anthropology* 19:194–212. https://doi.org/10.1111/j.1835-9310.2008.tb00122

2010 *The Lihir Destiny: Cultural Responses to Mining in Melanesia.* Canberra: ANU E Press. http://doi.org/10.22459/LD.10.2010

Ballard, Chris

2013 "It's the Land Stupid!" The Moral Economy of Resource Ownership in Papua New Guinea. In *The Governance of Common Property in the Pacific Region,* edited by Peter Larmour, 47–66. Canberra: ANU E Press.

Ballard, Chris, and Meredith Wilson
2012 Unseen Monuments: Managing Melanesian Cultural Landscapes. In *Managing Cultural Landscapes,* edited by Jane Lennon and Ken Taylor, 130–153. Oxford: Routledge.

Bani, Ernest
2008 Environmental Impact Assessment Report for Commercial Subdivision (Shefa Permit No 117/07) at Mangaliliu West Efate, Shefa Province, Republic of Vanuatu. Bani's Environmental Consultants.

Banivanua Mar, Tracey, and Penelope Edmonds
2010 Introduction: Making Space in Settler Colonies. In *Making Settler Colonial Space,* 1–24. London: Palgrave Macmillan.

Banner, Stuart
2005 Preparing to Be Colonized: Land Tenure and Legal Strategy in Nineteenth-Century Hawaii. *Law & Society Review* 39:273–314. https://doi.org/10.1111/j.0023-9216.2005.00083.x
2009 *How the Indians Lost Their Land: Law and Power on the Frontier.* Cambridge, MA: Harvard University Press.

Bear, Laura, Karen Ho, Anna Lowenhaupt Tsing, and Sylvia Yanagisako
2015 Gens: A Feminist Manifesto for the Study of Capitalism. Editors' Forum: Theorizing the Contemporary. *Society for Cultural Anthropology,* 30 March. https://culanth.org/fieldsights/gens-a-feminist-manifesto-for-the-study-of-capitalism [accessed 31 March 2021]

Bedford, Stuart, Patricia Siméoni, and Vincent Lebot
2017 The Anthropogenic Transformation of an Island Landscape: Evidence for Agricultural Development Revealed by LiDAR on the Island of Efate, Central Vanuatu, South-West Pacific. *Archaeology in Oceania* 53:1–14. https://doi.org/10.1002/arco.5137

Beliso-De Jesús, Aisha M, and Jemima Pierre
2020 Special Section: Anthropology of White Supremacy. *American Anthropologist* 122:65–75. https://doi.org/10.1111/aman.13351

Bell, Diane
2002 "Writing in the Eye of a Storm": Response to Gaynor Macdonald's Review Article on *Ngarrindjeri Wurruwarrin. Australian Journal of Anthropology* 13:219–223. https://doi.org/10.1111/j.1835-9310.2002.tb00201.x

Benjaminsen, Tor A, and Espen Sjaastad
2002 Race for the Prize: Land Transactions and Rent Appropriation in the Malian Cotton Zone. *The European Journal of Development Research* 14 (2): 129–152. https://doi.org/10.1080/714000423

Berry, Maya J, Claudia Chávez Argüelles, Shanya Cordiz, Sarah Ihmoud, and Elizabeth Velásquez Estrada
2017 Towards a Fugitive Anthropology: Gender, Race, and Violence in the Field. *Cultural Anthropology* 32:537–565. https://doi.org/10.14506/ca32.4.05

Blomley, Nicholas
1998 Landscapes of Property. *Law and Society Review* 32:567–612.
2003 Law, Property, and the Geography of Violence: The Frontier, the Survey, and the Grid. *Annals of the Association of American Geographers* 93:121–141. https://doi.org/10.1111/1467-8306.93109

2005 Remember Property? *Progress in Human Geography* 29:125–127. https://doi.org/10.1191/0309132505ph535xx

2013 Performing Property: Making the World. *Canadian Journal of Law and Jurisprudence* 26:23–48. https://doi.org/10.1017/S0841820900005944

Bolton, Lissant

1998 Chief Willie Bongmatur Maldo and the role of Chiefs in Vanuatu. *The Journal of Pacific History* 33:179–195. https://doi.org/10.1080/00223349808572869

1999 Women, Place and Practice in Vanuatu: A View from Ambae. *Oceania* 70:43–55. https://doi.org/10.1002/j.1834-4461.1999.tb02988.x

2003 *Unfolding the Moon: Enacting Women's Kastom in Vanuatu.* Honolulu: University of Hawai'i Press. https://doi.org/10.1515/9780824865405

2009 *Women and Customary Land Tenure in Vanuatu: The Influence of Expatriate Thinking.* Port Vila: Vanuatu Cultural Centre.

Borras, Saturnino M, Jr, and Jennifer Franco

2010 Towards a Broader View of the Politics of Global Land Grab: Rethinking Land Issues, Reframing Resistance. *Initiatives in Critical Agrarian Studies (ICAS)* Working Paper Series No 001.

Bratrud, Tom

2021 Asserting Land, Estranging Kin: On Competing Relations of Dependence in Vanuatu. *Oceania* 91 (2):280–295.

Bridge, Captain Cyprian

1882 Letter to the Western Pacific High Commission, 16 August. Correspondence, Western Pacific Archives (WPA), University of Auckland.

Brodkin, Karen, Sandra Morgen, and Janis Hutchinson

2011 Anthropology as White Public Space? *American Anthropologist* 113:545–556. https://doi.org/10.1111/j.1548-1433.2011.01368.x

Burnett, Mark, Charlie Parsons, and Jeff Probst, executive producers

2004 *Survivor: Vanuatu—Islands of Fire. Survivor* television series 9. Aired 15 September–12 December on CBS.

Butler, Judith

1990a Gender Trouble, Feminist Theory, and Psychoanalytic Discourse. In *Feminism/Postmodernism,* edited by Linda Nicholson, 324–340. New York: Routledge.

1990b *Gender Trouble: Feminism and the Subversion of Identity.* London: Routledge.

Capell, A

1938 The Stratification of Afterworld Beliefs in the New Hebrides. *Folklore* 49:51–85. https://doi.org/10.1080/0015587X.1938.9718729

Connell, Raewyn, and James W Messerschmidt

2005 Hegemonic Masculinity: Rethinking the Concept. *Gender & Society* 19:829–859. https://doi.org/10.1177/0891243205278639

Cotula, Lorenzo

2013 The New Enclosures? Polanyi, International Investment Law and the Global Land Rush. *Third World Quarterly* 34:1605–1629. https://doi.org/10.1080/01436597.2013.843847

Cotula, Lorenzo, Nat Dyer, and Sonja Vermeulen

2008 *Fuelling Exclusion? The Biofuels Boom and Poor People's Access to Land.* Rome: International Institute for Environment and Development.

Cummings, Maggie
2013 Looking Good: The Cultural Politics of the Island Dress for Young Women in Vanuatu. *The Contemporary Pacific* 25:33–65. https://doi.org/10.1353/cp.2013.0007

Davis and Campbell Solicitors
1906 Letter to the Director, French New Hebrides Company, Vila, Efate Presbyterian Archives (PA), Mitchell State Library, New South Wales (NSW).

Davis, Heather, and Zoe Todd
2017 On the Importance of a Date, or Decolonizing the Anthropocene. *ACME: An International Journal for Critical Geographies* 16 (4):761–780.

Deininger, Klaus W
2003 *Land Policies for Growth and Poverty Reduction: A World Bank Policy Research Report.* Washington, DC: World Bank Publications.

Delisle, Jennifer Bowering
2003 Surviving American Cultural Imperialism: *Survivor* and Traditions of Nineteenth-Century Colonial Fiction. *The Journal of American Culture* 26:42–55. https://doi.org/10.1111/1542-734X.00072

Demian, Melissa
2007 Land Doesn't Come from Your Mother, She Didn't Make It with Her Hands: Challenging Matriliny in Papua New Guinea. In *Feminist Perspectives on Land Law,* edited by Hillary Lim and Anne Bottomley, 155–171. Abingdon: Routledge-Cavendish.

Derrida, Jacques
1990 Force of Law: The "Mystical Foundation of Authority." In *Deconstruction and the Possibility of Justice.* Special issue of *Cardozo Law Review* 11:920–1045.

Don, Alexander
1927 *Peter Milne (1834–1924): Missionary to Nguna, New Hebrides, 1870 to 1924, from the Presbyterian Church of New Zealand.* Dunedin: Foreign Missions Committee, Presbyterian Church of New Zealand.

Dvorak, Greg
2008 "The Martial Islands": Making Marshallese Masculinities between American and Japanese Militarism. *The Contemporary Pacific* 20:55–86. https://doi.org/10.1353/cp.2008.0029

Erskine, John Ephinstone
1853 *Journal of a Cruise among the Islands of the Western Pacific, including the Feejees and Others Inhabited by the Polynesian Negro Races, in Her Majesty's Ship Havannah.* London: John Murray, Albemarle Street.

Facey, Ellen E
1981 Hereditary Chiefship in Nguna. In *Vanuatu: Politics, Economics, and Ritual in Island Melanesia,* edited by Michael R Allen, 295–313. Sydney: Academic Press.

Farran, Sue
2002 Land Leases: Research: Ministerial Leases in Efate, Vanuatu. *Journal of South Pacific Law* 6. http://www.paclii.org/journals/fJSPL/vol06/6.shtml [accessed 17 June 2022]

Federal Committee of Presbyterian Missions
1886 Petition to Queen Victoria, Victorian Assembly of the Presbyterian Church, PA, Mitchell State Library, NSW.

Field, Michael

2011 "Shell" Operation Shuts after Crime Links Exposed. *NZ Stuff,* 7 June. http://www.stuff.co.nz/auckland/local-news/5107131/Shell-operation-shuts-after-crime-links-exposed [accessed 11 May 2021]

Filer, Colin

1997 Compensation, Rent and Power in Papua New Guinea. In *Compensation for Resource Development in Papua New Guinea,* edited by Susan Toft, 156–189. Port Moresby: PNG Law Reform Commission; Canberra: The Australian National University.

2006 Custom, Law and Ideology in Papua New Guinea. *The Asia Pacific Journal of Anthropology* 7:65–84. https://doi.org/10.1080/14442210600554499

2007 Local Custom and the Art of Land Group Boundary Maintenance in Papua New Guinea. In *Customary Land Tenure and Registration in Australia and Papua New Guinea: Anthropological Perspectives,* edited by James F Weiner and Katie Glaskin, 135–173. Asia-Pacific Environment Monograph 3. Canberra: ANU E Press. https://doi.org/10.22459/CLTRAPNG.06.2007.08

2011a New Land Grab in Papua New Guinea. *Pacific Studies* 34:269–294.

2011b The New Land Grab in Papua New Guinea: Case Study from New Ireland Province. Discussion paper 2011/2. State Society and Governance in Melanesia, School of International Political Strategic Studies, The Australian National University.

2012 Why Green Grabs Don't Work in Papua New Guinea. *Journal of Peasant Studies* 39:599–617. https://doi.org/10.1080/03066150.2012.665891

Filer, Colin, Siobhan McDonnell, and Matthew G Allen

2017 Powers of Exclusion in Melanesia. In *Kastom, Property and Ideology: Land Transformations in Melanesia,* edited by Siobhan McDonnell, Matthew G Allen, and Colin Filer, 1–55. Canberra: ANU Press. https://doi.org/10.22459/KPI.03.2017.01

Fingleton, Jim

2005 Introduction. In *Privatising Land Tenure in the Pacific: A Defence of Customary Tenures,* edited by Jim Fingleton, 1–6. Discussion Paper Number 80. Canberra: The Australia Institute.

Fiske, Shirley

2009 Global Change Policymaking from Inside the Beltway: Engaging Anthropology. In *Anthropology and Climate Change: From Encounters to Actions,* edited by Susan A Crate and Mark Nuttall, 277–291. Walnut Creek, CA: Left Coast Press, Inc.

Fitzpatrick, Daniel

2005 "Best Practice" Options for the Legal Recognition of Customary Tenure. *Development and Change* 36:449–475. https://doi.org/10.1111/j.0012-155X.2005.00419.x

Forsyth, Miranda

2009 *A Bird That Flies with Two Wings:* Kastom *and State Justice Systems in Vanuatu.* Canberra: ANU E Press. http://doi.org/10.22459/BFTW.09.2009

2014 Navigating the Mythscape of Biodiversity and Associated Traditional Knowledge in Pacific Island Countries. Paper delivered at the Traditional Knowledge Book Symposium, Griffith University, Brisbane, 28 March.

Foster, Robert J
2007 The Work of the New Economy: Consumers, Brands, and Value Creation. *Cultural Anthropology* 22:707–731. https://doi.org/10.1525/can.2007.22.4.707
Foukona, Joseph
2015 Urban Land in Honiara: Strategies and Rights to the City. *The Journal of Pacific History* 50:504–518.
Foukona, Joseph D, and Matthew G Allen
2017 Urban Land in Solomon Islands: Powers of Exclusion and Counter-Exclusion. In *Kastom, Property and Ideology: Land Transformations in Melanesia,* edited by Siobhan McDonnell, Matthew G Allen, and Colin Filer, 85–110. Canberra: ANU Press. https://doi.org/10.22459/KPI.03.2017
Garae, Len
2013 Dinh Says They'll Die in the Country. *Vanuatu Daily Post,* 19 January.
Garanger, José
1982 *Archaeology of the New Hebrides: Contribution to the Knowledge of the Central Islands.* Translated by Rosemary Groube. Oceania Monograph Series 24. Sydney: University of Sydney.
Geddie, John
1848 Diary. Australian Presbyterian Board of Missions, Sydney, NSW.
1868 Petition by John Geddie to the Governor of New South Wales, the Earl of Belmore, London Missionary Society, Box 31.
Geoffrey Gee and Partners and Ashurst
2014 *Vanuatu Property Investment Guide: Hospitality Edition 2014.*
Gewertz, Deborah B, and Frederick K Errington
1999 *Emerging Class in Papua New Guinea: The Telling of Difference.* Cambridge, UK: Cambridge University Press. https://doi.org/10.1017/CBO9780511606120
Gibson-Graham, J K
1996 *The End of Capitalism (As We Knew It).* Oxford: Basil Blackwell.
Golub, Alex
2007 Ironies of Organization: Landowners, Land Registration, and Papua New Guinea's Mining and Petroleum Industry. *Human Organization* 66:38–48. https://doi.org/10.17730/humo.66.1.157563342241q348
2014 *Leviathans at the Gold Mine: Creating Indigenous and Corporate Actors in Papua New Guinea.* Durham, NC: Duke University Press. https://doi.org/10.1515/9780822377399
Gosarevski, Steven, Helen Hughes, and Susan Windybank
2004 Is Papua New Guinea Viable *with* Customary Land Ownership? *Pacific Economic Bulletin* 19 (3):133–136.
Graeber, David
2009 *Direct Action: An Ethnography.* Oakland, CA: AK Press.
Griffiths, John
1986 What Is Legal Pluralism? *The Journal of Legal Pluralism and Unofficial Law* 18 (24):1–55. https://doi.org/10.1080/07329113.1986.10756387
Guiart, Jean
1964 Marriage Regulations and Kinship in the South Central New Hebrides. *Ethnology* 3:96–106. https://doi.org/10.2307/4617558

2004 Retoka Revisited and Roymata Revised: A Retort. *The Journal of the Polynesian Society* 113:377–382.

2009 Notes on Lelepa Island. Unpublished manuscript, provided to Chris Ballard. Canberra: The Australian National University. Copy in author's files.

2013 *Cultures on the Edge: Caught Unwittingly between the White Man's Concepts of Polynesia Opposed to Melanesia.* Papeete: Te Pito o te Fenua.

Hale, Charles R

2006 Activist Research v. Cultural Critique: Indigenous Land Rights and the Contradictions of Politically Engaged Anthropology. *Cultural Anthropology* 21 (1): 96–120. https://doi.org/10.1525/can.2006.21.1.96

Hall, Derek, Phillip Hirsch, and Tania Murray Li

2011 *Powers of Exclusion: Land Dilemmas in Southeast Asia.* Honolulu: University of Hawai'i Press.

Haraway, Donna

2016 *Staying with the Trouble: Making Kin in the Chthulucene.* Durham, NC: Duke University Press. https://doi.org/10.1215/9780822373780

Harvey, David

2003 *The New Imperialism.* Oxford: Oxford University Press.

Hau'ofa, Epeli

2008 *We Are the Ocean: Selected Works.* Honolulu: University of Hawai'i Press. https://doi.org/10.1515/9780824865542

Hromek, Danièle Siân

2019 The (Re)Indigenisation of Space: Weaving Narratives of Resistance to Embed Nura [Country] in Design. PhD thesis, University of Technology Sydney.

Hughes, Helen

2003 Aid Has Failed the Pacific. *Issue Analysis* 33. https://www.cis.org.au/publication/aid-has-failed-the-pacific/ [accessed 17 June 2022]

Hutchinson, R J S

1970 Native Court Held at Pango at 1400 Hours on 26 March 1970 before R.J.S. Hutchinson, President, and Assessors, G. Kalsakau and P. Piolapa. Port Vila, British New Hebrides National Service. British Residency nat/cdi/civ-2/70. File no. bd1/214/6, Land Matters Pango Box 5, National Archives of the Republic of Vanuatu.

Hviding, Edvard

2003 Contested Rainforests, NGOs, and Projects of Desire in Solomon Islands. *International Social Science Journal* 55:539–554. https://doi.org/10.1111/j.0020-8701.2003.05504003.x

Ignatieff, Michael

2003 *Human Rights as Politics and Idolatry.* Princeton, NJ: Princeton University Press.

Imada, Adria L

2011 Transnational *Hula* as Colonial Culture. *The Journal of Pacific History* 46:149–176. https://doi.org/10.1080/00223344.2011.607260

Independent State of Papua New Guinea

1974 Land Groups Incorporation Act 1974.

IPCC, Intergovernmental Panel on Climate Change

2019 *Special Report on Climate Change and Land.* Available from https://www.ipcc.ch/srccl/ [accessed 13 May 2021]

Jacka, Jerry
2015 *Alchemy in the Rain Forest: Politics, Ecology, and Resilience in a New Guinea Mining Area*. Durham, NC: Duke University Press. https://doi.org/10.1215/9780822375012

Jobson, Ryan Cecil
2020 The Case for Letting Anthropology Burn: Sociocultural Anthropology in 2019. *American Anthropologist* 122:259–271. https://doi.org/10.1111/aman.13398

Jolly, Margaret
1992a Custom and the Way of the Land: Past and Present in Vanuatu and Fiji. *Oceania* 62:330–354. https://doi.org/10.1002/j.1834-4461.1992.tb00361.x
1992b Specters of Inauthenticity. *The Contemporary Pacific* 4:49–72.
1994 *Women of the Place:* Kastom, *Colonialism and Gender in Vanuatu.* Amsteldijk: Harwood Academic Publishers.
1996 Women's Rights, Human Rights and Domestic Violence in Vanuatu. *Feminist Review* 52 (1): 169–190. https://doi.org/10.1057/fr.1996.14
2000 Woman Ikat Raet Long Human Raet O No? Women's Rights, Human Rights and Domestic Violence in Vanuatu. In *Human Rights and Gender Politics: Asia-Pacific Perspectives,* edited by Anne-Marie Hilsdon, Martha Macintyre, Vera Mackie, and Maila Stivens, 124–146. London: Routledge. https://doi.org/10.1057/fr.1996.14. Updated and expanded version of prior publication in *Feminist Review* 52 (1996): 169–190. https://doi.org/10.2307/1395780
2008 Moving Masculinities: Memories and Bodies across Oceania. *The Contemporary Pacific* 20:1–24. https://doi.org/10.1353/cp.2008.0010
2012a Introduction—Engendering Violence in Papua New Guinea: Persons, Power and Perilous Transformations. In *Engendering Violence in Papua New Guinea,* edited by Margaret Jolly, Christine Stewart, and Carolyn Brewer, 1–46. Canberra: ANU E Press. http://doi.org/10.22459/EVPNG.07.2012
2012b Material and Immaterial Relations: Gender, Rank and Christianity in Vanuatu. In *The Scope of Anthropology: Maurice Godelier's Work in Context,* edited by Laurent Dousset and Serge Tcherkézoff, 110–154. Methodology & History in Anthropology Series. New York: Berghahn Books.
2016 "When She Cries Oceans": Navigating Gender Violence in the Western Pacific. In *Gender Violence & Human Rights: Seeking Justice in Fiji, Papua New Guinea & Vanuatu,* edited by Aletta Biersack, Martha Macintyre, and Margaret Jolly, 341–380. Canberra: ANU Press. https://doi.org/10.22459/GVHR.12.2016.08

Jolly, Margaret, Helen Lee, Katherine Lepani, Anna Naupa, and Michelle Rooney
2015 Falling Through the Net? Gender and Social Protection in the Pacific. UN Women Discussion Paper 6, September. Available from http://www.unwomen.org/en/digital-library/publications/2015/9/dps-gender-and-social-protection-in-the-pacific [accessed 7 April 2021]

Jubilee History of Presbyterian Church of Victoria
1888 PA, Mitchell State Library, NSW.

Kahn, Miriam
2000 Tahiti Intertwined: Ancestral Land, Tourist Postcard, and Nuclear Test Site. *American Anthropologist* 102:7–26. https://doi.org/10.1525/aa.2000.102.1.7

2003 Tahiti: The Ripples of a Myth on the Shores of the Imagination. *History and Anthropology* 14:307–326. https://doi.org/10.1080/0275720032000156479

2014 "Invest in Your Love": Romantic Desires, YouTube Videos, and the Online Marketing of Tahiti. *Tourist Studies* 14:144–163. https://doi.org/10.1177/1468797614532181

Kalontano, A, C Vatu, and J Whyte

2003 *Assessing Community Perspectives on Governance in the Pacific*. Suva: Foundation of the Peoples of the South Pacific International.

Kawa, Nicholas C, José A Clavijo Michelangeli, Jessica L Clark, Daniel Ginsberg, and Christopher McCarty

2019 The Social Network of US Academic Anthropology and Its Inequalities. *American Anthropologist* 121:14–29. https://doi.org/10.1111/aman.13158

Keesing, Roger M

1982 Kastom in Melanesia: An Overview. *The Australian Journal of Anthropology (Mankind)* 13:297–301. https://doi.org/10.1111/j.1835-9310.1982.tb00994.x.

Kenneth, Dorosthy [Dorosday], and Henlyn Silas

1986 Vanuatu: Traditional Diversity and Modern Uniformity. In *Land Rights of Pacific Women,* edited by Cema Bolabola, Dorosday Kenneth, Henlyn Silas, Mosikaka Moengangongo, Aiono Fana'afi, and Margaret James, 67–85. Suva: Institute of the South Pacific, University of the South Pacific.

Kirksey, Eben

2012 *Freedom in Entangled Worlds: West Papua and the Architecture of Global Power.* Durham, NC: Duke University Press. https://doi.org/10.1515/9780822394761

Kirsch, Stuart

2018 *Engaged Anthropology: Politics beyond the Text.* Oakland: University of California Press. https://doi.org/10.1525/california/9780520297944.001.0001

2002 Anthropology and Advocacy: A Case Study of the Campaign against the Ok Tedi Mine. *Critique of Anthropology* 22:175–200. https://doi.org/10.1177/03075X02022002851

Kraemer, Daniela

2020 Planting Roots, Making Place: Urban Autochthony in Port Vila Vanuatu. *Oceania* 90 (1):40–54. https://doi.org/10.1002/ocea.5239

LANDBACK

2021 LANDBACK Manifesto. https://landback.org/manifesto/ [accessed 7 Sept 2021]

Latai, Latu

2016 Covenant Keepers: A History of Samoan (LMS) Missionary Wives in the Western Pacific from 1839 to 1979. PhD thesis, The Australian National University.

Lawrence, Salmah Eva-Lina

2013 Gender and Development in Papua New Guinea: Matriliny and Indigenous Best Practice in Gender Relations. MA thesis, Deakin University.

2014 Revisiting "Those Massim Women": Could the Discourse of Gender Equality in PNG Learn from the Massim Experience? Paper prepared for ARC

Laureate project, Engendering Persons, Transforming Things: Christianities, Commodities and Individualism in Oceania. Canberra: The Australian National University.

Layard, John
ca 1915 Notes. Cambridge Library of Anthropology and Archaeology (CLAA).

Leouve, Captain A
1898 Letter to Minister for the Navy. Inwards Correspondence, Western Pacific High Commission (WPHC).

Lepani, Katherine
2012 *Islands of Love, Islands of Risk: Culture and HIV in the Trobriands.* Nashville: Vanderbilt University Press. https://doi.org/10.2307/j.ctv16759zt
2015 "I Am Still a Young Girl if I Want": Relational Personhood and Individual Autonomy in the Trobriand Islands. *Gender and Person in Oceania.* Special issue of *Oceania* 85:51–62. https://doi.org/10.1002/ocea.5073

Lepowsky, Maria
1994 Women, Men, and Aggression in an Egalitarian Society. *Sex Roles* 30:199–211. https://doi.org/10.1007/BF01420990

Levitt, Peggy, and Sally Engle Merry
2011 Making Women's Human Rights in the Vernacular: Navigating the Culture/Rights Divide. In *Gender and Culture at the Limit of Rights,* edited by Dorothy Hodgson, 81–100. Philadelphia: University of Pennsylvania Press. https://doi.org/10.9783/9780812204612.81

Li, Tania Murray
2010 Indigeneity, Capitalism and the Management of Dispossession. *Current Anthropology* 51:385–414. https://doi.org/10.1086/651942
2012 What Is Land? Anthropological Perspectives on the Global Land Rush. Paper presented at the International Conference on Global Land Grabbing II, Cornell University, Ithaca, 17–19 October.
2014 What Is Land? Assembling a Resource for Global Investment. *Transactions of the Institute of British Geographers* 39:589–602. https://doi.org/10.1111/tran.12065

Ligo, Godwin
2012a Forari Sublease Best for Landowners. *Vanuatu Daily Post,* 10 January.
2012b Vanuatu Land Developer Assaulted over New Project. *Vanuatu Daily Post,* 18 January.
2015 Telukluk Outlines Five Lands Ministry Priorities. *Vanuatu Daily Post,* 27 June.

Ligo, Joe
2011 *Report of Complaints of Alleged Corruption in the Ministry of Lands and the Department of Lands.* Port Vila: Ministry of Lands.

Lindstrom, Lamont
1997 Chiefs in Vanuatu Today. In *Chiefs Today: Traditional Pacific Leadership and the Postcolonial State,* edited by Geoffrey White and Lamont Lindstrom, 211–228. Stanford, CA: Stanford University Press.
2008 Melanesian *Kastom* and Its Transformations. *Anthropological Forum* 18:161–178. https://doi.org/10.1080/00664670802150208

LiPuma, Edward
1994 Sorcery and Evidence of Change in Maring Justice. *Ethnology* 33:147–163. https://doi.org/10.2307/3773894

1998 Modernity and Forms of Personhood in Melanesia. In *Bodies and Persons: Comparative Perspectives from Africa and Melanesia,* edited by Michael Lambeck and Andrew Strathern, 53–79. Cambridge, UK: Cambridge University Press. https://doi.org/10.1017/CBO9780511802782.003

1999 The Meaning of Money in the Age of Modernity. In *Money and Modernity: State and Local Currencies in Melanesia,* edited by David Akin and Joel Robbins, 192–213. Pittsburgh, PA: University of Pittsburgh Press.

LJ Hooker Vanuatu

2014 Efate Havannah Harbour-Havannah Estates Fantastic Investment High Growth Area. Real Estate Efate.

2021 Havannah Harbour - ID: 158119: Elite Waterfront Block. Property listing. https://www.ljhooker.vu/Listing.aspx?Id=ef09f002-a832-4746-a6b2-717b6764040a [accessed 7 Sept 2021]

Low, Setha M, and Sally Engle Merry

2010 Engaged Anthropology: Diversity and Dilemmas. An Introduction to Supplement 2. *Current Anthropology* 51 (S2):S203–S226. https://doi.org/10.1086/653837

Luders, David

2001 Retoka Revisited and Roimata Revised. *The Journal of the Polynesian Society* 110:247–287.

MacClancy, Jeremy

1983 Vanuatu and Kastom: A Study of Cultural Symbols in the Inception of a Nation State in the South Pacific. DPhil thesis, Oxford University.

Macdonald, Daniel [Rev]

1875 *The Labour Traffic versus Christianity in the South Sea Islands.* Melbourne: ML Hutchinson.

1878 *The Labour Traffic Versus Christianity in the South Sea Islands.* Melbourne: ML Hutchinson.

1887 Letter to the Foreign Mission Committee, 17 August. Western Pacific Archives (WPA), University of Auckland.

1893 Journal of the *Dayspring. Annual Report of the New Hebrides Mission, 1893–1902.* PA, Mitchell State Library, NSW.

1898 Journal of the *Dayspring. Annual Report of the New Hebrides Mission, 1893–1902.* PA, Mitchell State Library, NSW.

Macintyre, Martha

2012 Gender Violence in Melanesia and the Problem of Millennium Development Goal No. 3. In *Engendering Violence in Papua New Guinea,* edited by Margaret Jolly, Christine Stewart, and Carolyn Brewer, 239–266. Canberra: ANU E Press. https://doi.org/10.22459/EVPNG.07.2012.08

Macpherson, C B

1962 *The Political Theory of Possessive Individualism: Hobbes to Locke.* Oxford, UK: Oxford University Press.

Macpherson, C B, editor

1978 *Property: Mainstream and Critical Positions.* Toronto: University of Toronto Press. https://doi.org/10.3138/9781442627918

Maetala, Ruth

2008 Matrilineal Land Tenure Systems in the Solomon Islands: The Cases of Guadalcanal, Makira and Isabel Provinces. In *Land and Women: The*

Matrilineal Factor: The Cases of the Republic of the Marshall Islands, Solomon Islands and Vanuatu, edited by Elise Huffer, 35–72. Suva: Pacific Islands Forum Secretariat.

MANLEP Investment Ltd

2011 Minutes of MANLEP Investment Ltd, 27 June. Copy in author's files.

Marx, Karl

1887 *Capital: A Critique of Political Economy. Volume I, Book One: The Process of Production of Capital.* Translated by Samuel Moore and Edward Aveling, edited by Frederick Engels. https://www.marxists.org/archive/marx/works/download/pdf/Capital-Volume-I.pdf [accessed 9 April 2021]. Originally published as *Das Kapital: Kritik der politischen Oekonomie, vol 1.* Hamburg: Verlag von Otto Meisner, 1867.

McDonnell, Siobhan

2013 Exploring the Cultural Power of Land Law in Vanuatu: Law as a Performance that Creates Meaning and Identities. *Intersections: Gender and Sexuality in Asia and the Pacific* 33. http://intersections.anu.edu.au/issue33/mcdonnell.htm [accessed 8 April 2021]

2015 "The Land Will Eat You": Land and Sorcery in North Efate, Vanuatu. In *Talking it Through: Responses to Sorcery and Witchcraft Beliefs and Practices in Melanesia,* edited by Miranda Forsyth and Richard Eves, 137–160. Canberra: ANU E Press. https://doi.org/10.22459/TIT.05.2015.08

2017 Urban Land Grabbing by Political Elites: Exploring the Political Economy of Land and the Challenges of Regulation. In *Kastom, Property and Ideology: Land Transformations in Melanesia,* edited by Siobhan McDonnell, Matthew G Allen, and Colin Filer, 283–305. Canberra: ANU Press. https://doi.org/10.22459/KPI.03.2017.09

2018 Selling "Sites of Desire": Paradise in Reality Television, Tourism and Real Estate Promotion in Vanuatu. *The Contemporary Pacific* 30:413–437. https://doi.org/10.1353/cp.2018.0033

2020 Other Dark Sides of Resilience: Politics and Power in Community-Based Efforts to Strengthen Resilience. In *Naturalising Disaster in the Pacific,* guest edited by Chris Ballard, Maëlle Calandra, and Siobhan McDonnell. Special issue of *Anthropological Forum* 30:55–72. https://doi.org/10.1080/00664677.2019.1647828

McDonnell, Siobhan, and Ralph Regenvanu

2022 Decolonization as Practice: Returning Land to Indigenous Control. *AlterNative: An International Journal of Indigenous Peoples* 18 (2):235–244.

McDougall, Debra

2011 Church, Company, Committee, Chief: Emergent Collectives in Rural Solomon Islands. In *Managing Modernity in the Western Pacific,* edited by Mary Patterson and Martha Macintyre, 121–146. St Lucia: University of Queensland Press.

McGarry, Dan

2016 Coming Clean. *Vanuatu Daily Post,* 6 April. https://dailypost.vu/opinion/editorials/coming-clean/article_73b04fea-d42a-5194-b989-69f0fa17d3bd.html [accessed 11 May 2021]

Mera Molisa, Grace

1983 Custom. In *Black Stone: Poems,* 24–25. Suva: Mana Publications.

Merry, Sally Engle
1988 Legal Pluralism. *Law and Society Review* 22:869–896. https://doi.org/10.2307/3053638
1999 *Colonizing Hawai'i: The Cultural Power of Law.* Princeton, NJ: Princeton University Press.
2001 Changing Rights, Changing Culture. In *Culture and Rights: Anthropological Perspectives,* edited by Jane K Cowan, Marie-Bénédicte Dembour, and Richard A Wilson, 31–55. Cambridge, UK: Cambridge University Press. https://doi.org/10.1017/CBO9780511804687.004
2006a New Legal Realism and the Ethnography of Transnational Law. *Law & Social Inquiry* 31:975–995. https://doi.org/10.1111/j.1747-4469.2006.00042.x
2006b Transnational Human Rights and Local Activism: Mapping the Middle. *American Anthropologist* 108:38–51. https://doi.org/10.1525/aa.2006.108.1.38
2009 Relating to the Subjects of Human Rights: The Culture of Agency in Human Rights Discourse. In *Law and Anthropology: Current Legal Issues, Volume 12,* edited by Michael Freeman and David Napier, 385–407. Oxford: Oxford University Press. https://doi.org/10.1093/acprof:oso/9780199580910.003.0015

Merry, Sally Engle, and Donald L Brenneis
2003 *Law & Empire in the Pacific: Fiji and Hawai'i.* Oxford: James Currey Publishers.

Meyer, Manulani Aluli
2014 Indigenous and Authentic: Hawaiian Epistemology and the Triangulation of Meaning. In *Handbook of Critical and Indigenous Methodologies,* edited by Norman K Denzin, Yvonna S Lincoln, and Linda Tuhiwai Smith, 217–232. Thousand Oaks, CA: Sage Publications. https://doi.org/10.4135/9781483385686.n11

Miller, J Graham
1981 *Live: A History of Church Planting in the New Hebrides, Now the Republic of Vanuatu to 1880.* Book 2. Sydney: Presbyterian Church of Vanuatu.
1987 *Live: A History of Church Planting in the Republic of Vanuatu.* Book 5. Sydney: Presbyterian Church of Vanuatu.
2001 *Live: A History of Church Planting in the New Hebrides to 1880.* Book 1. Sydney: Presbyterian Church of Vanuatu.

Monson, Rebecca
2010 Women, State Law and Land in Peri-Urban Settlements on Guadalcanal, Solomon Islands. *Justice for the Poor Briefing Note* 4 (3). http://www-wds.worldbank.org/external/default/WDSContentServer/WDSP/IB/2010/05/07/000020953_20100507115121/Rendered/PDF/544240Briefing1Guadalcanal1SolIslds.pdf [accessed 9 April 2021]
2011 Negotiating Land Tenure: Women, Men and the Transformation of Land Tenure in the Solomon Islands. In *Traditional Justice: Practitioners' Perspectives Working Papers* 1:1–21. Rome: International Development Law Organisation.
2012 Hu Nao Save Tok? Women, Men and Land: Negotiating Property and Authority in the Solomon Islands. PhD thesis, The Australian National University.

Moreton-Robinson, Aileen

2013 Towards an Australian Indigenous Women's Standpoint Theory, A Methodological Tool. *Australian Feminist Studies* 28 (78):331–347. https://doi.org/10.1080/08164649.2013.876664

Mormor, Kalkot

2005 Strange News: The Story of My Life from Birth. Unpublished paper. Mangaliliu Village, Vanuatu. Copy in author's files.

Morrell, W P

1960 *Britain in the Pacific Islands.* Oxford: Clarendon.

Mosko, Marc

2010 Partible Penitents: Dividual Personhood and Christian Practice in Melanesia and the West. *Journal of the Royal Anthropological Institute* 16:215–240. https://doi.org/10.1111/j.1467-9655.2010.01618.x

Mosse, David

2005 *Cultivating Development: An Ethnography of Aid Policy and Practice.* London: Pluto Press.

2015 Misunderstood, Misrepresented, Contested? Anthropological Knowledge Production in Question? *Focaal: Journal of Global and Historical Anthropology* 72:128–137. https://doi.org/10.3167/fcl.2015.720111

Nakata, Martin, Victoria Nakata, Sarah Keech, and Reuben Bolt

2012 Decolonial Goals and Pedagogies for Indigenous Studies. *Decolonization: Indigeneity, Education & Society* 1 (1):120–140.

Narayan, Kirin

1993 How Native Is a "Native" Anthropologist? *American Anthropologist* 95:671–686. https://doi.org/10.1525/aa.1993.95.3.02a00070

Naupa, Anna

2017 Making the Invisible Seen: Putting Women's Rights on the Agenda. In *Kastom, Property and Ideology: Land Transformations in Melanesia,* edited by Siobhan McDonnell, Matthew G Allen, and Colin Filer, 305–326. Canberra: ANU Press. https://doi.org/10.22459/KPI.03.2017.10

Naupa, Anna, and Joel Simo

2008 Matrilineal Land Tenure in Vanuatu: *Hu I Kaekae Long Basket?* Case Studies of Raga and Mele. In *Land and Women: The Matrilineal Factor: The Cases of the Republic of the Marshall Islands, Solomon Islands and Vanuatu,* edited by Elise Huffer, 73–119. Suva: Pacific Islands Forum Secretariate.

Neil-Jones, Marc

2011 Ligo Alleges "Dirty Deals" at Samoa Point. *Vanuatu Daily Post.*

O'Connell, Daniel Patrick

1968 Condominium of the New Hebrides. *The British Yearbook of International Law* 43:1–145.

Patterson, Mary

2006 Finishing the Land: Identity and Land Use in Pre- and Post-Colonial North Ambrym. In *Sharing the Earth, Dividing the Land: Land and Territory in the Austronesian World,* edited by Thomas Reuter, 323–344. Canberra: ANU Press.

Peluso, Nancy Lee

2012 What's Nature Got to Do with It? A Situated Historical Perspective on Socio-natural Commodities. *Development and Change* 43:79–104. https://doi.org/10.1111/j.1467-7660.2012.01755.x

Peluso, Nancy Lee, and Christian Lund
2011 New Frontiers of Land Control: Introduction. *Journal of Peasant Studies* 38:667–681. https://doi.org/10.1080/03066150.2011.607692
Peters, Julie Stone
2008 Legal Performance Good and Bad. *Law, Culture and the Humanities* 4:179–200. https://doi.org/10.1177/1743872108091473
PG IT Consulting and MMA Consulting
2017 *Vanuatu Paradise.* Originally at: http://vanuatuparadise.com/en/investment/why-invest-in-vanuatu. No longer available.
Philibert, Jean-Marc
1982 Will Success Spoil a Middleman? The Case of Etapang, Central Vanuatu. In *Middlemen and Brokers in Oceania,* edited by William L Rodman and Dorothy Ayres Counts, 187–208. Ann Arbor: University of Michigan Press.
Polanyi, Karl
1944 *The Great Transformation: The Political and Economic Origins of Our Time.* Boston: Beacon Press.
Porter, Raewyn, and Rod Nixon
2010 Wan Lis, Fulap Stori: *Leasing on Epi Island, Vanuatu.* Justice for the Poor Research Report, September. Washington, DC: World Bank Group. https://doi.org/10.1596/27601
Powell, Dana E
2018 *Landscapes of Power: Politics of Energy in the Navajo Nation.* Durham, NC: Duke University Press. https://doi.org/10.1215/9780822372295
Presbyterian Church of Victoria
1886–1908 Correspondence in Relation to the Havannah Harbour Land Case, PA, Mitchell State Library, NSW.
Presbyterian Mission New Hebrides
1864–1892 Annual Report of the Missionary Ship *Dayspring,* Nos. 1–38, which later became the *Annual Report of the New Hebrides Mission, 1893–1902.* PA, Mitchell State Library, NSW.
Rawlings, Gregory E
1999a Foundations of Urbanisation: Port Vila Town and Pango Village, Vanuatu. *Oceania* 70:72–86. https://doi.org/10.1002/j.1834-4461.1999.tb02990.x.
1999b Villages, Islands and Tax Havens: The Global/Local Implications of a Financial Entrepôt in Vanuatu. *Canberra Anthropology* 22:37–50. https://doi.org/10.1080/03149099909508347
2002 "Once There Was a Garden, Now There Is a Swimming Pool": Inequality, Labour and Land in Pango, a Peri-urban Village in Vanuatu. PhD thesis, The Australian National University.
2012 Statelessness, Human Rights and Decolonisation: Citizenship in Vanuatu, 1906–80. *The Journal of Pacific History* 47:45–68. https://doi.org/10.1080/00223344.2011.647397
Regenvanu, Ralph
1999 Afterword: Vanuatu Perspectives on Research. *Oceania* 70:98–100. https://doi.org/10.1002/j.1834-4461.1999.tb02992.x
2011 *Welkam Toktok* (Welcome Speech). In *Working Together in Vanuatu: Research Histories, Collaborations, Projects and Reflections,* edited by John Taylor and Nick Thieberger, 125–132. Canberra: ANU E Press. http://doi.org/10.22459/WTV.10.2011

2013 Response to Letter to the Editor of 17 April. *Vanuatu Daily Post,* 23 April.

Regenvanu, Sethy John

1980 The Land. In *Vanuatu,* 66–81. Christchurch, NZ: University of the South Pacific.

Republic of Vanuatu

1980 Constitution.

1983 *Land Leases Act* (Cap 163).

1988 *Land Reform Act* (Cap 123).

2000 *Strata Titles Act* (Cap 266).

2001 *Customary Land Tribunal Act* (Cap 271).

2006a *National Council of Chiefs* (Organisation) Act (Cap 183).

2006b *Preservation of Sites and Artifacts Act* (Cap 39).

2008 *Family Protection Act 2008* (Act No 28 of 2008).

2013a *Custom Land Management Act* (No 33 of 2013).

2013b *Strata Titles (Amendment) Act* 2013 (No 8 of 2013).

Rigney, Lester-Irabinna

1999 Internationalization of an Indigenous Anticolonial Cultural Critique of Research Methodologies: A Guide to Indigenist Research Methodology and Its Principles. *Wicazo Sa Review: Emergent Ideas in Native American Studies* 14 (2):109–121. https://doi.org/10.2307/1409555

Rio, Knut

2002 The Sorcerer as an Absented Third Person: Formations of Fear and Anger in Vanuatu. *Social Analysis* 46 (3):129–154. https://doi.org/10.3167/015597702782409284

Rodman, Margaret

1995 Breathing Spaces: Customary Land Tenure in Vanuatu. In *Land, Custom and Practice in the South Pacific,* edited by R Gerard Ward and Elizabeth Kingdon, 65–108. Cambridge, UK: Cambridge University Press. https://doi.org/10.1017/CBO9780511597176.004

Rodman, Margaret C

1992 Empowering Place: Multilocality and Multivocality. *American Anthropologist* 94:640–656. https://doi.org/10.1525/aa.1992.94.3.02a00060

Rodman, Margaret Critchlow

1987 *Masters of Tradition: Consequences of Customary Land Tenure in Longana, Vanuatu.* Vancouver: University of British Columbia Press

2001 *Houses Far from Home: British Colonial Space in the New Hebrides.* Honolulu: University of Hawai'i Press.

Rodman, William L, and Dorothy Counts

1983 Introduction. In *Middlemen and Brokers in Oceania,* edited by William L Rodman and Dorothy Counts, 1–33. Ann Arbor: University of Michigan Press.

Rooney, Michelle Nayahamui

2017 "There's Nothing Better than Land": A Migrant Group's Strategies for Accessing Informal Settlement Land in Port Moresby. In *Kastom, Property and Ideology: Land Transformations in Melanesia,* edited by Siobhan McDonnell, Matthew G Allen, and Colin Filer, 111–158. Canberra: ANU Press. https://doi.org/10.22459/KPI.03.2017

Rose, Carol M
1994 *Property and Persuasion: Essays on the History, Theory, and Rhetoric of Ownership*. Boulder, CO: Westview Press.

Rousseau, Benedicta
2008 "This Is a Court of Law not a Court of Morality": *Kastom* and Custom in Vanuatu State Courts. *Journal of South Pacific Law* 12 (2): 15–27.
2017 The Achievement of Simultaneity: Kastom and Place in Port Vila, Vanuatu. *Journal de la Société des Océanistes* 144–145:37–50. https://doi.org/10.4000/jso.7692

Ryle, Gerard
2011 Inside the Shell: Drugs, Arms and Tax Scams. *Sydney Morning Herald,* 15 May. www.icij.org/offshore/geoffrey-taylor [accessed 11 May 2021]

Salesa, Damon
2014 The Pacific in Indigenous Time. In *Pacific Histories: Ocean, Land, People,* edited by David Armitage and Alison Bashford, 31–52. Basingstoke, UK: Palgrave Macmillan.

Sawyer, Suzana
2004 *Crude Chronicles: Indigenous Politics, Multinational Oil, and Neoliberalism in Ecuador.* Durham, NC: Duke University Press. https://doi.org/10.1215/9780822385752

Scheper-Hughes, Nancy
2009 Making Anthropology Public. *Anthropology Today* 25 (4):1–3. https://doi.org/10.1111/j.1467-8322.2009.00674.x

Scott, James C
1998 *Seeing Like a State: How Certain Schemes to Improve the Human Condition Have Failed.* New Haven, CT: Yale University Press.

Scott, Michael W
2007 Neither "New Melanesian History" nor "New Melanesian Ethnography": Recovering Emplaced Matrilineages in Southeast Solomon Islands. *Oceania* 77:337–354. https://doi.org/10.1002/j.1834-4461.2007.tb00020.x

Scott, Sue, Milena Stefanova, Anna Naupa, and Karaeviti Vurobaravu
2012 Vanuatu National Leasing Profile: A Preliminary Analysis. *Justice for the Poor Briefing Note* 7 (1). Port Vila: World Bank.

Shange, Savannah
2020 Discussion in *Transforming Anthropology,* Instagram Live, 3 September. https://www.instagram.com/p/CEpV3mgppgh/ [accessed 3 Sept 2021]

Sikor, Thomas, and Christian Lund
2009 Access and Property: A Question of Power and Authority. *Development and Change* 40:1–22. https://doi.org/10.1111/j.1467-7660.2009.01503.x

Sikor, Thomas, and Daniel Müller
2009 The Limits of State-Led Land Reform: An Introduction. *World Development* 37:1307–1316. https://doi.org/10.1016/j.worlddev.2008.08.010

Simo, Joel
2005 *Report of the National Review of the Customary Land Tribunal Program in Vanuatu.* Port Vila: Vanuatu National Cultural Centre.
2010 Land and the Traditional Economy: "Your Money, My Life." *Hu I Kakae Long Basket Blong Laef?* In *In Defence of Melanesian Customary Land,* edited by Tim Anderson and Cary Lee, 40–44. Sydney: AID/WATCH.

Simo, Joel, and Howard Van Trease
2011 *Report on the Activities of the Vanuatu Customary Land Tribunal and the 2001 Act.* A review commissioned by the New Zealand Agency for International Development for the Government of the Republic of Vanuatu, Port Vila.

Simpson, Audra
2007 On Ethnographic Refusal: Indigeneity, "Voice" and Colonial Citizenship. *Junctures: The Journal for Thematic Dialogue* 9:67–80.
2014 *Mohawk Interruptus: Political Life across the Borders of Settler States.* Durham, NC: Duke University Press.

Slatter, Claire
2006 *The Con/Dominion of Vanuatu? Paying the Price of Investment and Land Liberalisation—A Case Study of Vanuatu's Tourism Industry.* Auckland: Oxfam New Zealand.

Smith, Linda Tuhiwai
1999 *Decolonizing Methodologies.* New York: Zed Books.
2005 On Tricky Ground: Researching the Native in the Age of Uncertainty. In *The Sage Handbook of Qualitative Research,* edited by Norman K Denzin and Yvonna S Lincoln, 85–108. Third edition. Thousand Oaks, CA: Sage Publications.

Smith, Rachel E
2017 From Colonial Intrusions to "Intimate Exclusions": Contesting Legal Title and "Chiefly Title" to Land in Epi, Vanuatu. In *Kastom, Property and Ideology: Land Transformations in Melanesia,* edited by Siobhan McDonnell, Matthew G Allen, and Colin Filer, 327–356. Canberra: ANU Press.

Sope, Barak
1974 *Land and Politics in the New Hebrides.* Suva: South Pacific Social Sciences Association.

Speed, Shannon
2007 *Rights in Rebellion: Indigenous Struggle and Human Rights.* Stanford, CA: Stanford University Press.

Stan and the Earth Force
2013 Stan & The earth force (My land my life) live in Dumbea N-C 2013x. YouTube video, 4:43. Uploaded 19 August. https://www.youtube.com/watch?v=sJw9tDY0itM [accessed 9 April 2021]

Stead, Victoria
2017 *Becoming Landowners: Entanglements of Custom and Modernity in Papua New Guinea and Timor-Leste.* Honolulu: University of Hawai'i Press. https://doi.org/10.1515/9780824856694

Stocking, George W
1992 *The Ethnographer's Magic and Other Essays in the History of Anthropology.* London: University of Wisconsin Press.

Strathern, Marilyn
1988 *The Gender of the Gift: Problems with Women and Problems with Society in Melanesia.* Berkeley: University of California Press. https://doi.org/10.1525/california/9780520064232.001.0001
1992 *Reproducing the Future: Essays on Anthropology, Kinship and the Reproductive Technologies.* Manchester, UK: Manchester University Press.

1996 Cutting the Network. *Journal of the Royal Anthropological Institute* (NS) 2:517–535. https://doi.org/10.2307/3034901

2004 Losing (Out on) Intellectual Resources. In *Law, Anthropology, and the Constitution of the Social: Making Persons and Things,* edited by Alain Pottage and Martha Mundy, 201–233. Cambridge, UK: Cambridge University Press. https://doi.org/10.1017/CBO9780511493751.007

Sydney Morning Herald

2006 Investigators Turn to Treasure Islands. 9 September. https://www.smh.com.au/business/investigators-turn-to-treasure-islands-20060909-gdocqg.html [accessed 25 Aug 2021]

Sykes, Karen

2007a Interrogating Individuals: The Theory of Possessive Individualism in the Western Pacific. *Anthropological Forum* 17:213–224. https://doi.org/10.1080/00664670701637669

2007b The Moral Grounds of Critique: Between Possessive Individuals, Entrepreneurs and Big Men in New Ireland. *Anthropological Forum* 17:255–268. https://doi.org/10.1080/00664670701637727

Tamaira, A Marata

2010 From Full Dusk to Full Tusk: Reimagining the "Dusky Maiden" through Visual Arts. *The Contemporary Pacific* 22:1–35. https://doi.org/10.1353/cp.0.0087

Taylor, John P

2006 The Ways of the Land-Tree: Mapping the North Pentecost Social Landscape. In *Sharing the Earth, Dividing the Land: Territorial Categories and Institutions in the Austronesian World,* edited by Thomas Reuter, 299–322. Canberra: ANU Press. http://doi.org/10.22459/SEDL.10.2006

2008a Changing Pacific Masculinities: The "Problem" of Men. *The Australian Journal of Anthropology* 19:125–135. https://doi.org/10.1111/j.1835-9310.2008.tb00117.x

2008b *The Other Side: Ways of Being and Place in Vanuatu.* Pacific Island Monograph Series. Honolulu: University of Hawai'i Press. https://doi.org/10.21313/hawaii/9780824833022.001.0001

2008c The Social Life of Rights: "Gender Antagonism," Modernity and *Raet* in Vanuatu. In *Changing Pacific Masculinities,* edited by John P Taylor. Special issue of *The Australian Journal of Anthropology* 19:165–178. https://doi.org/10.1111/j.1835-9310.2008.tb00120.x

2015 Sorcery and the Moral Economy of Agency: An Ethnographic Account. *Oceania* 85:38–50. https://doi.org/10.1002/ocea.5072

2016 Two Baskets Worn at Once: Christianity, Sorcery and Sacred Power in Vanuatu. In *Christianity, Conflict, and Renewal in Australia and the Pacific,* edited by Fiona Magowan and Carolyn Schwarz, 139–160. International Studies in Religion and Society Series 26. Leiden, The Netherlands: Brill Publishers. https://doi.org/10.1163/9789004311459_009

2017 Pikinini in Paradise: Photography, Souvenirs and the "Child Native" in Tourism. In *Touring Pacific Cultures,* edited by Kalissa Alexeyeff and John Taylor, 361–378. Canberra: ANU Press. https://doi.org/10.22459/TPC.12.2016.24

Taylor, John, and Nick Thieberger
2011 Editors' Introduction. In *Working Together in Vanuatu: Research Histories, Collaborations, Projects and Reflections,* edited by John P Taylor and Nick Thieberger, xxv–xxx. Canberra: ANU E Press. http://doi.org/10.22459/WTV.10.2011

Taylor, John, and Nick Thieberger, editors
2011 *Working Together in Vanuatu: Research Histories, Collaborations, Projects and Reflections.* Canberra: ANU E Press. http://doi.org/10.22459/WTV.10.2011

Teaiwa, Teresia
1994 bikinis and other s/pacific n/oceans. *The Contemporary Pacific* 6:87–109.

Thomas, Julian
1887 Letter to Sir Charles Mitchell, Governor of Fiji and High Commissioner to Western Pacific, 20 July. Western Pacific Archives, University of Auckland.

Thomas, Nicholas
1992 The Inversion of Tradition. *American Ethnologist* 19:213–232. https://doi.org/10.1525/ae.1992.19.2.02a00020

Thompson, Roger C
1970 Australian Imperialism and the New Hebrides, 1862–1922. PhD thesis, The Australian National University.
1981 Natives and Settlers on the New Hebrides Frontier, 1870–1900. *Pacific Studies* 5:1–18.

Toa, Evelyne
2011 New MANLEP Joint-Venture at Havannah Harbour. *Daily Post,* 3 May.

Todd, Zoe [zoetodd]
2016 An Indigenous Feminist's Take on the Ontological Turn: "Ontology" Is Just Another Word for Colonialism. *Journal of Historical Sociology* 29:4–22. https://doi.org/10.1111/johs.12124
2018 Should I Stay or Should I Go? *Anthro{dendum},* 12 May. https://anthrodendum.org/2018/05/12/should-i-stay-or-should-i-go/ [accessed 3 Sept 2021]

Tonkinson, Robert
1981a Church and Kastom in Southeast Ambrym in Vanuatu. In *Vanuatu: Politics, Economics and Ritual in Island Melanesia,* edited by Michael R Allen, 237–267. Sydney: Academic Press.
1981b Sorcery and Social Change in Southeast Ambrym, Vanuatu. *Social Analysis* 8:77–88.
1982a Kastom in Melanesia: Introduction. *The Australian Journal of Anthropology* 13:302–305. https://doi.org/10.1111/j.1835-9310.1982.tb00995.x
1982b National Identity and the Problem of Kastom in Vanuatu. *The Australian Journal of Anthropology* 13:306–315. https://doi.org/10.1111/j.1835-9310.1982.tb00996.x

Tor, Roselyn, and Anthea Toka
2004 *Gender, Kastom & Domestic Violence: A Research on the Historical Trend, Extent and Impact of Domestic Violence in Vanuatu.* Port Vila: Department of Women's Affairs.

TransPacific
2011 Letter to Lelema Council of Chiefs, 29 November. Copy in author's files.

Trask, Haunani-Kay
1991 Lovely Hula Lands: Corporate Tourism and the Prostitution of Hawaiian Culture. *Border/Lines* 23 (July).
Trau, Adam M, Chris Ballard, and Meredith Wilson
2014 *Bafa Zon:* Localising World Heritage at Chief Roi Mata's Domain, Vanuatu. *International Journal of Heritage Studies* 20:86–103. https://doi.org/10.1080/13527258.2012.712981
Tsing, Anna Lowenhaupt
2000 Inside the Economy of Appearances. *Public Culture* 12:115–144. https://doi.org/10.1215/08992363-12-1-115
2003 Natural Resources and Capitalist Frontiers. *Economic and Political Weekly* 38:5100–5106. https://doi.org/10.2307/4414348
2005 *Friction: An Ethnography of Global Connection.* Princeton, NJ: Princeton University Press. https://doi.org/10.1515/9781400830596
2015 *The Mushroom at the End of the World: On the Possibility of Life in Capitalist Ruins.* Princeton: NJ: Princeton University Press. https://doi.org/10.2307/j.ctvc77bcc
Tuck, Eve, and K Wayne Yang
2012 Decolonization Is not a Metaphor. *Decolonization: Indigeneity, Education & Society* 1 (1):1–40.
2014a R-Words: Refusing Research. In *Humanizing Research: Decolonizing Qualitative Inquiry with Youth and Communities,* edited by Django Paris and Maisha T Winn, 223–248. Los Angeles: SAGE Publications.
2014b Unbecoming Claims: Pedagogies of Refusal in Qualitative Research. *Qualitative Inquiry* 20:811–818. https://doi.org/10.1177/1077800414530265
Tuck, Eve, Marcia McKenzie, and Kate McCoy
2014 Land Education: Indigenous, Post-Colonial, and Decolonizing Perspectives on Place and Environmental Education Research. *Environmental Education Research* 20:1–23. https://doi.org/10.1080/13504622.2013.877708
UNDRIP
2007 United Nations Declaration of the Rights of Indigenous Peoples (A/RES/61/295).
UNESCO, United Nations Educational, Scientific and Cultural Organization
1972 Convention Concerning the Protection of the World Cultural and Natural Heritage. Paris, 16 November. https://whc.unesco.org/archive/convention-en.pdf [accessed 19 Dec 2022]
2008 Examination of Nomination of Natural, Mixed and Cultural Properties to the World Heritage List—Chief Roi Mata's Domain (Vanuatu). Decision 32 COM 8B.27. https://whc.unesco.org/en/decisions/1488/ [accessed 17 October 2022]
United Nations General Assembly
1979 Resolution 34/180, "Convention on the Elimination of All Forms of Discrimination against Women [CEDAW]," 18 December. New York. www.ohchr.org/EN/ProfessionalInterest/Pages/CEDAW.aspx [accessed 30 March 2016]
Uperesa, Lisa
2016 A Decolonial Turn in Anthropology? A View from the Pacific. Savage Minds: Notes and Queries in Anthropology, 7 June. *Decolonizing Anthropology* 6.

Van Fossen, Anthony B
2012 *Tax Havens and Sovereignty in the Pacific Islands.* Brisbane: University of Queensland Press.
Van Trease, Howard
1984 The History of Land Alienation. In *Land Tenure in Vanuatu,* edited by Peter Larmour, 17–30. Suva: Institute of Pacific Studies, University of the South Pacific, and University of the South Pacific Extension Centre.
1987 *The Politics of Land in Vanuatu: From Colony to Independence.* Suva: University of the South Pacific.
Vanuatu Daily Post
2013 Letter to the Editor. 17 April.
Vaturisu Council of Chiefs
2007 Vaturisu Customary Land Laws. Number 7 Conference, Efate Council of Chiefs, Imere Village Efate Vaturisu Kastomari Land Loa. *Namba 7 Konfrens blong Efate Vaturisu Kaonsel Blong Ol Jifs: Imere Vilij 12–16 February.*
VNSO, Vanuatu National Statistics Office
2009 *2009 National Census of Population and Housing—Data Collected for Lelepa Island.* Port Vila: National Census Office.
2016 *2016 Mini Census Report* (Shefaa [*sic*]). Port Vila: National Census Office.
2020 *2020 National Population and Housing Census: Basic Tables Report—Volume 1.* Noumea: Pacific Community. Available from https://sdd.spc.int/digital_library/vanuatu-2020-national-population-and-housing-census-basic-tables-report-volume-1 [accessed 15 December 2022]
von Benda-Beckmann, Franz
2002 Who's Afraid of Legal Pluralism? *The Journal of Legal Pluralism and Unofficial Law* 34 (47):37–82. https://doi.org/10.1080/07329113.2002.10756563
von Benda-Beckmann, Keebet
1981 Forum Shopping and Shopping Forums: Dispute Processing in a Minangkabau Village in West Sumatra. *The Journal of Legal Pluralism and Unofficial Law* 13 (19):117–159. https://doi.org/10.1080/07329113.1981.10756260
von Benda-Beckmann, Franz, Keebet von Benda-Beckmann, and Melanie Wiber
2006 The Properties of Property. In *Changing Properties of Property,* edited by Franz von Benda-Beckmann, Keebet von Benda-Beckmann, and Melanie Wiber, 1–39. Oxford: Berghahn Books.
Vuti, A, J Simo, G Mavromantis, J Kanawi, and Don Patterson
2005 *Review of the Customary Land Tribunal.* Port Vila: NZAID.
Wagner, Roy
1967 *The Curse of Souw: Principles of Daribi Clan Definition and Alliance in New Guinea.* Chicago: University of Chicago Press.
1977 Analogic Kinship: A Daribi Example. *American Ethnologist* 4:623–642. https://doi.org/10.1525/ae.1977.4.4.02a00030
Wardlow, Holly
2002 Headless Ghosts and Roving Women: Specters of Modernity in Papua New Guinea. *American Ethnologist* 29:5–32. https://doi.org/10.1525/ae.2002.29.1.5
2006 *Wayward Women: Sexuality and Agency in a New Guinea Society.* Berkeley: University of California Press. https://doi.org/10.1525/9780520938977

2019 With AIDS I Am Happier Than I Have Ever Been Before. *The Australian Journal of Anthropology* 30:53–67. https://doi.org/10.1111/taja.12304

Weiner, James F, and Katie Glaskin

2007 Customary Land Tenure and Registration in Papua New Guinea and Australia: Anthropological Perspectives. In *Customary Land Tenure and Registration in Australia and Papua New Guinea: Anthropological Perspectives,* edited by James F Weiner and Katie Glaskin, 1–14. Asia-Pacific Environment Monograph 3. Canberra: ANU E Press. https://doi.org/10.22459/CLTRAPNG.06.2007.01

Welcome, Leniqueca A

2020 After the Ash and Rubble Are Cleared: Anthropological Work for a Future. *American Anthropologist,* 28 May. https://www.americananthropologist.org/commentaries/welcome-after-the-ash [accessed 3 Sept 2021]

West, Paige

2006 *Conservation Is Our Government Now: The Politics of Ecology in Papua New Guinea.* Durham, NC: Duke University Press. https://doi.org/10.1215/9780822388067

2016 Introduction. In *Dispossession and the Environment: Rhetoric and Inequality in Papua New Guinea.* New York: Columbia University Press.

White, Geoffrey M

1992 The Discourse of Chiefs: Notes on a Melanesian Society. *The Contemporary Pacific* 4:73–108.

Whyte, Kyle

2017 Indigenous Climate Change Studies: Indigenizing Futures, Decolonizing the Anthropocene. *English Language Notes* 55 (1–2):153–162.

Wolfe, Patrick

2006 Settler Colonialism and the Elimination of the Native. *Journal of Genocide Research* 8 (4):387–409.

World Bank

2011 *Jastis Blong Evriwan* (JBE): Vanuatu. *Pacific Islands Justice for the Poor: Promoting Equity and Managing Conflict in Development.*

Wright, Alexis

2016 What Happens When You Tell Somebody Else's Story? *Meanjin Quarterly,* Summer. https://meanjin.com.au/essays/what-happens-when-you-tell-somebody-elses-story/ [accessed 7 April 2021]

Zoomers, Annelies

2010 Globalisation and the Foreignisation of Space: Seven Processes Driving the Current Global Land Grab. *Journal of Peasant Studies* 37:429–447. https://doi.org/10.1080/03066151003595325

Zorn, Jean

2012 Engendering Violence in the Papua New Guinea Courts: Sentencing in Rape Trials. In *Engendering Violence in Papua New Guinea,* edited by Margaret Jolly, Christine Stewart, and Carolyn Brewer, 163–196. Canberra: ANU E Press. https://doi.org/10.22459/EVPNG.07.2012.05

Index

Page numbers in **boldface** indicate illustrations.

About the Author

Siobhan McDonnell is an Australian settler of European and Bermudan (African) descent. She is a lawyer and anthropologist with over twenty-five years of experience working with Indigenous people in Australia and Oceania on land rights, displacement, gender, and climate change issues. She is a senior lecturer at the Crawford School of Public Policy, Australian National University. In 2013–2014 Siobhan was the legal adviser to the minister of lands in Vanuatu, and the principal drafter of the land laws and constitutional amendments detailed in this book, designed to provide better land rights for custom landowners and end the era of ministerial land grabs over customary and state land. Siobhan's commitment to the practice of engaged anthropology means that she produces research that contributes to high-impact policy and legal outcomes across a range of areas. Since 2019 she has been an international negotiator on climate change issues for Pacific Island governments.

OTHER VOLUMES IN THE PACIFIC ISLANDS MONOGRAPH SERIES

1 *The First Taint of Civilization: A History of the Caroline and Marshall Islands in Pre-Colonial Days, 1521–1885,* by Francis X Hezel, SJ, 1983
2 *Where the Waves Fall: A New South Sea Islands History from First Settlement to Colonial Rule,* by K R Howe, 1984
3 *Wealth of the Solomons: A History of a Pacific Archipelago, 1800–1978,* by Judith A Bennett, 1987
4 *Nan'yō: The Rise and Fall of the Japanese in Micronesia, 1885–1945,* by Mark R Peattie, 1988
5 *Upon a Stone Altar: A History of the Island of Pohnpei to 1890,* by David Hanlon, 1988
6 *Missionary Lives: Papua, 1874–1914,* by Diane Langmore, 1989
7 *Tungaru Traditions: Writings on the Atoll Culture of the Gilbert Islands,* by Arthur F Grimble, edited by H E Maude, 1989
8 *The Pacific Theater: Island Representations of World War II,* edited by Geoffrey M White and Lamont Lindstrom, 1989
9 *Bellona Island Beliefs and Rituals,* by Torben Monberg, 1991
10 *Not the Way It Really Was: Constructing the Tolai Past,* by Klaus Neumann, 1992
11 *Broken Waves: A History of the Fiji Islands in the Twentieth Century,* by Brij V Lal, 1992
12 *Woven Gods: Female Clowns and Power in Rotuma,* by Vilsoni Hereniko, 1995
13 *Strangers in Their Own Land: A Century of Colonial Rule in the Caroline and Marshall Islands,* by Francis X Hezel, 1995
14 *Guardians of Marovo Lagoon: Practice, Place, and Politics in Maritime Melanesia,* by Edvard Hviding, 1996
15 *My Gun, My Brother: The World of the Papua New Guinea Colonial Police, 1920–1960,* by August Ibrum Kituai, 1998
16 *The People Trade: Pacific Island Laborers and New Caledonia, 1865–1930,* by Dorothy Shineberg, 1999
17 *Law and Order in a Weak State: Crime and Politics in Papua New Guinea,* by Sinclair Dinnen, 2001
18 *An Honorable Accord: The Covenant between the Northern Mariana Islands and the United States,* by Howard P Willens and Deanne C Siemer, 2001
19 *Colonial Dis-Ease: US Navy Health Policies and the Chamorros of Guam, 1898–1941,* by Anne Perez Hattori, 2004
20 *Imagining the Other: The Representation of the Papua New Guinean Subject,* by Regis Tove Stella, 2007
21 *Songs from the Second Float: A Musical Ethnography of Takū Atoll, Papua New Guinea,* by Richard Moyle, 2007

22 *The Other Side: Ways of Being and Place in Vanuatu,* by John Patrick Taylor, 2008

23 *Jean-Marie Tjibaou, Kanak Witness to the World: An Intellectual Biography,* by Eric Waddell, 2008

24 *Repositioning the Missionary: Rewriting the Histories of Colonialism, Native Catholicism, and Indigeneity in Guam,* by Vicente M Diaz, 2010

25 *Cultures of Commemoration: The Politics of War, Memory, and History in the Mariana Islands,* by Keith L Camacho, 2011

26 *Colonialism, Maasina Rule, and the Origins of Malaitan* Kastom, by David Akin, 2013

27 *The Kanak Awakening: The Rise of Nationalism in New Caledonia,* by David Chappell, 2013

28 *Remaking Pacific Pasts: History, Memory, and Identity in Contemporary Theater from Oceania,* by Diana Looser, 2014

29 *God Is Samoan: Dialogues between Culture and Theology in the Pacific,* by Matt Tomlinson, 2020

30 *Sweat and Salt Water: Selected Works,* by Teresia Kieuea Teaiwa, compiled and edited by Katerina Teaiwa, April K Henderson, and Terence Wesley-Smith, 2021